Sydney Loch was born in Ealing in in 1905. An Anzac veteran, Loch ~~wrote the once banned, but now~~ classic, account of Gallipoli, *To Hell and Back*. In 1922, Loch and his wife, Joyce, worked as aid workers in Thessaloniki, helping many Greeks escape from Turkey and later rescued thousands of Polish and Jewish children from the Nazis during World War II, setting up a refugee camp in Haifa. After the war, they moved to Thessaloniki, where Loch died in 1955.

Tauris Parke Paperbacks is an imprint of I.B.Tauris. It is dedicated to publishing books in accessible paperback editions for the serious general reader within a wide range of categories, including biography, history, travel, art and the ancient world. The list includes select, critically acclaimed works of top quality writing by distinguished authors that continue to challenge, to inform and to inspire, These are books that possess those subtle but intrinsic elements that mark them out as something exceptional.

The Colophon of Tauris Parke Paperbacks is a representation of the ancient Egyptian ibis, sacred to the god Thoth, who was himself often depicted in the form of this most elegant of birds. Thoth was credited in antiquity as the scribe of the ancient Egyptian gods and as the inventor of writing and was associated with many aspects of wisdom and learning.

ATHOS

The Holy Mountain

Sydney Loch

TPP

TAURIS PARKE
PAPERBACKS

New paperback edition published in 2017 by Tauris Parke Paperbacks
An imprint of I.B.Tauris & Co. Ltd
London • New York
www.ibtauris.com

Text used for this edition published in 1957 by Lutterworth Press

Cover image: Xenofontos Monastery, Mount Athos, Greece © Travis Dove /
National Geographic Creative / Bridgeman Images

ISBN: 978 1 78453 799 9
eISBN: 978 1 78672 193 8
ePDF: 978 1 78673 193 7

A full CIP record for this book is available from the British Library
A full CIP record is available from the Library of Congress

Library of Congress Catalog Card Number: available

Typeset in Perpetua by OKS Prepress Services, Chennai, India
Printed and bound by CPI Group (UK) Ltd, Croydon, CR0 4YY

MIX
Paper from
responsible sources
FSC® C020471

My thanks are due to the monk Meletios Sikiotes, of Karyes, for the great trouble he has taken in preparing the copy of Byzantine music shown in plate 5; Mr. and Mrs. Basil Deed for their valuable assistance with proof-reading and indexing, and the map; the Rev. C. E. Hampton for his help in cataloguing and sorting films, and for the photograph of Zographou in plate 10; Mr. Gerald Palmer for the photograph of the Holy Mountain in plate 1; and the Greek Government Information Office for the photograph of the view from Iviron in plate 10.

J. M. L.

Contents

List of Illustrations

Introduction

Books in several languages have been written round the history and legends, the artistic and literary treasures of the Holy Mountain; and during the last fifty years five or six have appeared in English. Is there room for a book with a different approach?

I have lived on the doorstep of the Holy Mountain for the past twenty-five years, and claim to know it as do few other laymen. Therefore I have chosen to attempt to record the heart of Athos through the everyday life of that womanless land. That heart started to beat at the dawn of Christianity, and this community, which can claim to be the world's oldest democracy, was already well established when William the Conqueror landed in England. The astonishing thing is how little time has changed it. It is the Past, with all the old enthusiasms. Wars, revolution, evolution, and scientific research have not stripped it of its form; but it remains to-day as it was when, full of zeal at the direct message from Christ, monks crept into the caves and became the first hermits.

To-day the zeal is still there; but the monks are in danger of dying out, for the world no longer breeds solitaries, or only in unimportant numbers. Statesmen, kings, and generals no longer desert thrones to become monks, so that the monks of to-day are for the most part simple men. And the pilgrims of to-day are tourists, usually on the run from an austerity they never suspected.

The peasants from the neighbouring land-starved villages have their thoughts and eyes upon the Holy Mountain to ease their situation. In the past, reverence for the church would have made such thoughts impossible; not so now, and old monks feel with a certain urgency that they must find a new generation of novices, or they may find themselves homeless. They founded a school at Karyes in 1953, hoping to stimulate an interest in Athos by providing an excellent education for boys "from the world". They naturally hope that a few of these boys may be tempted to remain on as novices; but it is not expected.

The majority of monks are from peasant stock, and few men of education now don the habit. The present monks understand the peasant point of view. They understand land-hunger; but at the same time they feel they are the keepers of a tradition that is a direct legacy from the past, and they know that their lands, carefully built up out of the stony wastes by their own toil through centuries, could not feed more than a handful of people. On the other hand they, through devotion, have preserved something that would vanish from the world if Athos ceased to be.

To the monks their ikons are powerful personalities. You have only to listen to their gossiping in their hours of relaxation to realize this, and faintly to understand what a tremendous impact Christianity made on the human heart in the first days. Monks think of their saints as superbeings who take a lively interest in the thoughts and works of each one of them. Quick to comfort, quick to rebuke; keeping careful watch, and functioning through their ikons. I have written the history of the ikons as nearly as possible as the monks tell it, for only so can the reader glimpse the atmosphere in which the Holy Mountain is wrapped.

It calls for a writer more able at words to picture the sheer beauty of the Mountain. To convey the altering feeling of morning, or high noon; of afternoon, and deep midnight; of the golden scores of stars puncturing the sky. But I give ground to no one in appreciation of what Athos offers. The disciplining heat or cold does not matter, nor the giddy paths, for everlasting beauty is spread under sun or across snow. Let the sunlit or moonlit sea be sleepy or lively, or turned by winter into threatening wind-piled waters, beauty continues mistress of the Mountain. There is always the returning opportunity of entering ancient churches or lowly chapels; or stopping at the crosses or holy springs that are at every crossroad; hours of invitation for the worshipper or the man troubled in spirit in a land in which a feeling for God is ever existent.

SYDNEY LOCH

1

The Wall: Chromitsa Metorchi

I SHOULDERED A RUCKSACK and was off to the Holy Mountain, after storm
had turned the long summer into autumn and coloured the leaves. Others
had already skimmed through the libraries and studied the murals and
church treasure, but few of them had much time to spend there, and many
no tongue to talk with. Time and the language are two essentials if a true
scene is to be painted of what may soon be a lost world; for the tired old
men who now people it must soon disappear.

The Mountain is a range which runs south-east for thirty miles from
Xerxes' Canal; a sea-chafed peninsula called the Holy Mountain of Athos
and, in pagan days, Akte. Two kilometres wide at the canal, it broadens to
ten, with a long backbone rising into peaks of roughly five hundred, six
hundred, six hundred and fifty, eight hundred and fifty, and a thousand
metres, and finally the marble summit of Athos itself, 2,039 metres or
6,670 feet of grey-white crystalline limestone.

The village I lived in consisted of ninety cottages. It was called
Prosphori, after the huge stone Byzantine building rising on rocks from
the sea, which became my home. The village was built after the first
World War, under the League of Nations scheme for the exchange of
populations between Greece and Turkey. Until then the Tower had
been an outpost of the monastery of Vatopedi, and was the last point
on the peninsula to which women could go. In its modern form it was
built by Andronikos the Second about seven hundred years ago, but is
suggested to have had a much earlier foundation than that. Certain
stones may even run back to ancient Dion, believed to have been on
this site.

The villagers came from the Princes' Isles, near Istanbul, and from distant inland Caesarea, and they looked on themselves as two distinct tribes. Each despised the other.

Farmers received a cottage, olive trees, and a few acres to cultivate. Fishermen were given a cottage, olive trees, fewer acres, and a promise of fishing gear. The islanders arrived speaking Greek and Turkish; but not all Caesareans knew Greek. They were moved under a ruling that all members of the Eastern Orthodox Church in Turkey were to be considered Greeks, an instance of the Greek Church's ability to keep the nationality of a group in being. Some had lived for so many generations in Turkey that touch with Greece, even to the language, had been lost, but their priests kept them Christians and Greeks.

The outstanding thing about all the villagers was their poverty and the poverty of their acres. Yet as years passed some became "rich" in public opinion, owing to their ability to seize every opportunity which offered, to their superior energy, and to less numerous offspring. The monasteries had work to offer to wood-cutters, charcoal-burners, fishermen, and workmen, which considerably eased an intolerable situation.

Cocks, donkeys, and dogs crowed, brayed, or barked at dawn, ending the heavy sleep that followed, the unrolling of mattresses across the floor at nightfall. Families stood up half clothed, shook themselves like horses, chased away sleep with a wash at the well, and were ready for the day. In winter a few rags were pulled over summer's tatters, and coarse socks drawn over bare feet. Firewood was not a great concern with the peasants. Though mule after mule dropped loads at our door, we were never warm while winter winds drove the sea against our rock; but cottage rooms were small and heated by a handful of twigs or charcoal. We burned away a fortune in our lamps, but never defeated the shadows sufficiently for comfortable reading; while the villager, watching a supper pot in the ashes, obtained enough light from a little lamp nailed to the wall.

The head of each household either wrested a living with the plough from a few acres of stony ground, or with net, trident, and hook from the waters washing the long base of the Holy Mountain. Holdings became split up as children received marriage portions, and parents became necessarily poorer. The ploughman tramped at his lonely work, the wife baked, the

PLATE I *The Holy Mountain, which dominates the monastic world of Athos*

PLATE 2   *The Wall: the land frontier of Athos, beyond which: "no female animal or beardless person" may venture*

girls went to the well for water, and the grandmother pegged the goat out to pasture, otherwise the old woman was free to gossip along the traffic-less street, spindle in hand, in the sunshine of most of the year.

The promontory of Athos, forbidden to woman and female animals, continued beyond the wall for twenty-five miles until ending in the Holy Mountain, and touched village life more closely than the normal world which stretched for a hundred miles in the other direction to Salonika. As a centre which provided work, villagers disappeared there for months on end. They turned up with cupboards and tables for their cottages from decayed Russian buildings, or smuggled sugar for their wives. Strings of mules passed in and out at night with swarms in bee-skeps. Some of the villagers had relations who had taken the vows; others occasionally let a room to a monk on medical leave, usually to enable him to get a milk diet, denied to him on the Mountain.

There may have been two hundred square miles of reserved territory; but so rugged was it, so impenetrable most of it, so amazing a world, that it seemed more extensive, and entered village talk a hundred times a day.

It was after three when I set out, and too late to get anywhere beyond the Russian farm of Chromitsa. The last swifts of the year rushed screaming round the Tower, their clamour following me.

A path left the village between a vineyard and some veronica bushes and ran over a headland. It dipped to a pasture and led across a red hillside to a rivulet's sandy mouth. From there it turned inland among cistus and erica, towards slopes of pine, and wound round the ruins of Frankokastron, about which no more seems known than that the Latins built the castle at the start of the thirteenth century, when Athos was taken into the kingdom of Salonika after the occupation of Constantinople during the fourth Crusade. From this base the western barons plundered the peninsula, sown at that time with numerous small monasteries; but they failed to force the Roman rite on the Greek monks in the few years before the kingdom of Salonika passed away.

The path ran on round the ruins and through an olive-grove, within sight of a house and garden near the seashore, looked after by three elderly Russian monks. Sunlight, broken up in the olive-branches, fell through in showers, warming the turf. Birds might suddenly trill, birds might fly; but the trill failed, wings passed through boughs and quiet returned. In spring this grove was full of nightingales and crested hoopoes. The track petered out in a stream-bed, dry half the year, along the other side of which crumbled a low and endless wall under a hill of olives.

It was the boundary of the Virgin's Garden. Women might go no farther. The Mother of God, the Panayia, the All-Holy, had said so. Neither might female animals cross the wall; for, as was pointed out nearly a thousand years ago by St. Paul of Xeropotamou, the unseemly spectacle of mating must not offend souls intent on their daily purification.

There was another time of day over the wall; at sunset most monastery clocks pointed at twelve, and the calendar had retrograded thirteen days, Gregorian giving way to Julian. Should it be August 19 when the walker's foot left the streambank, his leg came down beyond the wall on August 6, feast of the Transfiguration, and that dawn the grapes had been blessed on the Mountain top, after an all-night vigil. The womanless land ran on south-east for twenty-five miles.

Women came as far as this wall in the autumn to strip the olive-trees, and herd-girls occasionally scrambled a few steps beyond the wall to use the well; on the sly, for the monks rigidly enforced the Panayia's command against women.

Tradition on the Mountain relates that the Virgin sailed from Joppa to visit Lazaros, who had been hunted to Cyprus by the Palestinian Jews who were prejudiced by his four-day death. She sailed from Joppa with St. John, and the ship was blown out of its course to pagan Athos, the home of false gods and an oracle of Apollo. The vessel anchored near the port of Klement, close to the present monastery of Iviron, and the Virgin walked ashore and was recognized at once, for even the idols admitted their own falseness and broke themselves to bits. The Virgin blessed the Mountain before leaving it, and declared it to be her garden and forbidden to other women.

The monks are historically correct in claiming the peninsula to have been populated in pre-Christian days. Herodotus mentions cities there;

but when the first of historically-accepted hermits, Peter the Athonite, found his ship miraculously rooted in the sea off Karavostasi (the Bay of the Standing Ship) as a heavenly direction that his voyage was over, and was watched by the ship's company climbing up that savage ravine at the peninsula end to the fifty years of solitude that ended in canonization, the land was considered uninhabited.

The possibly tenth-century record of Peter the Athonite makes him a captive of Arabs at Samara on the Tigris. He neglected a vow to become a monk, and called on St. Nicholas and St. Simeon from prison, promising to mend his sin. They permitted his escape. He sailed for the Levant after ordination; but the ship was blown out of its course and stood still in the sea off Athos until he climbed the pass to the cave which he occupied for fifty years. The Virgin—or St. Nicholas in another version—tells him in a vision that this is the wilderness where the rest of his life is to be spent.

A hunter discovered him near the end of his life and, moved by an old man's sanctity, vowed to follow the ascetic life after saying farewell to his family. However, when the converted hunter arrived the next year with a little band of followers he found the future saint already dead.

Bones to attract pilgrim wealth were on a cave floor, but they were not left for the wild beasts to crack. One can skip the shabby details of the story of the monks of Klementos, where Iviron stands to-day, who took the relics from the finders by force.

The inference is that the Mountain was thought to be uninhabited when Peter the Athonite went ashore about A.D. 840, though the monastery of Klementos had come into being by the time he died fifty years later.

Eighteen-year-old Euthymios had found the Mountain by then. He was born near Ankyra in 823, and left wife and child to God's care in order to practise religious exercises and learn obedience in the humblest services. An anchoret's life drew him to Athos, where he became head of a community about 862. He twice made his home on a pillar. The record of his wandering life suggests numerous solitaries and hermit settlements on the Mountain and throughout Chalkidhiki in the second half of the ninth century.

A certain John Kolovos, who was at one time with Euthymios, founded the monastery of Kolovou about 875; according to one account to the north of Erissos, according to another on the Megale Vigla, well inside the wall. Kolovou lasted for a century, first as protector of the neighbouring hermits against the Erissiotes, later as oppressor of those ill-organized recluses. The monastery stooped to forgery to get its way, became inhospitable, and in the last quarter of the tenth century came to an end in a struggle with the Great Lavra, founded by Athanasios in 963, a monastery reigning on the Mountain to-day.

Athanasios, a rich man's son, appeared on Mount Athos as a peasant, intending to lose his identity. The few monks already settled there lived in communities, or apart as solitaries, under a ruler, the "Protos" or "First", who had hermitages and cells in his gift. In 972 the seat of the Protos was transferred to Messi, or the "Middle", which changed its name to Karyes, and was the scene of gatherings for the three great feasts of Christmas, Easter, and the Falling-asleep-of-the-Virgin. Athanasios was presently discovered by Nikephoros Phokas, friend of his youth and soon to be Emperor, who offered treasure to build a monastery on the lines of Mount Kymina, where Athanasios had spent his novitiate. The Great Lavra stands to-day at the peninsula's end where the saint founded it with eighty monks in 963. The hermit system had probably outlived its usefulness. In any case the period of primitive anchorets, pluckers of fruit and grubbers of weeds, raisers of humble huts roofed with grasses, was passing away. Athanasios angered the old-fashioned by constructing buildings, making harbours, and importing oxen for hauling and ploughing. He was accused of bringing "the world" to the Mountain; but complaint of abuse of power failed, and victory went to Athanasios and the rule of the Studium, introduced from Mount Kymina. Other monastic houses on the Lavra model rapidly came into being.

The traveller crossing the wall will be more at home if he knows modern Greek and Russian; will find more meaning in his surroundings if on nodding terms with Byzantine history and able to appreciate the austere, detached ikonography. If he can, he should develop fortitude to remain between hanging and standing in a church stall through the night-long vigil until dawning day brings relief and causes the monks to consider a meal.

The path beyond the wall turned sharply uphill through a second olive-grove, then entered macchie which clothed the mountainous slopes.

This thick scrub harboured hares, pig and martins. The spidery path passed uphill between arbutus branches and Judas trees. Myrtle, erica, manna ash, and cyclamen presently hemmed in a mule-trough protected by a shrine to St. Panteleimon, patron of doctors, the only hint that man passed up and down here. A hard-bitten local poacher looked sharply up from drinking at the spring. The gendarmes were said to have marked him down, for he was believed to own the mantraps which occasionally caught stray cattle. Most villagers were tempted to shoot deer, and nobody paid for a gun-licence; but only a rogue risked maiming cattle or a wandering man on the lonely ranges.

He glanced at my rucksack and then at the sun, observing:

"You'll hardly get to Chilandari to-night."

"To-morrow," I said, glad to pull up. "They'll put me up at the top of the hill to-night."

"What a place to stay at!"

"There'll be a bed and a meal."

"What a place! Now the gold they hide at Vatopedi!" he sighed, passing to the richest monastery like a buccaneer thinking of Spanish galleons. "Twelve underground rooms. Full. A man standing in one of them for a minute would come out as full as a bee."

"No layman's ever seen one gold piece. And no monk either, if you listen to them."

"Believe a monk," he sneered. "How long'll you be away from the village?"

"Let's say a week."

"If I bring in a wild pig next week?"

"I'll gladly take a leg."

He straightened up as I moved on.

"Believe a monk," he repeated. "I had a friend knowing all about that gold."

The road lost pitch after running over a wooden bridge spanning a chain of pools. Trees to the left concealed a kitchen garden, in past days half the size of a meadow, then the stable, barns, and outbuildings of the pretty outpost, Chromitsa, came into sight.

Up to the 1914–18 World War the great Russian monastery of St. Panteleimon, near Daphne, led the Mountain in numbers of monks and wealth, overflowing into sketes, and forming colonies of kelliotes at the Mountain end. (A skete is a dependency of a monastery, governed by a prior. A kelli is an establishment of two to six monks, living in a cottage which contains its own chapel.) The Russian monks were said to be six thousand at one time, and this healthy, sheltered outpost I was approaching, high over the sea in a pine-grove, had been built as a general hospital for Russians, and was equipped with wards, surgeries, and storerooms. The collapse of Tsarist Russia in 1917, followed by the atheistic reign of the Bolsheviks, dried up the stream of Russian funds and Russian monks to the Mountain; and year by year death reduced the numbers already there, for very few novices arrived to fill empty places. The disused hospital decayed, and the monks farming the neighbourhood became further reduced by being called in to larger centres to fill vacant places, until the elderly men left could no longer carry out their work. The whole region was in decline.

I drew breath outside the watchman's cottage. A Cossack officer, flotsam of the 1917 revolution, once occupied the place. But he moved and thought too quickly for his masters, the peasant monks. Watchman's work, carried out to nocturnal ecclesiastical chanting, upset him to the point of sending him over the wall with gifts of fruit and vegetables for me. He would stay a few minutes to laugh at his fate, and then disappear into the tavern. His masters—kindly men—might have overlooked lapses beyond the wall; but there were songs of the "world" from his cottage, and a slower, letterless substitute soon patrolled in his place.

Our unrealized farewell was during a grape-harvest. He dropped down beside me in some bushes at a dip where an old wild boar came out to feed in spite of the iron gongs beaten by patrolling monks. Vineyards were spread widely in the moon's milky light, and flat sea shone a thousand feet below. The Cossack made the night cry out with campaigning tales of Reds and Whites. His slanting eyes caught the moonlight as he spoke of prisoners bound with paraffin-soaked ropes. His companions lighted those living dancers, who twirled away blazing.

We separated in the end, and he passed on his toes to another ambush, alert, himself again. The last seen of him by me.

An oil-mill stood just beyond the cottage, and a monk with resigned eyes, in a threadbare habit, the steward Basil, turned the mill-stone round a basin in the twilit interior by clucking at a circling horse. The place reeked of crushed olives, and a bank of fruit, fifty feet long, had to be skirted to reach him.

In forsaking the world for the Mountain, Basil had hoped to put off responsibility as a man removes his coat. He had taken vows of obedience, and could avoid further decisions. Then the unexpected happened, and a superior had been withdrawn to another place, and he was left to direct a group of elderly men on this undermanned farm. Life had played him a trick.

"Don't stop the horse, Father. I want to go on to Chilandari in the morning, and stay here to-night. May I?"

He checked the horse and stood between accompanying me to the guestmaster and going on with the work, and we might have stood like this to sundown.

"I see you're busy. I'll sit in the sun."

"There's this to finish," he mumbled, beginning a new clockwork shuffling after the horse.

"You're having a good olive year."

"We shan't do without."

The sun, low down, shone over leagues of sea and still warmed this lofty land. A row of elderly monks were knocking olives off the trees with long canes, and a noisy band of boys swept the black fruit into baskets. The boys, as "beardless" men, had no right there; but the wall was near, olive-picking the busiest season, and a parent in charge. The monks directed the shrill, darting boys, who saved them stooping.

The hospital decayed in the background. Thirty-two or thirty-three monks now occupied cells intended for scores of men. Not half the seventeen thousand olive-trees on the books were still cultivated, and the vineyards were deteriorating.

The neglected monks let their greying hair hang round their shoulders, instead of knotting it under the bonnet, and rolled in knee-high leather boots to the field-work they were insufficient for. Nor were they expecting help, but recognized that twilight leads to night.

The single Russian workman still with them sat on a bench at the gates, nursing his fiery poll between freckled, red-haired hands.

"Last night they gave me a bad fish. It kept me vomiting all day," he volunteered, making a place for me. "Because these people know no difference between fresh and bad fish, they expect others not to. God has kissed them!"

A large, soft monk puffing from beating trees came up to ask me where I was going.

"To Chilandari."

"Three or four hours' march," he said. "I've never been there, for they say an hour away from here nothing marks the path."

"Nothing does," the workman agreed, lifting his head out of his hands again. "For a year now I've been saying, 'One day you must climb up there and do strangers a kindness by fastening a wooden hand to a rock to show the way.' But one year can become a second, and a man not hear it go by. That wooden hand still has to be cut out."

He let his red-whiskered head fall to the ears between his fists, and the monk shouted mildly at two boys quarrelling over a basket.

A weather-beaten villager, elderly but with an edge to him, perched sideways on a jogging mule, bore past us on the way down to the village, drumming the animal's ribs with his sandalled feet. He came from Zographou, where he worked for a merchant with a timber concession. A sugar-bag of lemons and oranges jerked at the saddle, and a raki bottle showed out of a torn coat pocket. He ran the mule round us, and pulled up to take in the activity under the trees. The raki had made a prophet of him.

"Make the most of your olives while there's time, good Fathers," he urged cheerfully, "for we're coming up here soon. There's not enough room for us down there any longer, and you're too few now to use these fine trees and vineyards. They'll be calling you into Panteleimon soon. We old fellows'll stay down there, where we've made it a bit easy for ourselves, and our married boys and girls'll make a fine colony in these empty buildings."

Villagers were playing with this idea, which was unlikely to be considered by the Government. The Russian labourer kept his head buried, and the monks looked as if an answer might be resolved. But they were too long growing annoyed, amused, or witty. The old ruffian took another gulp at his bottle and called: "On with the day's work, Fathers. The better these trees are looked after, the more olives they'll give us later on." He swung the bit of his head-chain above the mule's long ears, drummed its ribs again, and was off at a rough amble.

"He'll have that animal breaking its knees on the stones if he takes it down the slope like that," observed a monk, leaning on his long cane to watch him bump away. "More raki in his stomach than sense in his head."

This hospital farm lacked historic interest. The church of St. Mary was dated 1880, and the other buildings 1881. Tucked away off one of the corridors was the chapel of Tatiana, and Platon, existing when the Russians bought the property from the Greeks. Oil and garlic from the kitchen had permeated stairs and corridors; but the church was polished and swept.

The sun left the oleander bushes, and the clock stood at twelve. Basil, the steward, had already passed into the court with baskets on both arms, ordering the monks to stack their long canes under a cypress.

I stood looking down into the darkening court from a window above the gate. A reader was to be heard in the refectory, and later the monks drifted back on the way to their cells. One slippered old man with a saucer was followed by a line of trotting cats like a tail to him. He clucked, they mewed, and tail and body disappeared into the dingy building.

I looked round at the sound of steps. Metrophanes, the guestmaster, was bringing in the supper tray, supported against his chest. He carried it into the bedroom, where a bench joined a table under the window. Mattresses softened the wood, and there was a heavy quilt. He went into the quilt question as he put the tray down.

"Shall I get you out blankets?"

"It's early yet for a cold night," I said. "Tikhon the priest seems missing. Where is he?"

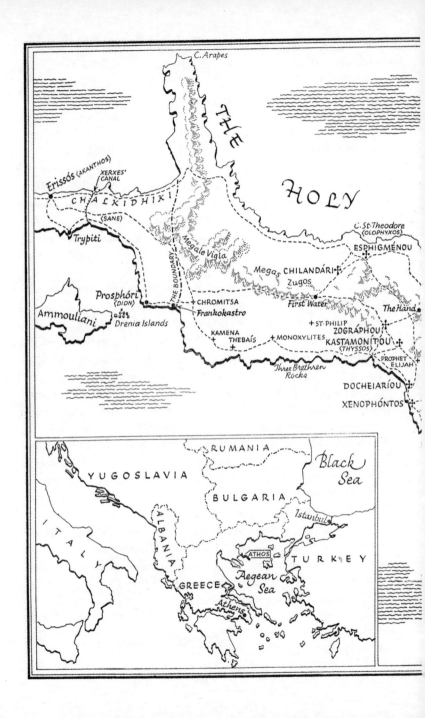

Monasteries .... ✝ SIMÓPETRA
Dependencies .... + PROPHET ELIJAH
Other places .... • Daphne
Old Greek names .... ⟨DION⟩
Paths .... - - - - - -

N

W   E

S

SCALE 1:100 000
Kilometres
0   5   10   15

MOUNTAIN

• Abbots Rock

✝VATOPÉDI

✝ST·DIMÍTRIOS
+BOGORÓDITSA

✝PANTOKRÁTOROS

OF

✝STAVRONIKÍTA

ST·
ANDREWS✝
KARYÉS✝ ✝KOUTLOUMOUSÍOU
✝IVÍRON

PANTELEÍMON ✝PHILOTHÉOU •Mylopotámou
(ROUSSIKÓ)   KARAKÁLLOU
⟨CLEONAE⟩

ATHOS ⟨ACTE⟩

✝XEROPOTÁMOU

PROVÁTA

• Daphne

• Morphonoú

C. Chelona

+LÁKKOU

✝SIMÓPETRA   GREAT LAVRA✝

CROSS OF KOUKOUZÉUS
+ Cave of the Wicked
+GREGORIOU   THE PEAK   ST·GEORGE+ Dead
           2039 M▲   +PRODRÓMOU C. Akrothos

DIONYSÍOU✝ •Kerasiá
    ✝ST·PAUL'S   KARAVOSTÁSI

+ST·NEILOS
+KAPSOKALÝVIA
Spring of Akakios
Island of Christophoros

NEW SKETE   +ST·ANNE'S
        ST·BASIL✝

LITTLE ST·ANNE'S✝ ✝KATOUNÁKIA
             ✝KAROÚLIA

C. Pinnes ⟨NYMPHAEUM⟩

-MANN-

"Called to Panteleimon, where Anophrios has died. Have I given you enough?"

"I'll never get through that trayful."

Metrophanes backed out, and left me to eat. In the jumble on the tray were a glass of raki, a meatless rice pilau, a decanter of red wine, two small fish, aubergine, and good black bread. What there was must have taken some collecting in this poor place. Hours afterwards the clock struck seven, or I a.m. as the outside world reckoned time, and there broke out on the windless night the sound of mallet-taps on the wooden semantron. A veiled monk moved up and down the dark court, mallet in right hand and slender sounding-board in left, calling the others to church.

2

Chilandari: the Idiorrhythmic Monastery of Chelandion

I STARTED AT EIGHT o'clock in the morning, without breakfast. The monks give two meals, one about ten-thirty, and supper towards seven, but the guestmaster produces a farewell glass of raki, a spoonful of jam, a glass of water, and a cup of Turkish coffee, for the early starter. The experienced guest tosses the raki down, swallows the jam, drinks the water, and drops the soiled spoon into the empty tumbler. Coffee is sipped during the final five minutes. A beginner hardly benefits; the veteran feels ready.

I walked away over dewy ground, leaving Metrophanes bent in farewell. The wild direction was upwards and to the left, and the path rubbed out half the time. The track finally rose a thousand feet above Chromitsa, which had long passed out of sight. Then there opened out a view of the true Mountain, shouldering through white, rolling clouds at the end of leagues of rough ridges. A track runs on at this point, which leads the walker down into a green basin where a hermit once dug a vegetable plot. The true path leads up nearly invisibly over decaying granite rocks to a view of both seas, divided by miles of desolate land tumbling down almost to sea level at Xerxes' Canal, where Xerxes the Persian, descending on Greece about 480 B.C., is said to have cut a canal for his ships in order to avoid Akte's fearful head, after Mardonios had lost a fleet there twelve years before.

With the Drenia Isles on the right, and the Holy Sea on the left, the lonely advance was across country covered with macchie, an empty mountainous land, where a dead body could lie unfound. The sea-like cry

of moving pine-trees went mewing before me and followed wailing after,
where the land was not too poor for trees; and the way was often coloured
by arbutus bushes, loaded with ripening strawberry-red, crimson, yellow,
and orange fruit. This desert was the country of the first hermit saints,
Euthymios and Athanasios, who shared it with wild beasts. It took a couple
of hours to cross, but the path finally led into trees ending in vineyards
where a ramshackle farmhouse stood near a willow leaning over a spring
called "First Water".

. I drank under a cloud of fluttering martins, both legs nosed in turn by a
surprisingly good-natured fawn Vlach dog, a pup, though nearly to my
hips. These savage shepherd dogs are said to have been obtained in Albania
for use in the Roman arenas, and were introduced into Rumania by Roman
legionaries. Nomad shepherds bring them to the hills round Prosphori at
the start of winter. They will come a long way to look a stranger over, and
the walker blundering near a fold in the shepherd's absence may as well try
the traditional method of saving himself by squatting in the middle of the
circling brutes as any other.

The dog's master came out of the cabin wearing a monk's bonnet and
black homespun breeches buttoned down the legs—a tall, forbidding
fellow, who gathered up an armful of brushwood and stalked over to an
open-air oven, taking no notice of me, though he had probably been alone
for days. He finally unbent sufficiently to tell me he was a Macedonian
from Serres, and the monk in charge of these vineyards and the beehives in
sight, which increase to fifteen thousand skeps between April and October.
The monasteries own a third of the hives, using the wax for church
candles, and mules bring the other swarms at night from villages beyond
the wall, which pay rent for the bee-range.

"There must be jackals round here," I said.

"Swarms of them."

"What about wild pigs?"

"They still leave us enough grapes. There are roebuck and a few red
deer. I've startled stags like horses in those trees in cold weather."

"How about wolves?"

"Not one for five or six years now. They worked this way during the
war of 1914, and left again."

"One killed a cow near Prosphori six winters ago, and I've heard of none since then. They can't like crossing the narrow neck of the Canal."

"The last one howling round here had the voice of a steamer."

"You've a good guard coming on in this pup."

"He should be useful in a year or two," the monk admitted, looking first the pup's way, and then half-menacingly towards the beehives he guarded, which covered acres of ground.

The Macedonian concentrated on the blazing brushwood in his oven as I walked away; he required nobody's companionship, and was a common type on the Mountain.

The sunny downhill track to Chilandari, through macchie and along pine-valleys, crossed a chain of brown water-holes a few minutes before the Serbian monastery's keep came in sight. Wilderness swept up to the range of buildings, to fall back harmlessly, like sea from a rock.

The road passed the blighted cypress monks claim St. Simeon planted, then ran into a summer gossiping-ground under colouring walnut-trees. A fountain trickled beside a kiosk. Cypresses, pines, and planes pressed round, and a lanky swineherd kept an eye on twenty hogs which rooted near a grazing horse.

I dropped on a bench in the frescoed gateway to get breath, and a muttering porter swept out and snatched my stick away. It is said that a Turk struck one of the ikons here more than a century ago, and this may have been the reason for the porter's action. He was off with it into his lodge like a jackdaw. Having won, he led me between the iron-sheeted gates into a court enclosed by storeyed buildings, where the pink-and-white katholikon, or principal church, stood isolated between cypresses. A bell at the bottom of the guest staircase brought Makarios trotting down to greet me, a man cut out for a guestmaster, clean, friendly, brisk, and fond of callers.

He led me to a divan under windows overlooking the court storeys below, and hurried off for the tray. The committee members soon came down the passage to make me feel more at home; both large, authoritative men, growing paunches from endless standing in church. One wanted my opinion on a yellowing ivory mug in his hand, an ornament of the committee rooms. He held it up to the light.

"A lot of work went into that carving, Elder," I said as the mug went round in a sunbeam, "work and talent. The effort of a considerable master."

"For deep drinking, aye?" the Serbian monk chuckled, spanning the heavy vessel with long, thick fingers. "Robbers may have brought it, and forgotten it when they left. The pirates of old were always quarrelling. They lived on each other when failing to live on us. Who knows how it came here? You've had a long walk?"

"Which started off with a climb."

"God made hills as well as plains. You must stay a day or two now we have you. But there won't be many to talk to this time. Most of us are out all day picking up olives."

They stayed a few minutes to make me feel settled in, for they were good hosts. These two men would not pick up the olives, that was work for lowlier monks. Their work was to direct, deal with finance, keep an eye on the stores, negotiate sales of produce or timber, and see no obstacles came in the way of the religious life of the group. In this idiorrhythmic house they were allowed to possess their own property, probably not much more than the furniture in their private quarters pf two or three small rooms. In idiorrhythmic houses guests were often invited to coffee in the committee rooms after the Sunday Liturgy. In a coenobitic house the equivalent was an invitation to eat with the monks in the refectory on Sunday.

Portraits of Serbia's national heroes hung on the walls. The coffin-shaped dining-room looked on to a wooded hillside. I sat down, the single guest, to a cabbage salad, stockfish, macaroni, salted herrings, slabs of white cheese, brown bread, fried potatoes, and a decanter of wine, any one of the dishes enough for a man. The guestmaster fingered single hairs in his black beard and offered suggestions in what order to take items. The traveller may occasionally strike a plate of cold, clammy beans as the guestmaster's sole offering, and when this happens in two or three successive monasteries, as it may during a fast, he usually flees the Mountain and touches on his sufferings in his resulting books and lectures; but most meals are of this substantial kind, and occasionally impressive ones have been put on in my honour. The good bread and invariable

PLATE 3   *Monks weighing chaff, Prosphori village;* (below) *the author's home, Prosphori Tower, "The Offering" of Andronicus the Second to the monastery of Vatopedi*

PLATE 4   *Olive-pickers at Chromitsa; and* (below) *Meletios of Vatopedi talking to a woman in the village of Prosphori*

presence of wine usually unite a haphazard assortment of edibles into a meal for a hungry man. The custom of spreading the entire offering on the table at the same time gives the sense of dining off *hors d'œsuvres*.

Makarios made the mistake of glancing all the time at the martyred ecclesiastics on the wall. He addressed the ceiling and punctured his remarks with: "What is man and his life on earth?" Then he made the statement that a few years before Chilandari had eighty monks, and now forty-three. "Another twenty years and ... !" He left the rest to me.

The shadow of melancholy had fallen over this ancient house, ranking fourth on the Mountain. It received few visitors now, although so many raiding parties in bygone centuries had swarmed over the meadow-land which led peacefully to the shore. As a Slav house it was left in the cold by the Greek houses. Their turbulent histories were in the bones of these separate Balkan people, and too easily penetrated through the all-covering skin of the Eastern Orthodox Church.

The monastery lacked novices, and had grown poorer through the expropriation of its rich lands beyond the frontier by the Greek Government. The nearest and last to go had been taken by our villagers, after the expropriation order had gone through in Athens. News came to the village ahead of the official announcement. The men, without waiting a day, crossed the rough country to where the monks were ploughing, laid claim, and, when the monks resisted, started a hand-to-hand struggle. They won and remained in possession.

Makarios soon became cheerful and brisk again, and suggested the macaroni, then the salt fish.

"Athos has a long history," he reflected aloud, "and long histories go up and down. There've been periods in the past when novices seemed falling off. Numbers always revived again. Try the cheese. It's sheep cheese—better than goat."

The sun had set, we were behind walls needing scaling-ladders. Frequent pirate raids have taught monks to value walls, and every house shuts the gates at sunset, and reopens them at sunrise. Chilandari has a refinement of this rule, resulting from an Easter morning that has become legendary. A thousand Latin pirates streamed out of their ships to sack the monastery. A thousand! The monks crowded into church and prayed before the wonder-working ikon, the Virgin-of-Three-Hands. A mist rose over the meadow-land, filling it with shapes and the damp of death. The raiders lost their bearings, and before long panic-stricken men had mistaken comrades for foes and set to work on them with sword and spear. A thousand warriors struggled together in an eddying white mist! Three repentant raiders still lived when the monks turned over the clammy dead, and they were admitted to the monastery, where their portraits decorate the refectory as converts.

The attack took place at dawn on Easter Sunday, and started the custom of keeping the gates closed each Easter Sunday until after the Liturgy, as monks believe that will always be the monastery's vulnerable hour. Chilandari has always been a Slav house. Bulgar monks now outnumber the Serbians, who control it.

The heroic resistance to the Catalans early in the thirteenth century under Abbot Daniel, later Archbishop of Serbia, is historical; and Crusader, Saracen, pirate, and Turk have anchored their ships off the shore below. This was a powerful house in the thirteenth and fourteenth centuries, but was burned down in 1722, and not much more than the church and tower are of great age.

The origin claimed is interesting. Stephen Nemanja, Great Zupan of Serbia at the close of the twelfth century, had a son Rastko, who deserted his father's court for the Holy Mountain. Messengers were two years finding him, and in the end waited under the monastery's walls while the royal monk's robes were lowered to them, indicating that the prince they had come for was not returning to the world. Stephen Nemanja had fallen into a state of chronic melancholy for his absent son and, handing over the Serbia he had united to his second son, abdicated in 1196, and retired into the Serbian monastery of Studenica, which he had founded. From there he went to the Holy Mountain, to be shorn by the monk, his son, at Vatopedi.

Father and son, now the monks Simeon and Savvas, occupied cells in Vatopedi; but Simeon was still an emperor's son-in-law, and through his father-in-law, Alexios III, Angelos, who mounted the throne in 1195 by blinding and deposing his brother, he obtained a ruined monastic building in Vatopedi's gift, rebuilt it just before 1200, endowed it, and founded Chilandari with Vatopedi's Slav monks.

Savvas, the son, left the new monastery to become "Archbishop of all the Serbian lands", to crown two kings, and be canonized as a national saint; but Simeon, uniter of Serbia's State and Church, died in 1200 as a monk at Chilandari, and to-day the vine that brings fertility to barren women is rooted in his empty sarcophagus against the church's south wall. Pilgrims take the grapes home as raisins.

From the windows of the guest rooms the monastery looked as if it was in the bottom of a bowl full of trees; and clouds were drifting across the rim like smoke when I woke in the morning. Monks sat in a gallery, combing their long uncut hair forward and down their faces like women.

Makarios rattled spoons in the pantry, and produced a tray of jam and coffee in a few minutes.

"How did you sleep?"

"Never opened an eye."

He pressed a hand expressively to his hip.

"Those boards we like to call beds!" Then he passed to my breakfastless state:

"Will what's on the tray do until half-past ten? I've found a fish for breakfast."

I dropped the jam-spoon into the tumbler, and picked up the coffee-cup.

"Is the sun coming out on the flats, Father, if I wander that way?"

"Yes," he answered happily, like the good host he was, "these mists are lifting in ten minutes."

He glided back to the pantry and I strolled seawards, after crossing the eighteenth-century court sheltering orange and lemon bushes. The tall buildings, a century or so old, had been stamped in places with the symbolic cross and lances between the words "Jesus Christ Conquers". Two knobkerrie-like maces hung near the porter's lodge to beat a warning on the gates at closing time. The road went downhill through a shallow sea of leaves drifting off walnuts, mulberries, and planes. Jays screamed in the trees and pigeons whistled in flight over them.

Cypresses stood near the shrine of that ass which dropped dead on this spot after bearing the Virgin-of-Three-Hands from Serbia. A sanctuary lamp was burning, and the ceiling murals told the story.

Half a mile away was written the name of Stephen Dushan on a white shrine on the edge of a cypress grove: he who mounted a throne over the body of a throttled father, and carved an empire out, which the son he sired lost in a few years. The shrine stands on the traditional spot where the monks trooped to meet him five hundred years ago.

On the edge of the meadow-land beyond stood the early fourteenth-century tower attributed to Stephen Urosh II, called "Milutin" or "Child of Grace". Stephen Dushan's wife, Helen, is said to have climbed it to look at the monastery so closely bound to her house. A legendary Queen of Serbia also climbed it every year to gaze across tree-tops at her son. She had promised her first son to Chilandari should the curse of childlessness be removed, and he was stationed on the monastery's tower for her to see.

Everywhere under the olive-trees monks were in sight, beating the boughs with long canes, picking up fruit off the ground. One or two agile men were in the boughs, beating top branches. The olives begin to fall in October, and are left on the ground until there are enough to pay for gathering. But when the mills start crushing, the trees are beaten lightly with long canes to bring down the olives still remaining on the branches. It was rather hard work for heavy, elderly men—long hours, stooping, and a good deal of carrying—but they set their own pace, gossiped, enjoyed the good weather, and were grateful for the heavy crop. Monks enjoy being thankful to the Virgin.

The meadow-land stretched to the thousand-year-old ruins of St. Basil's, decaying on the seashore among tamarisk bushes. A spectacled monk stood among grazing bullocks alertly quartering the ground. It was Klement, the herbalist, without his mule and saddle-bags weighted with his handwritten copy of Dioscorides, in two heavy tomes. He looked like a frameless picture on foot. Klement was a monk from Dionysiou, more used to a saddle under him than a church pavement. He was flavoured with the opposing richnesses of the garlic he munched and the flowers and herbs he gathered for his salves and purges.

He heard me coming, flashed a glance through his spectacles, and went on peering about.

"Good-day," I said in his ear, adding, "aren't you a long way from home this morning?"

"The whole Mountain's my home, as you know," he answered, refusing to be interrupted.

"What's brought you so far?" I persisted, knowing he belonged to the other shore, though he travelled far with his cures, and was strongly opinionated about them. He only accepted an occasional present after a notable cure. "What do you expect to find round here?"

"A plant that should appear about now. It is to clear the gravel out of an elder of Pantokratoros."

"Does he suffer a lot?"

"The pain permitted that elder!"

"Shouldn't he see a doctor?"

"Is a doctor's advice better than mine?"

"What if you don't find your plant?"

"If it's not in this meadow, I know of another place. Those bullocks like it too much."

One had to accept Klement's valuation of himself. He did not warm to colleagues, and when a botanical party from Kew Gardens, covering Athos one spring, found him in this same meadow, he scorned their herbal attainments, though forced to accept their botanical qualifications. He said it was the herbalist who was useful to his fellows, not the botanist.

Klement was busy and uninterested in me, so I prepared to leave.

"Tell me how to get into St. Basil's over there," I said.

"What do you want inside?"

"To look at the murals again. But who can get in, with the place always locked?"

"God is bigger than we are. A carpenter's there to-day, and you'll find it unlocked."

It was true. The door stood open, and a carpenter sawed and hammered on a wooden balcony near a large-nosed monk, hammering too, and chatting over a shoulder to a clockmaker in search of work. He had come to the right part of the world for something to do. Clocks are usually out of order, owing to the Mountain's three systems of reckoning time. Eighteen of the twenty monasteries follow the old Turkish method of considering sunset twelve o'clock; Vatopedi falls in with the outside world in accepting noon as twelve, and Iviron counts sunrise as twelve, tracing the custom to the fire-worshipping Persians, said to have passed it to the Georgians, who brought the system to the monastery. Thus nineteen monastic houses fiddle with their clock-hands almost daily until the discouraged clocks give up.

I saluted the group as I passed into the crumbling church, which, with the root of the crumbled tower and some ruined cells, was all that remained. The place's claim to have been founded by St. Basileios, Metropolitan of Salonika, at the start of the tenth century, makes it noteworthy. It was bought by Chilandari as a ruin in 1326, and it is still a ruin, sitting like a toy fortress on an islet off the shore with the sea passage filled in.

After seeing the church I added myself to the group. The monk who was directing the carpenter and working with him put his tools down. We retreated a few yards from the hammering carpenter, and the clockmaker asked:

"Did you pass anyone on the way here?" He had a heavy frame, but was yellow with malaria.

"The herbalist Klement," I said, "and there are monks everywhere under the olive-trees."

"I mean my brother."

"Is he a monk?"

"How can he be a monk if he's a mechanic like me? He came to the Mountain four days ago to look for work, and telephoned from Karyes he was on the way here."

"He'll have looked in at Vatopedi or Esphigmenou," argued the monk, who sounded as if he had not been listened to as yet.

The clockmaker stepped nearer to me, holding me with his eyes.

"A stranger begins by straying off the path, and then finds how many places for an accident?"

"You'll find him at Esphigmenou or Vatopedi," the monk insisted.

"That's likeliest," I agreed. "Klement may know something, if you run across him."

"That man cures many ailments; but he didn't cure my grandmother when God took her sight away."

"Did he try?"

"He gave her a paste of leaves; but God wanted her that way. She's dead now; but before she died she sat in a corner and ate bread. For years she sat and ate bread."

It was uncertain whether the monk's glance of sympathy was for the grandmother or the clockmaker, whose melancholy lifted after the fashion of the mists that had drifted off the flats earlier. "They say it's full of caves round here," he remarked, "and that the monastery's name means Chilia Antra (the place of a thousand caves)."

"Chilioi Andres (the place of a thousand men)," the monk corrected sharply, referring to the thousand robbers killed in the mist.

"The learned believe Chilandari likely to mean the place of the men of the chelandion—a kind of ship," I said.

"What can I, a letterless man, say against that?" the clockmaker asked.

When Makarios saw me return he stepped out of the pantry with wine and raki to wash down the salt fish, stockfish, and grilled fresh fish he had arranged in an arc round my place at table. He pointed a sensitive finger at a bowl of beans in oil to indicate which of his courses to lead off with, and changed the angle of a salad, standing back to make up his mind whether the table's sense of invitation had been improved.

He was amused over Stephen Dushan's memorial.

"That Tsar came along and found hermits outside the monastery, where they had every right to be. 'Go inside before the sun sets,' he ordered. And he drove them all into the monastery where they had no right. But kings are like that. Shall I call you for vespers?"

"Do. And perhaps Silvester will let me look round the church afterwards."

"Lie down looking at our coloured roofs."

The divan was under windows high over the court, and there was the orange-and-maroon lichen on the slated roofs to look at until three o'clock vespers—nine by the monastery clocks.

Vespers was poorly attended because of olive-picking; but the few monks who tramped in venerated the Virgin-of-the-Three-Hands, and this ikon was specially censed.

Another aspect of this ikon was the Panayia, the All-HolyOne, and the church possessed several Virgins presenting other aspects. By venerating them all the monk felt himself closer to her, and his apprehension of the ever-presence of the Virgin and her mercies and warnings sharpened.

No stress of seasonal work interrupted the succession of church services, though they might be carried out with a skeleton choir and congregation, and absent workers turn for the time being from Marys to Marthas.

Silvester, the officiating priest, wearing the dignity of bulk, came over at a seaman's roll to shake hands, his Mongolian face creased with goodwill. He might be vague over the succession of centuries, but had no misgivings about the powers of his ikons, and Makarios was equally sure. They had healed, punished, saved from fire. A third monk, who scraped candle-grease off the pavement with a chisel-edged instrument fixed on a broom handle, went out, leaving us to our subdued voices and careful footfalls.

Some opinion claims for this late-thirteenth-century Slav church of Stephen Urosh II the finest exterior on Athos, though a pleasing pink-and-white ornamentation inclines to entice the eye into by-paths when it should be pursuing the integrity of architectural line.

The dedication is to the Presentation of the Virgin, and the feast November 21. The twelfth-century opus Alexandrinum pavement and green marble slabs, bordered with petals set in fours, is a century older than the rest of the building, remaining from the original church raised by the founder, St. Simeon (in the world Stephen Nemanja), and there are remains of the original marble screen. A journeyman hand painted much of the austerity out of the fourteenth-century "Macedonian" frescoes in restoring them a century ago; but the old detachment is still traceable and the firm, slender limbs still please. Some date these frescoes at the end of the thirteenth century.

The Virgin-of-the-Three-Hands was against the bishop's throne. The staff beside it is claimed to belong to the Emperor Andronikos Komnenos; learned exquisite, seducer of queens, statesman who was to turn murderer and tyrant, but in the hours of his prolonged death faced his torturers splendidly and, from the mangy camel's back where they had set him, looked out of the single eye left and wagged his shattered jaw, crying:

"Lord God, wherefore wilt thou break a bruised reed!"

The dark, wonder-working ikon, triply hung with chains of gold votive coins, jewelled crosses, and enamelled decorations, stared sternly into the church's gloomy distances, her third hand of silver at the Child's feet. In lay opinion a fourteenth-century work; but monks believe it to have been known as the Virgin-of-Guidance and to belong to the eighth-century Greek father, St. John of Damascus.

John had used his pen so boldly against the ikonoclast, Leo the Isaurian, that the emperor addressed letters to himself in John's forged handwriting, which pointed out the advantage of attacking John's patron, the Caliph, and sent them to that potentate, who severed John's hand for the treason, and hung it up to wither. In his agony John begged for the hand in order to bury it, for he thought that would diminish the pain, and this was allowed. He fell into prayer before the Virgin-of-Guidance, who promised in a vision to re-join hand and wrist, provided the hand was afterwards employed writing hymns to God's Mother. John pressed the mutilated stump to the picture's lips, and his hand and arm became one.

The awed caliph pardoned him, and John fixed a commemorative silver hand to the lower part of the ikon, where it is to-day. The ikon went with John to the desert monastery of St. Savvas near Jerusalem, and remained there for four hundred years, until given to Savvas, Archbishop of Serbia, joint founder of Chilandari. The archbishop took it to the Serbian monastery of Studenica, where it was until 1371, when the Turks crushed the country in the final battle of the Maritza. To save the ikon it was roped to an ass, and it guided the humble animal across mountain and through river until the weary beast dropped dead where the shrine is, half a mile from Chilandari's gates.

Makarios shaded a taper and showed me another Virgin that had caused a sceptical monk who carried her one Epiphany to over-balance into the sea, where he had barely time to gasp out a confession before sinking; and a third Virgin who lacked a hand that had flown off clouting a negligent sacristan. Silvester had put on his stole, and appeared with a board on which were two candles, which he set on trestles before the screen as a preliminary to sanctifying it. He then stood the reliquaries on it in a flashing row and bent to press his lips to them. We two joined him, and waited before the silver caskets, while he touched on each saint's life and the miraculous working of the relics. Makarios pressed his lips to the glass above the yellowed bones, crossed himself three times, stooped, kissed, and thrice re-crossed himself as he straightened up. He did not insist on my doing this, a Protestant.

Silvester's glance had kindled and his voice warmed during his recitation. Then, mixing up rather much speed with his veneration, he packed all away and led us across to the refectory, a deserted chamber with seating for several score of diners.

"We've these to show you," he said, pointing a plump hand at the murals telling St. Savvas' story. "They've been greatly admired. I'm finding Jonah."

Before I was far along the walls with Makarios, Silvester returned with a monk with a close-fitting, curling beard, who looked as massive as an Assyrian statue. This was Jonah, and he carried a substantial copper mug full of rose-coloured wine. I sipped it as I admired the murals.

The colour on the walls barely warmed the barn-like chamber, which needed a hundred munching monks to become alive; but the scenes we stared up at testified to the largeness of bygone days. The men at prayer up there, who had ruled and renounced, had written themselves clearly enough across their times for the script to be legible to a painter, and no mean one, who had swept his brush up and down here to keep the diners, in the intervals of masticating their beans, dwelling on men of wider example than themselves.

"And now the needlework," someone suggested, as we stood under the portraits of the three converted robbers of the miraculous mist. Then the courtly old librarian materialized on the threshold, his keys chained to his belt.

"You wish to see our books?"

"Father, how good of you."

"We're on the way upstairs," Silvester hinted.

The librarian merely opened both hands in acquiescence, and came upstairs.

In the upstairs room, behind glass, was an imposing needlework of Christ between Mary and John the Baptist, said to have been sent to this house as a gift of Ivan the Terrible of Russia. We filed up to it between ikons laid aside for one reason or another; and age-toned golds, blues, greens, ochres, clarets, and chocolates winked and gleamed from the neighbourhood of stern, smoke-darkened countenances. My interest in a panel under a cloth caused a monk in the neighbourhood to stir uneasily. I knew why; for under this cover lies the vanished ikon struck by the Turkish captain, of which the exposed ikon of Christ beside it is the companion picture.

Athos kept internal independence by capitulating to the Turks under Mured II in 1430, nor were the monks ill-treated by their conquerors during the four centuries that the Holy Mountain made part of the Turkish Empire. But in the Greek uprising of 1821 against Turkey many monks joined the revolutionaries, which was replied to by quartering a Turkish force of three thousand men on the monasteries for nine years. Four-fifths of the monks abandoned Athos, leaving buildings to decay and the cultivated land to revert to wilderness.

Three monks remained caretaking at Chilandari, and one day the Turkish captain declared he saw a supremely beautiful woman going into the church. He pretended to be scandalized and ordered the monks to search for her. She was nowhere to be found, and the rash captain struck at an ikon with his staff, declaring: "I saw this woman." His arm withered after striking the blow, and the staff became glued to the ikon's face, and could only be wrenched free by leaving the ferrule there. But the Panayia can forgive a repentant man, and the Turk had his arm restored. The wonder-working ikon has decayed since, and lies nursed in wrappings. Its interest is in connection with a miracle little more than a century old, and the ferrule's remains, which are oval and rise up from the wood, are more substantial than the usual paint-blisters in ikons of similar tradition. I have not presumed to touch the ferrule with an impious finger; but it has been within a foot or two of my eyes. This ikon has been mentioned as lost by other writers, I think because the monks are ashamed of showing a miracle-working ikon in such a condition.

The library was across the court in a twelfth-century keep. A stone basin for blessing the water on the first of each month stood between four cypresses. Labourers were raking newly gathered olives on the pavement of the court. There was a lean-to on shovels and rakes on my remarking:

"Where I come from they talk of crushing into January."

"We shall be done by Christmas," said the monk in charge.

"What of the man who owns no olive-trees?" asked one of the labourers with a touch of impudence. "When did olives on the trees benefit any but tree-owners?"

"You eat olives here while you pick for us," the monk pointed out. "Why haven't you trees?"

"Can I have trees if I have no land? Can I have land if myfather had seven children eating bread? I've five myself, and a wife good for more."

"Have you children?" asked Jonah of the refectory, turning to me.

"No, none."

Jonah glanced from the ragged father of five to the betterclad man, and said with an air of knowing what he was talking about, "God is like that."

The librarian produced his keys at the base of the seventeenth-century keep.

Presently I was unrolling Byzantine chrysobulls, signed in the imperial scarlet. I handled the sigilla or edicts of patriarchs, Serbian and Bulgarian parchments, and Turkish firmans or decrees; and finally I turned over the leaves of a magnificent gold-lettered, illuminated quarto St. John's Gospel on white parchment, said to have been presented in the second half of the twelfth century by the Emperor Andronikos Komnenos, though other opinion argues the monastery was not in existence then, and the book probably a fourteenth-century gift of Andronikos II Palaeologos.

"One is still able to take books down off the shelves in the way those originally putting them there intended. It's not yet a matter of passing a museum's turnstile to glance into showcases," I observed.

"A good deal's missing," someone said.

"Much got destroyed everywhere before man had a hunger for the past," the librarian answered spiritedly. "An Englishman once told me his country possessed many old castles until the farmers pulled them down to build sheds and walls." They waited for me to admit this was true. "Now you shall see something no visitor has," the librarian concluded and, producing a minute key, unlocked a steel case, and laid before me the original typikon, or regulations of this house, inscribed on a discoloured parchment. "No other visitor" may have been an exaggeration, but the favour was a compliment. Chilandari's monks had preserved this document for seven centuries, and could refer at first hand to the rules of their house as laid down in the dawn of its history.

"Our fires have done harm," the librarian went on; "but now most libraries are somewhere in safety." A mischievous smile enlivened the old face, not unlike another parchment. "It's said the lost books were sometimes thought useful for stuffing broken windows. And our dead housekeepers have been accused of taking parchments for covering their pots of preserves."

"A few with a business turn sold the books by weight, Father."

The smile flickered out.

"But all our losses aren't our own fault. Turkish soldiers quartered on us after 1821 destroyed many books making cartridges."

The libraries are cared for at last, and the volumes often fantastically over-valued. Professor Spyridon Lambros, the Greek authority, has catalogued most houses for Cambridge University. Though nothing known to antiquity, and since lost, was found, numerous rare and beautiful parchments and books remain on the Mountain, and certain unique memoirs and martyrologies must exist. A few score books still remain unentered, having turned up after the cataloguing.

We drifted from library to belfry, from belfry to the cells, waiting a call from Makarios, who had left the group to get supper. In a narrow room off the gallery I was handed raisins from the miraculous vine, shaken out of a copper kettle by the slipshod donor. One would have expected a woman to have been an academic conception in his mind, for he mentioned not seeing one for fifty years. He took the heavy kettle off the shelf with a grunt, shook out the raisins, and afterwards lowered two hooked fingers through the lid-hole to secure a slip of the vine, finally holding forward in his palm three raisins and the vine-slip.

"Husband and wife eat these grapes," he explained in a voice thin with age; "he two, she one. Soak the vine-slip in holy water and sip the water before meals during forty days of marital restraint. The sipping of the holy water must be accompanied by short prayers addressed to Jesus Christ and our St. Simeon. Twenty-five repetitions to Christ in the morning; at evening to St. Simeon. The prayers are on the paper the raisins are wrapped in." He turned away for the printed wrapping, saying, "You'll know someone in the world glad of help."

The tree feels the way to the sky, the root remaining where the seedling germinated; and these Slav monks, so long absent from their countries, still had their roots where they had grown up.

Serbia or Bulgaria was in the heart of every man in this ancient house; concealed in the monk was the nationalist, eager for home news from any chance stranger who could supply it, for, as they say in Greece: "Where the baby first sees the sun is his home."

The porter sounded his mace on the gate, sending a warning downhill to the monks under the trees, and presently a thin, slow stream of men came along the road, bent under heavy sacks of olives. The day was over; to be followed by night when the monks would be called to church. Their hours in church were their hours of prayer.

3

Esphigmenou: the Coenobitic Monastery of the Tight-Girdled One

MAKARIOS NOTICED A SPLIT in my rucksack next morning just as I was about to make a start. This sent him darting off for a cobbler's thread and awl. While I sipped a cup of coffee he settled himself on the divan and started to sew, pointing a moral by telling me of spare-time lessons taken from a cobbler. At the last minute he accepted a present for the church, something less for himself, and a trifle for the cook. We shook hands affectionately.

Esphigmenou can be reached in half an hour from Chilandari, though it is easy to lose the path, which leads to the thorny stretches of the Samareia hill. This has constantly attracted hermits, but is bad ground for softer men. The saddleshaped hill hides from sight the true road running round Milutin's tower into a valley where Esphigmenou's fine old vineyards grow. Paths continue on either side of the vines to the monastery, which is so close to the sea that winter storms shoot spray up the walls.

Esphigmenou: of the Tight-girdled One. Some think this is an allusion to the squeezed situation against the sea, which, however, ignores the flat country inland, while the ruins of the original house, destroyed by landslide, are in no way cramped. Others link the name with an early abbot, Theoktistos, reputed to have bound his waist tightly as a discipline.

The ruins of the original house are to be seen. It was crushed nearly a thousand years ago in an earthquake which shook down the neighbouring hillside. The ghastly night became legendary, and although so long ago they still speak of the many monks missing in the morning. One can understand why they chose the present site away from hills.

Monks and labourers were hoeing the fine old vineyards when I climbed high above them to look at the landslide's scar. Vegetation has covered the wound for centuries. The neighbourhood appealed to a hermit, Savvas, a generation ago, sufficiently to keep him for twenty-five years on the isolated hillface. It was a long, prickly business pushing up between trees and bushes to peer into the obscure hermitage, already doorless and with a martin's pads printed in the fireplace. The anchoret had lingered about the site to keep his mind on the mutability of fortune, and his crumbling hut continued to record it.

The monastery was some distance farther off, at the sea's nearest point, in flat country, soon rising into wooded hills. Outbuildings, a kitchen garden, stonework, quinces, walnut trees, and lusty acacias projected man's influence a little way into the wilderness, but very little. The stone walls meeting in the clock-tower, a deep frescoed porch, and a pool of moving water beautified the range of buildings. Inside were some picturesque balconies. Half the buildings were new, and little was two hundred years old, yet there is documentary evidence of Esphigmenou in the eleventh century. Followers of the Latin rite raided it in the thirteenth century; it was fireswept in the fifteenth century; pirates destroyed it in the sixteenth. It was rebuilt. The Turkish occupation following the 1821 uprising brought new trouble. However, a year or two earlier a Macedonian monk, Gregorios of Melnik, had found Russia a sympathetic land because of Esphigmenou's connection with the eleventh-century hermit Anton Petchersky of Kiev, who died in a cave here in 1073. Gregorios eventually returned with the means to raise a church, and the monastery was rebuilt and enlarged within twenty years.

A gaunt, active porter, caught by surprise away from the gate, was digging round the lemon-bushes in the court. He hurried forward and led me two steps at a time up the west stairway to hand me over to a bustling guestmaster, who had an air of authority which made him seem much taller than his probable five foot three. A resonant bass voice added to his personality. As he piloted me to the reception-room he bawled into the pantry for a tray, which was produced by a muscular, beard-sprouting novice, charmed at the chance of examining a foreigner at close range.

The guestmaster made a place for himself beside me on the divan, with the fuss of a hen settling on the nest.

"You aren't hot or dusty?"

"I've only come from Chilandari, though I left the track to look at Savvas's hermitage. Another winter or two will make a complete ruin of it."

"Why shouldn't it fall down? Nobody uses it."

"Nobody thinks of taking Savvas's place up there?"

"He'd have to get our abbot's permission, which he wouldn't give easily. There are all sorts; but while I'm on earth I'm spending my time with other men."

"This neighbourhood's attracted many hermits."

"Yes," the guestmaster agreed, with a touch of house pride, "we've even the cave of St. Antony of Kiev in the hill at the back. I would have given you a fish for supper, but the boats aren't going out now because of the olive-picking. You shall have eggs."

I murmured thanks, though it crossed my mind that this was too strict a house to bother with fowls, and nothing short of one of the miracles for which the Mountain was famous would make my supper eggs new-laid. We were still gossiping when a considerable master of the semantron came into the court three storeys below to call to vespers. His black cylindrical hat was draped in the long black veil, which fell over his cloak, or raso, of the same sombre colour. This in turn concealed the black cassock, drawn in with a leather belt, on the buckle of which was moulded Christ crucified.

The monk wore his garments with style, and there was style in the arc of his mallet sweeping to meet the slim sounding-board; style in the timing, in the staccato quality of the tapping, diminuendo and crescendo. He sounded the long, insistent series of taps three times, from distant stations. "Adam! Adam! Adam!" he called, first to things that creep, then to the four-footed; and rapped a third and final call to man, said to be the call of Noah to come into the ark and be saved.

PLATE 5 *A sheet of Byzantine music as still in use on Athos. Copied from an illuminated medieval manuscript*

PLATE 6   *An archway with murals, Chilandari Monastery; and* (below)
a part of the Apocalypse mural, Vatopedi

For five minutes the monks crossed to vespers, adjusting their veils; but I stayed where I was and, an hour afterwards, watched them re-cross in procession, from church to refectory, behind their white-bearded abbot, Athanasios, black staff in hand, and the ruler of this house. A few veiled figures in that slowly-moving stream were acquaintances. Most men had taken the habit for that sufficient reason, a feeling for God. At the same time others had arrived disappointed with the dissatisfying days that make up a man's life. A few had withdrawn where no woman could follow in anger against a woman.

This was a coenobitic house under an abbot, whereas Chilandari, following the idiorrhythmic rule, was directed by a committee. Monks were more in evidence here, moving in procession, using the refectory, where visitors joined them on Sundays and feast days. Each had a simple cell to be alone in. In the idiorrhythmic monasteries the more important monks had apartments of several rooms, where they made themselves as much at home as flat-dwellers in the "world".

I decided to wander round unattended, and descended stairways to the ground, led nose first to the olive-mill. Fires glowed under steaming cauldrons, and a walking horse turned the crushing stone by everlasting circling.

Labourers in sacking overalls worked in twilight. They filled the heavy woven goathair sacks with pulped olives before stacking them in the press. Three or four men ran a capstan round like sailors. The descending press squeezed rivulets of oil from the sacks into a cauldron of steaming water. The warm water separated the unclean oil, dirty particles sinking, the refined oil rising to the surface, where it left the cauldron by a pipe which joined a second cauldron of hot water, and the process was repeated. The oil was finally skimmed off the water with a ladle, and stored in cisterns and massive jars. The oily refuse of crushed stones and skins was further processed into soap.

The monk overseer spoke through a beard growing up to his eyebrows to complain about worm in the table olives, but admitted the quality of the cooking oil to be good.

"Yes," he agreed under my pressure, "our five thousand olive trees are bearing heavily."

"There's talk of a good orange season too?"

"Our only trees are in the court; they are a small thing."

The labourers stopped running the capstan round, and leant on the bars.

"Mr., they can't do here what the Russians did at Chromitsa," one called down to me. "When a viper bit a holy father there they sent for the Erissos doctor, and he made some injections and asked for his drachmas. When had they seen the drachmas he expected? Not in twenty years. He could take the money in oranges. They'd give him two thousand oranges, and what he couldn't carry away he could eat on the spot."

"Get on with the work," said the monk. "Aren't you in charge?"

"Some fathers set the wolf to watch the sheep," cried one man, as the three started running the capstan round again.

A sudden tap on the shoulder made me turn almost into the arms of Arsenios, an old acquaintance, who walked me out into the court past a cheerful group of young monks washing horse-mushrooms at a running stream. Arsenios was about forty years old, had close-set brown eyes at the top of a long, straight nose; an unsettled type, with a big toe in the world after years as a monk.

"I heard you were here," he said, lowering his voice. "Just as I was thinking of writing."

"To me? What about?" As he remained silent, I repeated: "What about?"

"We can talk later in your room."

"Why not now?"

"It's to do with gold," he said, lowering his voice more.

"Gold?"

He nodded this time out of caution.

I regretted not feeling startled or expectant, but this could only be another story of buried treasure, of which the land was full. There was reason for the local tribe of legend-mongers. Raiders had been up and down these coasts all through the peninsula's long history, bent on robbing the monks of their accumulating church treasure. Jewels, bullion and specie must have been buried for safety on many occasions, and left unrecovered. In addition, old pagan coins often came to light. Fascinating tales went round; nevertheless I felt able to wait until Arsenios was ready to tell his tale, and said:

"To-night in my room. And now what about looking up Gregorios, who'll be baiting his hooks?"

We started northwards round the big church dedicated to the Ascension, a building in Byzantine red-and-white stripes. The walk led us to a monk threading baits at a window on the sea-wall. In the room were buoys of gourds, lines, nets and anchors; and several boats were housed near a pretty watergate. Gregorios, as salted as any fisherman, invariably appeared at the window towards evening, baiting nightlines, and was always ready to let down a net into the water, though this left his stall in church unoccupied. He was a lover of all wild animals, and the fish in the sea outside his monastery, but he could dispatch all that came his way without uneasiness, for he was a born hunter. He had had enough of the olive season.

"I've to pick up with the others," he said. "None of the larger boats have gone out for days. Where are the rowers?"

"He knows the month by the fish he pulls out of the sea, as some men tell it by stars," Arsenios remarked, leading on past the refectory, where the smoke of Turkish fires had ruined the murals. We went into the scullery, for the kitchen was as dark as a cave. Kitchen and scullery were furnished with utensils as indestructible as the thick walls they hung upon, or were propped against. Jugs and drinking-beakers were of copper; coffee-mills of brass. Man-power was the basis of everything in sight; man-power plentiful and cheap. Tree after tree had been sawn up into stairways, flooring, and doorways by carpenters building for their own generation and several to come. Heavy iron nails, with heads like half-crowns, were driven inches into massive wooden beams. Those lengths of timber would stay in place. Acres of tiled or slated roofing had to be repaired after the heavy winter winds were over; winds that had swept and banged and shaken the buildings for days on end.

The monks who were washing the mushrooms now made part of a group washing up, out of which rosy old Father Chariton sorted himself, and caught my fingers in soft, wet hands.

"A year since you were here last," he began, as he straightened up. "It must be."

"About that."

"You find me the same? Not more bent?"

"Not a bit more."

He sent for a big mug of resinated wine, which I dealt with in an eddy in the tide of washers-up. Then word came along that supper was ready. Arsenios and Chariton—one ahead, the other behind—hurried me up flights of stairs, one striding, the other rolling, then along galleries and passages to the small dining-room, already half full of talkative monks.

A place had been laid for me beside a landscape painter, a tall, bent man from Athens. It crossed my mind that the joyless glance sent in my direction was that of the hunter sighting the quarry and intending to follow to the kill. Then a monk said in a half whisper:

"He has pictures to sell. This size, and this size." The monk's square hands indicated generous sizes. "And he expects as much as you can get a hundred and a hundred and fifty eggs for. I offered him fifty lemons to paint me a Virgin this size. Pay away a hundred and fifty eggs for a picture!"

"Or more than a sack of onions, Father," I suggested, after a lightning calculation. "For that's another approach to the problem."

"Your first time on the Mountain?" I asked, as I sat down beside him.

"My first. I landed at Daphne six weeks ago, and have been moving down the coast."

"A wonderful country to paint, isn't it?"

He agreed, adding, "But now the weather's breaking up, and I must be getting back to Athens."

"Once the weather breaks, it's another matter here. In Athens you've easy winters. The monks have learnt to pass our Macedonian midnights in church; but softer men must be sure of a bed."

Monks came and went, for they enjoy seeing guests. A severe, spectacled person ceaselessly slid the beads of a black rosary along their cord. He unbent sufficiently to discuss world affairs. The monks even of this rather out-of-way house were well informed on current events: years on the Mountain failed to cure many monks of strong political views; the tall black hat, veil, and cloak of the monastic habit never quite smothered the lively-minded Greek. The wine at table brightened my opinions on world affairs, and encouraged the painter. Then the strong bass of the guestmaster spoke of the glorious occasion when the Virgin landed a few miles lower down the coast at Iviron. This caused an intellectual to lean forward and assert:

"The Panayia has never appeared in flesh on this Mountain."

A worried silence followed, and the speaker continued in some haste: "She has appeared in vision to Athanasios, to Maximos, to Kosmas, to other fortunate men. But not in flesh."

The stir of monks crossing themselves passed round the room, and the spectacled monk's smile cut like the east wind.

The conversation changed to the neo-martyrs, St. Timotheos and St. Agathangelos.

Agathangelos was a lad before the mast, and the captain of the ship he sailed in threatened him with blows, until, at sight of the sword's naked blade, he foreswore Christ. He escaped to Esphigmenou, where he finally took the great habit, though as a former apostate he might only receive communion at the moment of death. He was informed in a dream that his melancholy would be cured by martyrdom. He sailed for Smyrna, with a priest to administer the last sacraments, and publicly renounced Islam to the Turkish authorities. He suffered by the sword on April 18, 1818.

A Thracian Turk carried the wife of Timotheos off to a harem, and to recover her and safeguard his daughter he embraced Islam. A spiritual unrest led him to enclose his wife in a nunnery, while he went to the Holy Mountain. In the quiet Virgin's Garden the voice of conscience loudened, and after being prepared for death by one of Esphigmenou's priests Timotheos went to Adrianople in 1820, rejected the Turkish faith and was executed.

We spent so long over supper that the guestmaster dismissed us to our bedrooms, booming good night down the passage after our heels. Arsenios came with me to my room, where we took turns staring down from a window to the lapping sea, storeys below. He appeared first on one side of me, then on the other.

"About that gold," I said, suddenly, giving him a lead.

"I thought of writing," he began. "Monks know nothing; but you may have heard if an instrument has been invented which finds gold under the ground?"

"I seem to remember reading something of the sort, though the whole world would be using it if there was much in it. A water-diviner once walked me in front of him with his fingers above my elbows, and certainly the twig in my hands nearly bent double at the spot where he said there was water."

"I'm taking you to St. Theodore's to-morrow. It's only forty oar strokes over the water, and if I'm missed from the olives and our abbot asks why, we'll say you wanted me to find you a certain flower; for a flower like flesh grows there. Four thousand gold coins are buried under those few olive trees, or in the rough country to the right."

"But, Father, I'm no more likely to find the place than you. Who buried the treasure?"

"Greeks held men up for ransom after the Turkish occupation in 1821. One died in prison, after telling of the gold. A fisher-boy dug there about thirty years ago until the monks sent him away. Monks are like that. They don't keep in mind four thousand gold coins for the monastery. You can suggest the best place to-morrow."

"And who's digging, if we find a likely spot?"

"It can't be done by daylight, or the digging would be stopped."

The realization that I wouldn't be called on for spadework under the abbot's eye made me feel easier. And the gates were locked from sunset to dawn, which seemed to rule out night work.

"I'll join you and have a look round to-morrow," I said, "and if we miss the gold, there's always the flower like flesh."

Arsenios looked disappointed in me, and left soon afterwards.

The novice who brought me coffee in the morning lingered to finger my pyjamas. He told me he still had the top half of his own, brought from "the world". The monks ate at eight o'clock, or two by the striking of their own clocks, and afterwards I sat down with the painter to fried eggs, white cheese, and macaroni soup. The spectacled monk, Damian, was already in his corner; but I obtained a true light on his quality only after coming on Arsenios, who waited to catch me in the passage.

"When do we start for St. Theodore's?" I asked, set up by breakfast.

"Damian has been to our abbot about us," Arsenios answered sulkily. "He heard we were going to St. Theodore's to find flowers like flesh, instead of olive-picking, and he went to Athanasios."

"And what did the abbot say?" I asked in some embarrassment.

"What Damian intended he should say. That I'm to pick up olives. Monks are like that. They're small men, and see only a short way."

"He thought you were getting out of picking up olives. He hadn't grasped the possible loss of four thousand gold coins."

"It would have been the same thing, if I'd mentioned the gold. He hasn't the imagination to believe in it. Well, there it is."

The sun came out and lured me on to a gallery where Chariton found me examining a burst shoe.

"We'll fix that," he exclaimed happily, and he swept me up and down stairs, travelling just ahead of me with his cloak, his raso, ballooning. He had shed his old feverish life of the world to the last scale, and like the sloughed serpent received a gleaming new skin for the outworn one. He declared that a dream led to his change of heart. He had seen a seashore in this dream, and rising beside it a monastery's walls, forming so clear a picture, and framing so insistent an invitation, that he set off in search. He was at that time in America. Finally he reached the Holy Mountain, and recognized Esphigmenou as the monastery of his dreams. He took the habit, but it took him a few years to break off all interest in the old life. He spoke of joy in church each morning in receiving the blessed bread, and kept an interest in racing form, for he had been a bookmaker in the world. He was a contented old man, anxious to perform a few kindnesses while there was time, and as separated from the worries that once besieged him as he was from the field-glasses and leather bag by which punters knew him.

We knocked at a door, and were called into a room festooned with clumsy black shoes, by a cobbler in homespun. He worked at a table littered with leather scraps and tins of nails. Though the room was under-lighted and the cobbler well into his seventies he stitched without glasses, and doubled over deftly to pull off my shoe and damp it.

"The monastery gives us this old man," said Chariton. "The monk gets new shoes made for him when necessary. A monk does work set him, and the monastery in return looks after him, and it leaves him time to remember God. You can't miss a service here like they do in the idiorrhythmic monasteries. The abbot makes his round in church for anyone missing, and asks about it afterwards: 'Why weren't you in church?

There's our sickroom for the sick man.' Our abbot, Athanasios, is a clever man. No, he hasn't many letters, but he has a head. The days are all the same here, and I never want to go outside again. I've been broke, cleaned out, ruined twice on the race-course in one day in the States. That can't happen here."

"How many monks has Esphigmenou?"

"Sixty-two or three all told."

Two other monks sat in a corner, and I suddenly recognized the monastic historian, Barlaam.

"Forgive me, Father. I didn't see who it was. Do you feel like letting me have an opinion?"

Barlaam's eyebrows lifted expressively in his intellectual face.

"This is it. The map places Herodotos' Olophyxos as those ruins off the road to Vatopedi marked as Old Village; but it can be argued Olophyxos stood nearer Chilandari."

Barlaam pursed his lips in thought.

"Old Village is the ruins of the Vlach settlement belonging to Alexios Komnenos's day," he explained. "The shepherds brought their women to live on the Mountain through laxity. Half the land went to Esphigmenou on their expulsion, and half to Vatopedi."

The monk who sat beyond him looked thoughtfully down his broad nose at these revelations; but the historian was not to be balked, and continued judicially, "There have been periods of spiritual decadence, followed by reform, all through the Mountain's history."

Descendants of these same nomad Wallachian shepherds Barlaam referred to still arrive in winter to pasture goats up to the Mountain's frontier. They have done it for a thousand years, once coming down from the Danube, and now from the Albanian frontier. The scandal Barlaam touched on developed in the eleventh century, and it took a hundred years to clear it up. Three hundred shepherd families invaded the Mountain with their women, the latter becoming so useful to the monks as housewives, and amiable as companions, that the frailer fathers had to be excommunicated in numbers, seriously depopulating the Mountain.

The way the cobbler tossed my tip into his nail-box made Chariton wince.

"We've so little use for money here," he whispered, as he pressed my arm comfortingly, and started to his feet to pilot me out between strings of new shoes and a heap collected for patching.

"To light a candle in church," I suggested, to repair my error.

We parted company outside, and I went on my way to see St. Antony's cave. Most of the monks were under the olive-trees, but two or three rolled out scalded wine-barrels to air in the court. I passed the painter sketching a stone bridge. The graceful span was just wide enough, lofty enough, and strong enough for the work of linking the banks of an unimportant stream.

"There's something very satisfying about this bridge," I said, pausing beside the painter, whose eyes were two slits as he worked. "Is it its economy?"

"I noticed it yesterday, and now the light's right. I won't be able to sell it. There's nothing to suggest where it comes from. Buyers must have a monk in pictures of the Holy Mountain. But few bits of building succeed like this little bridge."

"Some fathers are less graceful," I said. "May I have a look at your work later on?"

There might be something to take away, priced no higher than a sack of onions; for this lean fellow, expending canvas and paint on an unsaleable bridge, invited sympathy.

The cave, which I identified by an ikon of St. Antony, lay high up in the cliff's face, overlooking the sea. It was cheek by jowl with a second cave, which had been occupied by a hermit, Matthew, who died half a century ago. The wooden planks in the second retreat may have been his bed. The saint's cave drew me back to it, and I lingered, sobered by its austerity. A cottage, built in the days when the spot attracted Russian pilgrims, crumbled nearby. It was all so desolate, although monks gathered annually in the chapel above the two caves for St. Antony's festival.

Sea chafed the roots of the cliff far below where there was a third cave, once occupied by a nameless man from Constantinople, who left his bones in it. A rash passer-by once removed them, but as he immediately fell ill with a fever, he hurried them back again.

A hermit, Johannes, made a home here to his last day on earth. Then, having a premonition that life was lived out, the old man found his way down those difficult rocks to the monastery door, on which he knocked. The porter opened it to a dead body.

Why have a few dreamers the gift of wakening while the many slumber on?

Wakening to the transcendence of God. God in the stones, in the sky, in the trees. In the gnat. And the trumpeting elephant. On with the sandals. Down from the shelf with the script. Along the highway to reality.

Wakening to the Immanence of God. Realizing the presence of two extended arms, tirelessly held out. The inviting, untrembling arms of God. Closer, closer. And at last a kiss! To the desert! To the cave!

I started downhill, to be accosted at the bottom by a monk who raised a shaggy head over the kitchen-garden wall to ask me to meet an English-speaking labourer. We followed rows of cabbages to a cottage. The lay gardener came out, dressed in a sack over rags. He spoke fluent English. He was an oddly-built man, inches too short, light in flank, but with a barrel of a chest, heavy shoulders, and a beard from ear to ear which held its own with any on the Mountain.

The monastery gave this man bed, board, and a pittance in exchange for his labour. He had been an army sergeant in the Greek war with Bulgaria, and a merchant sailor in the first World War. He had helped in the attack on Gallipoli, and, strangely enough, so had I.

"Those good times!" he cried. "All those young men about! Those horses! Those fine ships! To their memory!" And he tipped his glass of raki down his throat.

"To their memory," I echoed, holding a glass of raki up to the window-light. "Those men and horses filing over Egypt's sands to the water-troughs. Why does youth steal away, with never a glance back?"

"The boys swam in the sea with the shells singing over them! Those good days! In 1916 I took a cargo for the Russian army, from England to Archangel. The sun was shining all night."

His face glowed, his mane of hair shook, then his fire turned to ashes, and I preserved myself against melancholy with the heel of the raki bottle.

I was on the painter's bed before vespers, capitulating to a picture of both sizes. He had developed a paint-saving technique by leaving gaps of bare canvas; but offered a generous surface for the buyer's drachmae. Later I got him to sketch a damaged burial tablet in the court, from the pagan town of

Aige, which the monks claimed to have been brought from a monastic farm on Sithonia.

The weather degenerated during the night, and it still poured at 5 a.m., with the sea rising against the wall. It was St. Luke's day, and there was additional ceremony, and so I went to the Liturgy. Though rain fell and the wind blew outside, priest and deacon moved in a golden light inside the church, and the chanting of the choirs mounted into the drum of the dome, and we freshmen of eternity undertook one more exercise in the schools. An autumn night had turned into a stormy dawn when the veiled monks advanced in procession from the choirs to receive the blessed bread, followed by the novices, and then by the labourers.

I examined the reputed seventh-century miniature mosaic of Christ, which some outstanding craftsman graded with sufficient cunning for the face to appear painted, rather than built up of marble fragments, in the light of this church. The masterpiece has survived the test of a German expert's magnifying glass. The sanctuary preserved a piece of the True Cross, set in a golden cross quickened by the white, crimson, and green fires of precious stones; and one of the reliquaries held the head of St. Agathangelos.

Nave was divided from narthex by a curtain on rings. This was replaced at important festivals with a cloth-of-gold embroidery brought down from the library; a sumptuous but unsuitably medallioned church decoration for which Napoleonic associations are claimed. Some see in it the Emperor's tent or canopy.

Most interesting among some three or four score parchments in the library was a damaged eleventh-century calendar of saints, full of lively illustrations.

I ran across Arsenios, sheltering in the open loggia from wind and rain. We waited for the morning meal, while he brooded over the neglected treasure. He said, as the clocks struck, "Once kings and generals competed to become monks, and made the monkish world noteworthy; men who had ruled states came to rule monasteries, and monks had experience of wealth and learning. But now men become monks when they're short of food. Our world's full of little men. Look at the way Damian went to our abbot about St. Theodore's. He'd report a fly if he knew it was female."

We crossed to the refectory, led by Athanasios handling his abbatial staff. He sat at the side of a side-table on week-days, and at the top of that table on Sundays. At festivals his place was at the head of the high table, the middle of the three in the room. A place was given me near him, among the elders. Monks of lower rank, the servants, labourers, and mendicants, were at a table on the other side of the gloomy, frescoed refectory.

Athanasios struck a bell to permit eating, and sounded it again at the meal's end. Nobody spoke, but a reader in the pulpit instructed us from the church fathers. The polished copper vessels winked. After grace at the second bell, we walked in procession to the church opposite for a brief thanksgiving; and no set work following, many monks withdrew for a siesta.

The Greek and Slav monks on the Mountain were different. The larger, blue-eyed Slavs were slower in movement, stronger voiced; suggested a reserve of physical power. The vivider, brown-eyed Greeks were full of vitality; shot instantly into mobility and out of it. While the Slav slowly made up his mind, the Greek gesticulated and leapt into thought. Goliath lived beside David.

The Slav devotion inclined to be by way of the heart, the Greek by way of the mind. The Slav understood reverence, dignity, music. The Greek sometimes became a little at home in his services. But the Russian owed his religion to the Greek. Strange that the individualistic Greek had proved so conservative in his Church, which had remained unchanged for more than fifteen hundred years. He found this a matter for pride.

4

Zographou: the Coenobitic Monastery of the Painter

I LEFT ESPHIGMENOU EARLY in the afternoon and climbed for half an hour in a spray of rain. I followed a cobbled road which led through macchie to a shrine and a cross. Flocks of wood-pigeons swept with a rushing sound along the hillsides. The Zographou road began falling after the cross, and passed under the Chilandari-Karyes telephone line, when it was time to keep an eye open for an inconspicuous path running righthanded towards a long, desolate valley.

I followed this, and tramped across sodden country where pig and jackal had left fresh tracks, and a rain-fed stream was perpetually in the way. Ash-trees had turned colour, and there was a last blue campanula. Then I stood still to give a black-and-orange salamander time to waddle across the road. The path lifted itself out of the wet soon afterwards, along forested slopes, and reached a point where the cypresses round Zo-graphou's chapel of the Annunciation stood up on the skyline. The track finally ran out into opener country, near a white shrine and its cypresses, a few hundred feet below the monastery.

Zographou looks best from the sea road, with its impressive stone walls rising from trees. It grows barrack-like closer at hand, and this approach from Esphigmenou presents the walker with the unweathered surfaces of squared stone less than a century old.

Vespers were rapped on the semantron while I was too far down the slope to be on time, and I cooled off on a coping in the inner court, among walnut trees dropping their leaves. The great sad leaves drifted off the boughs with the melancholy of time going.

Zographou's monks have not hesitated to trace their monastery's beginning back into a past more distant than probable, and claim as founders three nobles of Ochrida, Bulgaria's ancient capital, said to have taken the vows in the days of Leo the Wise, 886–912. Smyrnakes, Esphigmenou's historian, finds a mention of the monastery in a document of 980, which can be reconciled with the opinion that Zographou came into existence as a cell dependent on a house since crumbled away, and rose to sovereign rank towards the end of the thirteenth century, after benefits conferred by Andronikos II. But another tradition speaks of it as reduced to a cell through Michael VIII Palaeologos' ambition to reconcile Eastern with Western Church, which brought about the fall of the Empire of Nicaea, and placed Constantinople in his grasp.

In the four centuries leading up to the fall of Constantinople to the Turk, some thirty attempts were made to bring Greek and Latin churches into one communion, and an ephemeral union was effected three times. But the majority of Athonite monks never acquiesced in the Latin rite, choosing to suffer, and the crimes of the Unionists are still remembered.

Michael VIII found that one way to defend his empire against western authority was to negotiate with successive popes for a union of the Latin and Greek churches. Blowing hot and cold according to the military position and internal difficulties with his subjects, he finally induced John Vekkos, soon to be patriarch, to agree to the primacy of Gregory X, and won the consent of a number of bishops. In 1274 Gregory held an œcumenical council at Lyons, to which Michael VIII sent representatives, and on July 6 of that year the union of the Churches was achieved for the second time, in the face of strong hostility from Greek clergy and laymen. Athonite monks underwent various trials for their obstinacy, and a monument raised in Zographou court about 1872, to twenty-six martyrs burned by the Latinizers in a tower believed to have stood on this spot, adds history, though not beauty. In the same connection, the small eighteenth-century church nearby dedicated to the Falling-Asleep-of-the-Virgin affords an honourable place on the screen to the ikon known as the Virgin-of-the-Salutations.

The ikon also became known as the Virgin-of-the-Warning after a recluse of that day was warned by it to hurry to the monastery and inform any monks unprepared for martyrdom to flee without argument. He set off, to find the ikon ahead of him at the monastery gate. In spite of the hermit's warning and the ikon's miraculous journey, twenty-six monks refused to fly and withdrew into the tower, bearing the ikon up the stairs with them. The tower proved a death-trap, for the creatures of Michael VIII set it on fire, and the monks perished in the flames. Yet the ikon was hardly scorched when lifted out of the cinders, and to-day is on the screen of the smaller of the two churches in the court. Some say it controls forest fires.

Report speaks of Michael VIII restoring the house afterwards, and life returned to the monastery about 1500, though little can be pointed out that is two centuries old. The house became coenobion in 1850, has always been Slav, and numbers many Macedonians. It has suffered the loss of rich Bessarabian lands, but still owns valuable tracts of forest.

Vespers was ending as I walked quietly into the New Katholikon, or larger of the red-and-white churches in the cobbled court. Built at the start of the nineteenth century, and frescoed in 1817, it is dedicated to St. George, festival April 23. This large church, not a century and a half old, was mellowing ahead of time, the surrounding forest seeming to help it.

The stalls were half empty on account of field work under the olives. I drew near the south-east pillar supporting the ikon of St. George alluded to in the monastery's name. The house's three founders, the nobles Moses, Aaron, and John, failing to agree over the dedication of the monastery— whether to the Virgin, St. Nicholas or St. George—resorted to divine direction. They locked a wooden panel in the church, and fell into prayer outside. After praying for a long time they agreed to go in, and found the panel miraculously painted with St. George's picture. The divine direction was accepted, and the monastery dedicated to St. George, and called Zographou: of the Painter.

There are men to doubt most things, and a visiting Bishop, questioning the picture's miraculous origin, once poked a finger at the left cheek beside the nose. There it stuck. A knife was brought after tugging failed, and the unholy finger-tip left in the picture, where the pilgrim may stare at it to-day. Actually what is seen resembles a swirl of paint, and is less remarkable than the ferrule on Chilandari's ikon which was struck by the Turk. In lay opinion the ikon is likely to be fifteenth-century work and shows Italian influence.

A second ikon of St. George, against the north-east column, is said to have floated to the Mountain from distant Arabia on a lighted sea-way. Some relate that it landed below Vatopedi. There should have been no doubt for which monastery it was intended, only Zographou's monks could lift it; other monks found it of unearthly weight. Yet Vatopedi's greedy fathers demanded a trial, and an unbroken mule or ass was led out of the field, and the ikon roped to it. The beast, under heavenly direction, travelled to the ridge west of Zographou and, scrambling to the summit, fell dead, indicating the destination. Zographou's monks hurried the picture into the church, but it was found back on the ass's ridge on the morning, the process being repeated three times. Then St. George appeared to the abbot, and consented to the ikon's remaining in the church if the monks built a chapel on the ridge, and for certain feasts it is carried there.

The Virgin, She-Who-Answers-Prayer, a chancel mural, answered the thirteenth-century Bulgar, Kosmas, when he prayed to her to be directed along salvation's road. The monk heard Mother asking Son to clear up his uncertainty. "Kosmas must exchange the monastery's shelter for a hermitage," was the answer. The monk accepted the direction, penetrated into the gorge beginning a mile from the monastery, climbed the difficult precipice up to a shelving-in of rock, deprived some beast of a den, and settled there.

The big withered leaves still sailed gently groundwards from the walnut trees on my return that way after vespers. An airy, spacy mule-barn, on a rise, was full of munching animals, chained to mangers. I looked through the doorway just as a run of hoof-thuds broke out, and a squealing beast began spinning round in the half-light, flashing shod feet; it looked like half a dozen of them. Riot spread as new victims began kicking back and biting, and the shouts of two or three leaping muleteers, and the run of halter chains over wooden mangers, magnified the din. The solitary level voice belonged to a spectacled monk in charge, who had the courage and agility of his best helpers, and gave the orders establishing quiet.

The glossy animals were lazily munching again when I left, and in a matter of minutes I fell into a net spread by a bored gendarme, who had taken his belt off for the day, and unhooked his collar. This castaway risked breaking his neck by leaning over a balcony to attract me.

The civil police are quartered at Karyes under a commandant, and deal with non-ecclesiastical offences. Outside stations are at Lavra and Zographou, where a sergeant and his men keep an eye on the empty country to the frontier. They are woe-begone exiles in a womanless land, where alternatives to duty are communion with nature and opportunities to join the monks in church. Marriage is forbidden in the force to all below the rank of sergeant, and, though cheap living may afford separated sergeants some consolation, most gendarmes are bachelors in the position of star-crossed lovers. Card games must be played in secret, the upholders of law becoming lawbreakers on sitting down to a pack; musical instruments may never be touched. A Daphne gendarme I once knew brought a guitar to his exile, and turned to the solace of its strings on the first lonely evening. No sooner were the comforting bars of a cabaret melody vibrating on the quiet air of that little roadstead than the monk in charge arrived with a kilted ecclesiastical policeman at his heels to order the instrument back on its peg.

Our coffee attracted a second gendarme, who apologetically showed us a volume of sermons, the only book he could find after reading his newspaper from cover to cover. The three of us settled on chairs round an empty grocery box covered with coffee cups, raki glasses, and cigarettes. Powerful Slav monks were returning from work in a long, slow string bending under bulging, oil-stained sacks. They passed on to the nearer buildings, except for two, both empty-handed, who came over to us. One was the owner of a fan-shaped beard fading through every ruddy shade to grey. His companion was a rougher type. He picked up the gendarme's book of sermons without being able to read it, and seemed to sniff at it. The other monk glanced at the title and said to the borrower:

"If you run out of newspapers often enough, we'll end by making a wise man of you."

"Finished the last advertisements yesterday evening," the gendarme said ruefully.

"Well, talking won't get the olives spread. And on top of that the wine-barrels have soured." The monk now turned directly to me, "I've come to tell you to come in when the signal sounds for the gates closing. We'll see you get supper before long."

"Thanks, Father. What soured the wine-barrels?"

"Carelessness somewhere. Why do things happen?"

"I left them scalding barrels at Esphigmenou."

"There they've good wine, and look after it."

Both monks passed on out of sight. The forest, a valuable possession yielding this house a steady income from timber, increased the sense of isolation, which was, however, never quite absent from any house at close of day. Then each range of buildings, though standing for centuries on the spot, tended to become an isolated island in an ocean of rock and macchie. This feeling of isolation accentuated the need for self-sufficiency, and underlined the value of the bakers, doctors, dentists, smiths, and carpenters, now using their trades and practising their professions as monks.

The tempting flocks of heavy wood-pigeons sweeping strongly by in noisy rushes led talk to the local game, the pigs, hares, and protected roebuck, and I was asked for additional details of a notable shot, delivered by night in a melon-patch, which passed through a raiding pig to slay its twin on the farther side. We passed to snakes, for I wanted light on a serpent of python like dimensions said to exist on the Mountain. For three summers one was reported by a dry stream near Prosphorion. It constantly startled the peasants, though it never crossed my path, in spite of the fact that I constantly stalked it. A smith had joined the group, and he declared that a very large snake turned up from time to time near the fountain."

How thick?" I asked. His glance played about a fine young walnut tree.

"Not as big as some," he said after a judicial pause. "For two hundred drachmas I'll turn it into a belt for you."

"Well," I replied dubiously, finding myself less anxious to carry the remains of a moderate serpent round my waist than to look at an outsize living one, "you admit to larger. In any case, it must be hibernating."

"God will know that," said a muleteer, "but I know a goatherd like this right hand of mine knows this left hand. He grazed his goats near Lavra. Those goats had a way of going into a cave out of the sun, and every day or two a goat was missing. So he thought of looking inside, but the hair stood up on his dog's back every time he started to go in, so he thought: 'Now if I go in and find something there, what will it be? Why not stand out here where God has stood me? The ant grows wings and flies before it dies.' A hermit came by. 'Oh, a great snake lives in there,' the hermit said. 'Take your goats out.' 'See if you can get the goats out, Elder,' suggested the goatherd. 'The snake will be used to you, and God will give you a thousand years in an armchair for such a kindness.' 'I'm busy,' the hermit said, going on through the forest. So in went my friend, and at the black end of the cave was a coiled serpent with a goat in its teeth. Such eyes! Such scales! Na!" The speaker flung up his chin expressively.

The gendarme gave a despairing cry, and grasped the raki bottle.

"Fancy the fate of a man more likely to meet one of those than a girl!" he exclaimed.

Sunset, and the closing of the gates ended the discussion.

A bell tolled at seven o'clock (our 1 a.m.) for matins, and the rapping of the semantron in the next half-hour set off the jackals. They howled in waves.' The guestmaster's tray arrived with the dawn; and Serge, a pleasant old monk, led me from the tap where I was shaving to give an opinion on a pair of antique carpets in his cell. They had acquired their antiquity more from moth than age. There are unlikely to be valuable carpets on Athos to-day, inasmuch as an Armenian went round the Mountain some time ago doing even better than the genie of Aladdin by offering two new carpets for one genuinely old.

The path to Prosphori had stretches which needed daylight to travel over. The wall must be crossed before dark. I started early and skirted the hill the ass climbed with the ikon. Later the road dipped over a bridge, and inclined upward along a forested valley, and passed St. Kosmas' cave in half an hour. It is a shelving in of the cliff with a chapel glued beside it, overlooking thousands of tree-tops. I risked being late and left the road, to follow a faint track through scrub and timber to a concealed stream-bed; and afterwards shouldered uphill, still through saplings, to the iron ladders secured into the cliff-face. Though badly rusted, and flaking in my hands, they looked safe; and I pulled myself up, rung by rung, ladder by ladder, to the platform before the saint's deserted cave. Six hundred years ago he had stared from this eyrie over the tree-heads at leagues of other trees filling other valleys, after flight from a marriage arranged by his parents. The Virgin's words, addressed to him through the ikon She-Who-answers-Prayer, directed him here.

The rising road continued to a fork, the straighter prong at once descending, the second leading seawards over a ridge before taking me steeply down into country covered with macchie. Two charcoal-burners came to rest on axe and crowbar with lowering expressions. They turned their heads after me like owls. Men who stayed for months on the Mountain working in the forests grow as wild as the eagles and jackals whose company they keep. They devour acres of scrub for charcoal, but little harm is done. The wilderness returns to forest in a few years.

St. Philip's was in sight at one time on the opposite ridge, and then a jangle of bells loudened until a string of mules filed out of the bushes, steered by a couple of men sitting sideways and drumming the beasts' sides with their heels. There were boar tusks and blue beads on the mules' bell-straps, against the evil eye. I came soon afterwards to a farm-house at sea level which sheltered a handful of Zographou's monks. They kept a few hens, and I asked one, who offered me water, how many went to the foxes.

"There are enough for the foxes and for us," was his answer.

The few fowls on the Mountain are usually kept far from the monasteries. The female cat problem lies in the hands of charcoal-burners, and male cats are kept in the monastic barns and storehouses. Domestic animals, fattened on the grazing lands, must all be male.

The exacting walk, up and down slopes of decaying granite and across wastes, was in sight of the long sheet of blue sea, where porpoises cruised. An eagle slowly wound out patterns in the sky. The stony track passes the valuable vineyards of Monoxylites, Dionysiou's metorchi or farm.

It was good walking weather, with a threat of rain, and presently the sea blackened round the Three Brethren rocks, and waves began running out of the north-west. Clouds bundled over the sky, and the sea's far edge was threshed white by oncoming storm. A first puff of wind arrived, followed by a blast bending everything, after which I ran for a large tree, and arrived neck to neck with the storm, which came tearing after me over the rocks. The sky opened, rain hissed along the ground and spurted up. The groaning trees leaked faster. I hugged the lee, and then the squall swept on, and I continued marching, no worse than half drowned.

The path skirted vineyards and dipped past a distilling barn. I poked into it on the chance of a pick-me-up. Only a bat could see in the dark; but a raised, angry voice was a guide. An old Russian monk, like a gnome, was bowing and bobbing this way and that before three half-amused Greek listeners, saying: "'My Lord Abbot,' I shall say to him next time, 'it's work, work, work all day long for my kind with you. Run uphill there for me. Good! Now run higher. That's you, my Lord Abbot; but has a man ever been made like the angels on Jacob's ladder? . . .'"

I coughed, and four silent monks of the humbler sort waited for me to reach the boiler where they were distilling the season's raki from grape-skins. I call it raki, for one hears no other name for it; but technically it is cheepira, raki being an island product. The ouzo of the city café is a brew of similar origin, flavoured with aniseed. The Mountain's raki keeps a high standard.

One of the Greek monks cleaned out a liqueur glass with the ball of his thumb. He filled the glass from a long-necked bottle and handed it to me, remarking, with a nod towards the old Russian:

"Monks get angry, but forget again."

The first offering went down my throat without result; but a second began recovery, which the third completed.

There remained three hours' daylight, and I went on through the bushes, until I was immediately above the pretty Russian skete of Thebais. A few monks were still picking up olives under the trees at Kamena, once the squabbling ground of Kolovou monastery and the Erissiotes, who claimed the grazing rights.

"Has Basil sent you down to help?" I asked a monk from Chromitsa.

"There's always too much work for the two in the cottage at this time of the year," he answered as he straightened up into a gigantic pillar of a man. "Have you come far?"

"From Zographou. Not so many miles; but all ups and downs."

"Who can say why God wishes the land that way?"

The path narrowed and became very difficult as the light began to go out. It led high above a recluse's orange grove. But I crossed the wall in the afterglow into easy country. In Prosphori the villagers had gone into their cottages for the night, leaving their dogs in command of the roads.

5

Kastamonitou: the Coenobitic Monastery of the Man of Kastamoni

ANEMONES AND ERICA were in bloom by the New Year. The colder weather increased the red mullet. Mules loaded with firewood passed children dragging home brushwood for the ovens. On January 6 gusts of wind swept down from the whitened hills, blasts shaking and sucking at the windows. Flags flown for the Blessing of the Waters cracked joylessly over the cottage doors as the priest passed in procession to throw the cross into the sea at the shoreside service. Three swimmers raced into the icy water for it.

The day was Christmas Eve beyond the wall, and a boat had been tossing off the jetty from noon to take me to Kastamonitou for Christmas and the feast of St. Stephen. I was asked to wait for David, a committee-man from Kastamonitou, who had come to the village to buy fish. This delayed the start. He arrived on the jetty at last, wrapped in a double twist of crimson muffler which contrasted vividly with his black habit. He urged and directed an assistant who staggered under two heavy wooden boxes full of fresh fish.

The boat pitched and rolled into a blizzard from the moment of casting off, so much movement quickly paling the face of David's man, who passed from the sphere of usefulness. Abreast Chromitsa's arsenal the calendar retrograded from the Epiphany to Christmas Eve. David, who kept his colour well, peered critically into the boxes of half-frozen mullet, thrusting an energetic, weather-beaten face out of the crimson muffler. He was bleak with cold and disappointment.

"All I could get to add to thirty okes now at the monastery. We need a hundred and fifty, two hundred okes, or we'll be serving stock fish. But a catch in this weather!"

The white cone of the Mountain rose beyond leagues of snowfields. Then sleet drove us under the lee of the dodger for an hour's beating up the coast. We crouched without saying a word until David, miraculously informed, exclaimed:

"Manoli! Now there'll be fish!"

A broad-beamed boat was coming in sight through the moving snow-curtains. Three icicled rowers stood at the sweeps. There was no fish to hand over, but some bawled promises satisfied David, who brought his head back into the muffler, and remarked with assurance:

"St. Stephen will see we are sent fish."

He sank back under the lee of the dodger more satisfied. His energy, acumen, and readiness to go outside his monastery made him valuable, and eventually caused him to be monastic representative on the Holy Assembly, work which generally kept him in Karyes, and occasionally sent him to Salonika, and even Athens. One was drawn to his face in church—devout, sincere, glad. One was drawn to his face in repose—intelligent, sympathetic, ready. The noisy blast stung, the slow boat pitched and rolled; he sat intent on reaching the monastery and throwing himself into final preparations for the feast.

A prolonged manœuvre up to Kastamonitou's arsenal finally landed us, and we took refuge in Gerasimos's shoreside house. The resentful old man left his own stove to light one to keep us alive until mules came down from the monastery a thousand feet above. David, respected and feared by the indolent for his appalling energy, passed restlessly in and out of the humble rooms, raking the stove, looking for firewood, instead of depending on the caretaker, and glancing at the sky, out of which snow fell increasingly. He made the stove roar, then swept into another room for no better reason than to leave the one he was in, and Gerasimos said bitterly:

"The day after the feast the new committee is chosen. If he gets in again and I have him over me next year, I'll take off my raso and go back to sea, sixty years old though I may be."

Gerasimos, a monk of the humbler sort, was too fond of cigarettes, and his own ease, to be completely successful in a strict house, and he spent his days in exile down here, where he had no more church than he liked to make for himself, and no more work than to take messages from passing boats, and direct arrivals.

David re-entered in time to hear us mention the abundant olive crop, and became so charged with devotion that he sat down to repeat Kastamonitou's legend connected with their ikon, the Virgin-who-makes-reply-to-Man.

"Not a drop of oil in our jars after a ruinous olive year. Not a drop," he said with emotion. "Nothing to light the church lamps with on the eve of a festival. The lamenting sacristan continued praying to our Virgin for advice and help until he sank from weariness to the church floor. Then he heard her direct him to the oil jar under the pavement. He went there, and found the jar immediately under her full to the brim with oil. He took the great habit in gratitude. We've never gone without since, nor shall while our Virgin looks after us."

David's face glowed with his story. Gerasimos went out, to shuffle in with news of the mules, and some sharp advice about reaching the monastery before dark. David threw off a slight weakness, and was first through the door to glance over the animals for shortcomings. The weather had worsened; a high wind, charged with snow, howled in long gusts, and dark was coming on.

"Aren't you putting on more than that?" he demanded, rounding on Gerasimos, as the old man followed to see us off.

"I'm not going up at all," Gerasimos snapped.

"You are coming up."

"I'm coming up for St. Stephen's."

"You're coming up for Christmas. When were you in church last? A monk, and planning to miss Christmas. Don't let it become a matter for the abbot."

Gerasimos disappeared with anything but a festive look, to reappear in a newer raso, with a muffler round his throat and an umbrella under

an armpit. Four mules were standing outside, turning away from the
weather, and while the fish boxes were roped to one, the two monks and
myself settled in the wide, wooden saddles with variegated saddlecloths.
But pleasure in riding mules is lessened by the poor command a head-chain
gives. Gerasimos took over the muleteer's animal, leaving that individual
his two large feet.

The mules knew every step of the way to stables, and swung powerfully
uphill through olive-trees to a cobbled path in the forest. The monastery
owns five thousand olive-trees, and vineyards which produce up to four
thousand gallons of wine. David was at both ends of the procession at once,
and fell out with the muleteer, who had a string of complaints until
silenced by a command thrown back over the elder's shoulder, as the
climbing mule flung him about like a tossing boat.

"That's enough. Not a word more, if you don't want to be in trouble."

We rode always higher and through trees, the mules lifting us
forward into the snow-curtains which were discharged out of the sky.
Just before dark Kastamonitou's roofs, tower and walls came in sight
behind a grey flurry of snow. We rolled off the heaving beasts at a
mounting step, and tramped without sensation under the ikon above
the great gates, the monks crossing themselves, and I, as layman, taking
off my hat. We stumbled up flights of stairs, and along galleries blocked
by smiling and handshaking monks. A group of them pressed into a
bedroom with me, where a stove already roared, and stayed with me
until David was back again to share a supper of soup, macaroni, red
mullet, halva and wine, seated close to the stove in the same damp
habit. Tired out by two days of incessant preparation, but kept full of
enthusiasm for the festival, David looked after me better than himself,
taking every excuse to fork a fish off the common platter and shake it on
to my plate.

I was overwhelmed and soon begged:

"Look after yourself, Elder."

His answer was to sweep walls and corner with a glance.

"Who should be here and isn't," he pointed out, "is our new novice.
But what difference is there in any of the young men coming to the
Mountain to-day? They are all more punctual at meals than at prayers.

Where's Anton at this minute? Probably with his feet in the kitchen fire, instead of comforting travellers."

Food, wine, and the fiery heat of the small room finally had David nodding, until a disturbance in the passage caused him to sweep off down to the corridor, which was full of hurrying monks exhilarated over the hospitality which was being prepared.

Kastamonitou's earliest mention seems to be in the eleventh century. Latin Unionists of the thirteenth century are accused of razing the buildings; but in the following century the house was enriched by the Emperors Andronikos II and the Turk-harassed John and Manuel II of the Palaeologos family, and was repaired about 1360 by Anne the Philanthropic of Serbia, who gave the wonder-working ikon. In the fourteenth century the Serbian general, Raditch, carried out repairs before taking the vows under the name of Romanos.

Damage by fires, leading to extreme poverty in the seventeenth century, complete ruin in 1772, abandonment in the revolutionary troubles; such is the outline of Kastamonitou's story. But in 1819 came help from Vassiliki, the Christian favourite of the tyrant Ali Pasha, in the form of gifts which completed the guestroom wing. The monastery has a gold-and-silver copy of the Gospels sent by her in 1820. In 1853 the monks Simon and Joseph of Sinai came forward with funds, and undertook a seven-year tour of Russia, travelling with a copy of Iviron's Virgin-of-the-Gate, now in a chapel near the guestrooms, where the Macedonian monk, Meletios, has left behind a memorial to his industry and taste in the wood-carving and inlay work. Nearly all the present buildings have been built during the last two centuries, most of them dating after the 1821 revolt against the Turks, including St. Stephen's church, built between 1860 and 1871 of local marble, festival December 27.

I went to church at 5 a.m., snowflakes falling on my shoulders as I crossed the court. It was Christmas Day, and a group of tattered misfits, who had drifted here to partake of monastic hospitality, pressed round a stove in the eso-narthex. I was led on to a stall in the south choir, near ecclesiastics conducting the service under the central chandelier of a hundred burning candles, which had just been rocked, together with the smaller chandeliers and the blazing brass corona, in symbolism of the joyous dance of angels and saved round the heavenly throne. The golden glow swayed across the drum of the dome, driving and drawing shadows over the marble pavement, picking up the patine in the choir-stalls.

Against the south-east pillar was an ikon of St. Stephen, reputed to have arrived miraculously from Syria (Palestine in another account) early in the twelfth century, after ikonoclasts had cast it into the flames. An Adrianople shepherd, praying before this painting in 1844 for his flock's increase, was so delighted by the answer that he gave a hundred goats to the monastery.

"They didn't all come at one time," a monk told me.

"No," his neighbour agreed. "They arrived over several seasons."

The Virgin-who-makes-reply was against the bishop's throne, and a monk left his stall to point out the lamenting sacristan's place, though the church was new and the sacristan's experience is said to have taken place in 1080, on the eve of the recovery of St. Stephen's Relics. The oil-store is in a tunnel under the church pavement, and the miraculous jar, possibly pre-Christian, holds a share of the yearly oil crop, a sanctuary lamp distinguishing it from others in the row.

The ikons, monks, and restless group of poor were censed. The monks took oil before the rood-screen, the poor filed into the nave for the blessed bread; and finally the ceremonious formation of ecclesiastics and congregation broke up into an irregular crowd pressing forward to kiss the ikons.

The walk over the snow to the refectory was in the dark. There were two tables for eighty or a hundred, and a shorter high table for the abbot and his elders. Forty-five monks sat at one of the tables on the left, and as many poor guests at the right-hand one. The acreage of white walls was relieved by ikons at the far end, and an interesting mural near the reader's pulpit.

A lukewarm rice soup; baked fish; a small loaf; wine sipped to the drone of a homily. The abbot, Kyril, handsome, composed, uninterested in what he ate, ended the meal by sounding his bell; rose, bringing us to our feet; turned to the mural, setting the example; and at the "Amen" we passed into the church opposite, Kyril blessing us in turn at the refectory door before following to occupy his throne for a few minutes. We were free to disperse. The big vigil would begin to-morrow evening, leading from

St. Stephen's eve into St. Stephen's day. Mules had been sent to Karyes to bring Hierotheos, the bishop, and additional singers.

Eusebios the guestmaster came at daylight to see to my stove. He was a Korphiote, asthmatical, slow and kind.

"Those novices," he wheezed, "and he expects us to make a monk of him! I'll see he's along with firewood in five minutes." He poked and rattled, his solid back turned, and voicing his island's affection for Britain. British sailors were fond of the bottle, but paid their bills, which the French never did.

I rolled off the bed and brought a dazzling world into sight through the window.

"Perfect for your festival," I said, "but hard weather for the bishop."

"He'll find a way," Eusebios said.

"The day he settled here was a lucky one for the Mountain. He must preside at half your feasts."

"He's riding round the whole year. To-day it's Simopetra."

"Of course, their feast's the Nativity. He'll meet with deep snow up there."

"He'll be here some time to-morrow."

"This talk of a good man and his work is getting near home, Father. It's my turn with that poker." I crossed towards the stove, but stopped at the window for a glance at the sparkling world outside. Eusebios came padding over, and in a moment the outside purity passed like a spear-thrust into his heart.

"This happy day," he began, gently gripping my arm. "If the year knows a happier one, it's Easter morning. Christmas, reminding us of the body's birth. Easter marking the recleansing of the spirit."

The corona was rocked again at early vespers. I walked over to church from the airy bakery, leaving half a dozen lethargic cats looking after it. Later I shared red mullet with David, who swept in to munch a few mouthfuls with his mind on next day. He was pleased, as more fish had arrived, but another catch was needed. With a calm sea it was possible. He was full of speculation about the bishop's journey. He thought heavy snow would make the path straight to the sea from Simopetra too difficult, so mules had been sent to Karyes to wait for him there.

"And the snow between Simopetra and Karyes? Won't that path be obliterated too?"

"Not so bad; but it does mean two long exposed rides in deep snow."

"And the bishop no longer young."

"He will be here," said David with assurance.

David was tired but far from worn out. The novice failed to please. Seeing through his own back at one time, David said sharply:

"Leave those waiter's airs behind in the world, Anton. We want work here, not flourish." Then, having driven the novice out of the room, he continued: "Some leave us after three months, after six, after a year. They come expecting something else, they think monks don't work. We on our side get rid of many. The best are on trial two years; but the men we are not sure of are on trial much longer."

Snow fell all night, loading the motionless woods. I shirked the Liturgy in the knowledge of seventeen hours of vigil, beginning that evening. The cheerful sound of men shovelling a path from cells to church accompanied my clatter at the dead stove. Two mules turned in at the great gates loaded with large wooden boxes, and somebody called out that more fish had come. St. Stephen had seen to his feast. The spirit of success was in the air. Visitors were wading up through the drifts; three gendarmes from the outposts, in green greatcoats whitened with snow; one or two minor officials from Karyes, and later a black string of chanters from distant St. Anne's, who had descended their slopes and tossed along the coast, to ride on muleback up here. They were welcomed at the gate by monks in high spirits, made to stamp and shake the snow off, and hurried into the warmth. Two Russian priests from Panteleimon arrived with a party to help officiate. By eleven o'clock a big group sat on a divan running round the walls of a room prepared for serving coffee and wine; home monks waited on us.

My neighbour had taken the name of Lazaros at his shearing to remind himself he had risen to a second life on earth; but this duplication of Lazaros of Bethany had not cured him of a tendency to criticize, and when I spoke in a complimentary manner of an ikon-painter who served in church as a deacon, and praised his delivery, Lazaros said:

"He's not from here. He's from Smyrna. I don't like his provincial accent."

"He's a good ikon-painter," I said, somewhat deflated.

"Ikons aren't painted in church. Yes, he's a very good ikon-painter, few better on the Mountain," but he said it grudgingly.

At this minute an earth tremor startled us. There had been several in the foregoing week, a reminder of the September evening in 1932 when a part of Chalkidhiki had suffered earthquake and a heavy death-roll. The tremor went with the speed of a heartbeat. A singer from St. Anne's held a coffee-cup like a large white marble against his black beard.

"Erissos fell to the last house," he reminded us.

"A terrible little town it was at the time," I offered as my opinion. "People escaped from one house to be crushed under the next. A man could span the streets by opening out his arms."

The bearded row agreed gravely as they sipped their sweetened coffee.

"A man ran from one house without his baby," said the singer with the coffee-cup against his fanned-out beard. "Both parents ran back together. The front had fallen off the house, but the baby was still in the cot upstairs. The father crossed himself, seized the child, and was out of the house as the floor came down, followed by the roof."

"God held up the floor," somebody said, and there was the stir of pious agreement.

"In the 1905 earthquake a Katounaki kelliote said he was sick and wanted to put off his office; but the elder said the reading must be done. The kelliote went into the chapel. The earthquake threw down a rock which crushed the hut he'd just left."

A carillon crashing out on the frosty air brought us to our feet. The bishop's train had arrived on muleback. The feast must now succeed. The hardy old man passed directly into church for a brief thanksgiving, while rumour flew round that his mule had foundered to the belly in snow, over and over again.

Hierotheos, at one time bishop of Koritsa in Albania, had retired to the Mountain after falling out with the Albanian Government, which was determined to have the Liturgy celebrated in Albanian, instead of in the traditional Greek. Now, in retirement, he lived in a cottage and garden at

PLATE 7   *Tower, Chilandari Monastery*

PLATE 8   *An interior rich in murals, "Macedonian" school, Chilandari Monastery*

St. Anne's, and had become an old man without losing alertness, humour, and the air of a man used to taking the lead. We met as old acquaintances, saluting each other over late afternoon refreshments with a "good vigil".

"I've had a nap," he said, looking wide awake.

"They say you had a bad time on the road, Most Reverend One."

"It would have been better to have gone straight down to Simopetra's arsenal. In the end we had to leave the mule-road and go down to Daphne. When the wind drops the sea is warmer than the mountain-side."

"It's true, is it, that you've settled in at St. Anne's?"

"I've done what's wise. When I was at Mylopotamou there was the vineyard traditionally planted by our St. Athanasios, not readily to be given up. But the place lacks water. Now I've plenty. What's a man without his orchard? You must help with the fruit trees. I'm told you have good peaches at Prosphori."

"Half a dozen. You had no water. We've no land. The village hems us in against the sea. But I've a friend near Salonika who can supply the young trees."

The bishop, who was about seventy at this time, astonished everyone. He loved his garden like any old peasant, and like a peasant expected it to feed him in return for his attention. Devoted to the duty imposed on him by the church, he was at the beck and call of any monastery for annual festivals or special occasions. In high summer the Mountain is a paradise under its trees and beside the fountains, but it is a blistering land of rocky rises and descents for man and mule. Winter turned the Mountain into an enemy. Winds howled down precipices, raced across rocks, raised thunderous seas. Snow isolated colonies of men from other colonies. Within the limits of a mule's powers, Hierotheos passed from place to place in answer to a call for his presence. Vigils averaged fourteen hours, the present one would last seventeen; through them he sat enthroned, apparently beyond bodily needs. He was as careless of money as he was of the weather, and gave it away, together with the splendid fruit and vegetables he grew. Fifteen years later a selfless old man continued the same life. In his eighties he became a small man still shrinking, inclined to mumble, and not always easy to follow. The monks openly spoke of a saint among them, and if a saint can ever be "now and here" and not always "then and there", it may have been my unusual fortune to be slightly acquainted with one over a number of years.

A veiled deacon glided up to the bishop, and bowed over and over before him, until touching the floor with the knuckles of both hands. He asked him to bless the vigil now to begin. It was the outside world's 6 p.m., but not time for a general move to church. Instead, we filed into another room for a soup and fish supper, tramping straight from supper into church for great vespers, which turned into matins towards midnight when I was called out of church with the visiting monks for raki, jam, and coffee. The chandeliers had been lighted and the corona swayed; but otherwise there had been no unusual ceremonial. Hierotheos remained motionless throughout, on his throne, pastoral staff in hand. We returned to a glowing scene. Hierotheos, now in magnificent vestments, descended from throne to pavement to venerate, before exposing St. Stephen's relics; for the First Martyr's right hand is one of the two relics of that saint in this church. He paced over to the long sparkling rood-screen, halting where the golden candle-light poured over the wealth of his apparel, and there raised the flashing silver hand, enclosing the yellowed bones; turned it about before our scores of watching eyes; raised it yet higher to tempt our gaze upwards; and at last laid it back in the reliquary before the gates. The monks then advanced in turn to kiss St. Stephen's ikon attached to the south-east pillar, then the smaller ikon of the day, also a St. Stephen, next to cross to the reliquary to press their lips to the two relics, after removing hat and veil. As they raised their heads, a priest signed the cross on their foreheads in oil from the ikon lamps.

A handsome chair was placed to face the screen. Hierotheos seated himself, attended by priests and deacons, who settled a scarlet mitre on his head. The chanting swelled; the heavenly dance symbolized in rocking corona and swaying chandeliers passed in light and shadow across the pavement, found, lost, and re-found the silver-sheeted ikons, the silver lamps, reddened and warmed the double-headed eagles buckling the corona together, and redeemed the crudity of the ostrich eggs suspended from it. The slender wax tapers, held against their music by the veiled chanters, caused bearded mouths to open in a pool of honey-coloured light. Hours later dawn began entering palely through the snow-glazed windows, ever making a way more strongly into the building, devouring more of the mystery. Monks who had remained in church since early evening filled the same places, one or two hanging from the arms of their stalls, like dead soldiers from wire entanglements. A neighbour might know if his neighbour slept or remained awake. It is said a monk discovering a sleeper may place a lighted taper beside him and, by so much as that taper has burned down when the sleeper wakes, by so many must be increased his prostrations of repentance. I have not seen this; but have noticed monks wearied to the frontier of collapse.

The lesser and greater entrances of the Liturgy had taken place. After the lesser, expressing the entry of the Saviour of Man into the world on His mission of teaching, the Gospels had been elevated to the announcement "Wisdom, O believers", and the congregation at last rested in the stalls listening to the epistle.

Later the cherubic hymn had risen from the choirs, to be interrupted by the "great entrance", when the holy gifts were borne into the sanctuary. The slow-moving procession now symbolized the passage of the Saviour of Man to His Passion and death. The hymn continued in the choirs. Chalice and paten were set in the altar in secret; in secret the clergy fanned the holy elements with the aer, the veil which has covered them; in secret the priest elevated the paten with the words: "Holy things to the holy".

It was broad daylight when, in a final lively scene, seniors, juniors, and laymen, the monastic labourers and the meek, shuffling poor received the blessed bread from Hierotheos on his throne; and other wine-wetted bread was distributed among the devout in the north choir. So concluded a vigil which continued from 6 p.m. until 11 a.m., an exercise and discipline and joy drawing a hundred and fifty men together.

Visitors were now led upstairs to take the edge off their appetite with rahat lakoum, raki and coffee. Everyone was talkative and full of congratulations, and showered compliments on Kastamonitou's monks, as they steered about with refreshments.

In the refectory afterwards, Hierotheos seated the Abbot, Kyril, on his right at the high table, where he presided. A second table was prepared for monks of ordinary rank, a third for labourers, and there were forty poor present. Other poor tried to push inside, and clamoured when pushed out again. But the seats were all full and doors were temporarily closed on the disappointed. The disturbance ceased, but we were left regretful. Soup and various fish courses were supported by a sound wine, and the meal ended with saucers of a garnished kolivar, or memorial sweet, in memory of the founders of this house.

A thanksgiving in the refectory led to a second thanksgiving in the church opposite, from where we trooped upstairs for wine and coffee. Then everyone dispersed until vespers at 3 p.m., which vespers included a memorial service for the founders, and the dedication of a memorial cake borne ceremoniously into church for the bishop's blessing by a uniformed ecclesiastical policeman. We laymen in the choir held up tapers symbolizing the life on earth which burns away, and threw light on the books of the dozen ecclesiastics celebrating. Then we went upstairs to coffee where Hierotheos noticed me hesitating about accepting another glass of wine.

"Hold it just as if it were a flower," he urged me with a twinkle, "nothing more than a red flower in your hand."

"The red rose has faded, Most Reverend One," I pointed out presently, staring at the empty tumbler.

"The certain end of all flowers is to fade."

Fifty guests sat at supper that night in a private room. Hierotheos then thanked Kastamonitou's monks. He spoke gracefully, pointing out that the coenobitic rule this house followed had been introduced on the Mountain by St. Athanasios nearly a thousand years before, and he rounded off his brief speech by repeating Kastamonitou's own little fable from days when poverty had caused the house to neglect hospitality. A pilgrim had knocked at the gate, to be told to go to the next house by the porter as no alms could be afforded. Instead of moving on, the ragged fellow struck his nose with a forefinger and remarked:

"There can only be fools inside here to have let go the two brothers who lived for ages at Kastamonitou and brought about its wealth. The monks turned out one, and of course his twin left with him."

"I'd like to hear who those two brothers were," the porter grumbled.

"You turned out the one named GIVE, and of course the twin IT-SHALL-BE-GIVEN left with him."

Our applause rang to the ceiling, and somebody called for songs. The songs were choruses glorifying the patron saints of the monasteries supplying the visitors. For my turn, St. Andrew was chosen for Scotland's sake.

Early in the morning the reluctant mules were led over the snow to the mounting-blocks for the bishop and his following, who settled in their saddles after a ceremonious leave-taking of the abbot. David was as prominent in speeding the departing guests as he had been in receiving them. But when the bishop congratulated him he shook his greying head and refused all credit. The success, he said, was due to St. Stephen, who had looked after his own festival and the house dedicated to him. Monks skipped and scampered over the snow in mufflers, waving farewells and begging for news of mislaid travelling bags and umbrellas. Beard bored into beard to find a cheek to kiss, and the malicious mules laid back their ugly ears.

An hour later I was on shore, seeing off the St. Anne's singers, who drew away in a boat, flapping handkerchiefs after the fashion of parlourmaids shaking out table-cloths. A swell rolled in from the southeast, and the snowy peak of the Mountain rose out of clouds. Gerasimos led me into his house for a cigarette and a raki until a second craft should pass going to Prosphori.

6

Docheiariou: the Idiorrhythmic Monastery of the Superintendent of the Stores

Xenophontos: the Coenobitic Monastery of Xenophon

WINTER STORMS DROVE everything off the water, and when southerly swells rolled ahead of rising winds and caïques ran under shortened sails to the shelter of the Drenia Isles, leaving seas to mount and pound, kelliotes in their eyries became snowbound and cut off.

In January the first early flowers came out, anemones, followed by the star-of-Bethlehem. In March the swifts swept back from overseas to scream round the tower. In April, when the gorse and broom burned in golden glory, the sponge-boats returned to the gulf. On May I the priest blessed the cottages. Wreaths of flowers were above each door, and the villagers streamed from church to dance and picnic under the olives.

During the long Lenten fast there had been a spiritual refurbishing, and, as if to coincide with this, the cottages were whitewashed. On Good Friday the children gathered flowers for Christ's bier. Flags flew at half-mast.

The Cross was auctioned at night and carried in procession round the dark streets by the highest bidder. At midnight on Saturday Christ rose, to the cracking of eggs and spurting of crackers in church. Tapers were lighted at the holy fire, and nursed back to the homes to the ikon lamps. After the Liturgy the fortunate returned home to feast off Easter lamb. On Sunday morning the priest passed round the village in procession to the gunfire of weapon-owners. Judas swung from a bough until burnt by revellers. The Eastern Orthodox Church accents Christ's triumph over death rather than the sorrowful sacrifice for humanity.

May 9 found me on a bench of Docheiariou's kiosk beside Valerian the porter, Veniamin the guestmaster, a jobless tailor dangling a string of amber beads between his knees, and a lively little shepherd who had come striding easily up the slope some minutes before. The sea lazily turned its blues into greens, and back again into blues. Cock chaffinches sang against nightingales, and the air was drenched with the scent of bitter-orange-blossom.

The monastery rose at hand in impregnable walls, bearing frailer storeys, distempered in bright colours by the monks tenanting them. Domes and elegant chimneys were to be glimpsed higher up, and the sixteenth-century keep dominated the range of buildings. Tradition allows this monastery of forty men a tenth-century foundation by St. Euthymios, bursar of the Lavra (Docheiariou—of the Superintendent of the Stores), friend of St. Athanasios and later Abbot of Daphne, who built a church of St. Nicholas on a site above the present after pirates destroyed his own monastery. Monks bought the present site from Xenophontos about 1046, and dedicated the new monastery to St. Michael in recognition of an archangelic intervention on the opposite coast, of Sithonia.

Early benefactors were Eudochia and her sons, the unhappy Michael VII Dukas (1071–8), whose quaking empire shook him off his throne, and Andronikos. Centuries later an Alexander, Voivode of Moldo-Wallachia, restored the monastery, which had been deserted after piratical raids, in the second half of the sixteenth century. A retired bishop, Theophanes of Moldavia, supervised the work, and earned burial in the church.

We might have sat on where we were all the morning in the wonderful surroundings had not a pair of beggars, one limping, come up the slope. The guestmaster tossed away a lettuce-stalk he was eating and sent them to wait for rations under the chapel of Peter and Anophrios the Athonites, close by. They settled down in the warmth, and Veniamin clicked his fingers at an elderly tom cat which sidled near. He had kept his figure better than Valerian, and he got on with guests, including foreigners who knew no Greek. A jolly old friar of books they thought him, with his good nature, dumbshow, and culinary surprises, for few could roast a more masterly barbecue than he, which he did outside the guest-rooms for the November feast.

The elderly tom's complacency irritated the jobless tailor, who sneered: "Your cats are fatter than the two Christians you just sent over there."

"Peter and Anophrios were thinner after living on berries than the pair snoozing beneath them," the porter pointed out placidly, drawing attention to a mural of the emaciated saints with beards to their ankles.

"My old tom's worked harder clearing us out of rats than those two'll ever work for us," the guestmaster retorted.

"Hunger's a very wolf," the shepherd chirped, glancing from the beggars to the saints and back again.

The tailor curled his lip, baring yellow teeth. "There'd be less hunger if men themselves weren't wolves," he said. "Man's made like his master, Satan. They say the devil's lame, and one of that pair came here limping. Satan, the wolf-bitten one, still goes about."

"The devil was lamed," the shepherd stuttered in delight, "in trying to destroy the first sheep Christ created, by carving a wolf from a wild-pear stick. But was he able to make the wooden wolf alive? No, he must go to Christ for help. 'Lord Christ, tell me how to get this wolf alive?' 'Order the wooden wolf to wake up,' Christ said. But Satan didn't like something about Christ's smile. 'It's not so often God lies; better dig a hole as a precaution.' But he forgot to pull one foot in after him, and the moment the wolf came alive it jumped at Satan's foot and bit it through. That's how the devil's lame to this day."

The legend sickened the tailor, who looked down to the sea a hundred yards below.

"But the wolf wouldn't give up eating sheep, so the shepherds came to our Lord Christ to get rid of the terrible animal. 'Look here, you fellows,' said Christ. 'What have I given you those crooks for? Throw them as far as you can.' The shepherds threw their crooks, and hairy animals like the wolf himself jumped up where they fell. 'Now,' said our Lord Christ to these animals, 'you're dogs. Go, hunt the wolves and mind your masters' sheep.'"

The irritated tailor stood up, shooting his amber beads together with his hands.

"Where have you walked from?" Valerian the porter asked the shepherd. "There's been no boat this morning." "Gomation, above Deviliki."

"You've got good water there and goats in plenty."

"Water's there, there are trees, and the rich have goats. I set off yesterday and was walking half the night. How I've walked!"

"Where are you going?"

"I've business with you here."

"What's your business with us?"

"My father lent this monastery money when I was that high," the little shepherd chirped, holding his hand hip-high from the ground.

We all turned sufficiently to calculate the years that had passed.

"Twenty-eight years ago," the shepherd said helpfully. "I've come to ask for it."

"Why hasn't your father come?"

"Can he come if he's dead?"

"Didn't he think once of coming for it?"

"Does a man know all in his father's mind?"

"Haven't you thought of coming before?"

"Last Monday I said: 'It's time to settle the debt of your father that he'd have wished given back to you'."

"Have you witnesses?"

"My father told me Hierotheos, the monastic representative, knows all about it. And a lame monk since dead."

The porter had finished his questions, but Veniamin carried on:

"Hierotheos is inside, and so is Ignatios. You can see if one of them can find a reference in the books. We'll go inside and see. It'll be too hot in ten minutes for the birds to sing, and time to go, anyway."

"And I've not yet started for Xenophontos," said I.

"Let Athanasios and Anophrios, the saints over there, be witnesses I don't want to rake up a long-past trouble," the shepherd pleaded. "But why not ask the monastery to do some small kindness to my son on account of the debt to my father? To educate him. To start him in a trade."

"Ask Ignatios to look at his books," Veniamin repeated, and on second thought stood up. "Now come along; we'll find one of them for you."

He walked off with the shepherd through the gates, adding the active beggar to the party. I followed to retrieve a rucksack in the guest-quarters, and the tailor fell in beside me. He accepted monastic hospitality in the intervals of a leisurely search for work, and was recognizable at a hundred yards; a sallow man in a garment like an old frock-coat, a collarless shirt, worn sandals, and a string of large amber beads, who claimed to have suffered in wars, conflagrations, revolution, and famine.

"He lets thirty years go by, isn't that it?" he sneered, "and then remembers this debt."

"Amazing," I agreed; "but the collection may have been his father's job for the first twenty of them."

"His only for the last ten," the tailor said, taking my point.

"What's so amazing is that in this land there may prove to be some small benefit for him out of it. And it will only have cost him a walk."

We arrived at the gates and paused outside, the tailor driving his beads together behind his back.

"If the host sleeps, it's good manners for guests to follow his example," he observed, preparing to turn off where his lodging was. "These monks," he continued suddenly, swelling, "you've only to spit on one of them and he'll tell you it has rained. Have you noticed the piece of green marble let into the church pavement? They tell you it marks the spot where this boy they talk of was found. They haven't had the brains to put it in a more likely spot. They've put it just as near the centre of the church as they can without spoiling the eagle."

"Why shouldn't the boy have been found in the centre of the church?"

"Ah-bah! He'd have been found in any other place. But that likelihood doesn't come into their heads. Or maybe they know any place is good enough for taking in pilgrims."

"You can't have it both ways."

"Ah-bah!" The tailor turned to go off to his room.

The miracle of Sithonia occurred, according to tradition, during the rule of Abbot Neophytos, nephew of Euthymios, founder of the monastery. Basil, a shepherd on a monastic farm at Sithonia, found a pillar with the information that gold would be discovered by digging at its head. He dug where the pillar's shadow fell at sunrise, and unearthed an urn filled with treasure. He informed the Abbot of Docheiariou, who sent three monks with him to take the valuables to the monastery.

The monks were of the baser brethren, and in league with the devil. They persuaded the youth to return with them, saying the abbot would reward him; but when they had him in the boat they tied a lump of marble to his neck and pushed him overboard.

The boy had the presence of mind to call on the archangels Gabriel and Michael as he sank, and they snatched him up and laid him, wet with sea-water, on the pavement of Docheiariou's church.

A monk beating on the semantron for matins found the boy on the pavement, with the stone still on his neck. The terrified man ran to the abbot, but the abbot at first feared the trick of a demon, and it was not until his third visit, when the boy stood up and told him what had happened, that he was convinced. The semantron was rapped and the monks assembled.

The three thieves had hidden the treasure in a well by the shore, below the mortuary chapel. They then walked to the monastery and said the boy had lied and there was no treasure. The angry monks forced confession, expelled them from the monastery, and preserved the piece of marble which was tied to the boy's neck with the relics.

Murals round the holy well of the Archangels in the court depict other accounts of archangelic intervention on the monastery's behalf. There are lively illustrations of a monastic ship pursued by Saracens. Docheiariou's ship had an ikon of the Archangels, and they appeared as two white pigeons, lifted her from the sea, and set her down in water near a farm of St. Dimitrios on Longos. There the vessel was burnt to prevent capture.

Another monastic ship is shown freighted with corn, blown off its course to Barbary, where the people, who were suffering from famine, gave spices in exchange for the cargo on condition that these spices would not find their way to the Emperor in Byzantium, with whom the people of

Barbary were at war. The monks broke their vows and sailed to Constantinople, where they sold the spices profitably, helping the monastery through a lean period. Thereupon the men of Barbary sent raiders against the monastery. When they attacked in overwhelming numbers the Archangels appeared and led a spirited counter-attack of monks and routed them.

I passed through the gates in the deep wall, and took a path round the court between the holy well and the big, red church, which rose towards a picturesque jumble of buildings built over the natural hillside. Ramps led up to the pretty eighteenth-century guest-quarters in the south-east corner, from where a view of sea opened over domes, leaded and slated roofs, and slim chimneys.

The sixteenth-century church which fills the court is dedicated to the Holy Archangels (feast November 8). It is frescoed from dome to stalls with work dated 1568 and attributed to the Cretan Zorzi, one of the two masters of the famed Panselinos. It was restored work, but what the later and lesser hand left behind of the earlier flowed pleasingly and feelingly over the high, light interior. At the north end of the narthex one came on the tomb of the Bishop of Moldavia who oversaw the sixteenth-century restorations, and bodies of monks are laid on a bier beside it on the night before burial. An eighteenth-century wooden screen, vigorously and amusingly carved with Biblical scenes, further enriched the nave, and a fragment of dark green marble in the pavement marked the spot where the young labourer was laid by the archangels.

Probably older than the murals, since the date is 1547, was the refectory at the church's west end, beside the frescoed chapel of the Ready-Listener ikon, source of the legend of Neilos and the Smoky Virgin.

The chapel of the miracle is a closet, with a window in place of the original door which made it a passage. Along here in 1654 the monk Neilos would shamble, torch in hand, past the ikon on the way to the refectory, a fellow loutish enough to allow the smoke of his link to float in that holy face. But one day he heard a voice say:

"Never again come this way sullying my picture with your pine-torch!" He was witless enough to think it was a trick of the brethren, and the Virgin let him have days of grace, which he wasted. Then he went by a last time with the smoking torch. The voice spoke again, terribly: "Oh, unworthy to be addressed by the name of monk, how long do you intend to go on sullying me!" Simultaneously Neilos was blinded and collapsed on his face in front of the picture. But the Virgin tempers punishment with mercy, and the miserable man's entreaties were listened to. She addressed him a third time in healing him. "Monk, your prayer has been heard, and you shall see again as you used to, for I am the Ready-Listener."

The impressive keep rose from the highest point, strengthened with a long, corbelled machicolation. It had been restored in 1617. Among the parchments in the library at the top were an illuminated twelfth-century copy of the four Gospels, and an illuminated menology for November of the same century.

Living-quarters crowded all levels. Senior monks had secured the two or three apartments which caught the winter sun and shade in summer, and would be rooted there until death; but nobody had bad quarters. This house usually charmed visitors, so pleasantly situated a hundred yards above the shore, in touch with every passing boat. As an idiorrhythmic house it was ruled by two monks, Hierotheos and Ignatios, backed by a committee. Hierotheos was said to sweep the sea daily with a spy-glass set up in his headquarters, marking down everyone who passed. He was said to have kept a thirty-year record proving a state of dead calm on the water throughout every Good Friday. The ocean had formed the habit of going into mourning for Christ's crucifixion.

When I reached the guest-quarters, Hierotheos and Ignatios were under the wistaria, talking to the spectacled treasurer, a younger man; Hierotheos was short, deep-chested, with a formidable glance; Ignatios taller, scholarly, remote. The shepherd waited hopefully in the neighbourhood; but they were too busy complaining of the way new fishing companies swept up everything in the sea and carried it away to Salonika.

"If they sell us fish, we're asked to pay twice as much," said the treasurer.

"What fish do we get now?" Hierotheos asked. "They take on our local men, provided the whole catch is handed over, and those big nets sweep up everything."

"Another winter behind us," said Ignatios to me, drawing the spring air into his frail body. The treasurer glanced sharply over his glasses. He was a man who loved beauty, and his special love of all lovely things was birds. He wanted budgerigars, and I had promised him some.

"So you've still no young parrots for me?" he said, nodding at the darting swallows. "Our own wild birds are building."

"Mine refuse to lay."

"I read that in Australia, where they come from, those little parrots run through the grass feeding, and flash up into the air in flocks like a shower of rain in paradise. And you can't bring me one."

"God intended the fish in these waters for the men living along the shore near them, not to be carried hundreds of leagues away," Hierotheos harped. "Is that Manoli's boat?"

The four of us agreed the brown sail was Manoli's.

"He'll have something," Hierotheos said decisively. "He refuses to work for these companies."

"It doesn't lower his prices," the treasurer pointed out.

Veniamin was stirring a pot of beans when I lifted the rucksack off a kitchen peg. A hermit, bent with age, crept round the door to join us. He mumbled a blessing and stood humbly while Veniamin shot a generous stream of bread-crusts and vegetables into his homespun sack. He turned up here, or at Xenophontos, every week or two, to have the sack filled. The murals depict the solitaries as stern and humourless, though sometimes with an air of command, inasmuch as some left their shelters to rule monasteries. But in this case one of the meekest of old men had chosen to dwell apart in the limestone rocks.

In the case of a monk who has taken vows and feels drawn to a solitary's life, his abbot's permission must be obtained, nor will this be given if the abbot has doubts about the wisdom of the step; for once a monk becomes a solitary, he loses the right of return to his monastery except on rare occasions. Monastic houses bake the larger fragments of waste bread into rusks, which reach the hermitages as a stone-like indestructible offering for the hermit to steep among the herbs in his soup.

Veniamin had already dealt with the beggar, who had passed me on his way down with a bagful of odds and ends to join his lame companion.

I accepted a spoonful of fig jam, dropped the spoon into the empty glass, and walked out under the flowering wistaria.

"Why do you always go round alone?" asked Veniamin, following to see the last of me.

"I like it that way, I suppose."

"The Virgin goes with you," he said.

In five minutes my path crossed a gully gold with genista, scarlet with poppies, pink with valerian. Asphodel still held up starred branches near the last purple flowers on the Judas tree. The track disappeared into cistus bushes on the hillside.

A snort went off while I climbed, and a wild sow crashed out of sight. Then it was snort, snort, snort, and I had become the bogey of six or eight piglets, transfixing one at my feet. The small striped beast trembled there for a moment, snout quivering, slits of eyes glinting, bristles raised. The decorative stripes would fade as it grew. Its mind made up, it wheeled a halfcircle and shot after the rest, adding one more line of shaking boughs to the scrub.

In a few minutes Xenophontos appeared near the seashore. The big house is more fully seen from a boat; nevertheless this glimpse of towers, domes, and roofs was impressive. Its monks have declined from a hundred and thirty-five to fifty in a generation, leaving it half-empty. The path now passed steeply downhill below a crenellated wall from which guards had peered in past centuries, standing on a still existing chemin-de-ronde. The neighbouring hills pressed in and all living-rooms faced seawards for the breeze.

Xenophontos' monks pretend to a foundation by sixth-century St. Xenophon, but a more plausible founder is a later St. Xenophon, the eleventh-century noble of Byzantium, who won the attention of Nikephoros III Botaniates (1078–81) before the latter deserted his throne for a monk's cell. An abbot of St. George is mentioned in a document of 1010; and Basil II Bulgaroktonos (976–1025), who could dispense with learning and luxury but not the camp, is credited with benefactions. The tiny Church of St. Dimitri, now a chapel in the southeast corner of the Old Katholikon, probably predates the monastery, and may have inspired the foundation.

PLATE 9 . *Esphigmenou; the monastery of the "Tight-Girdled One"*

PLATE 10 *One of Zographou's Byzantine churches; and* (below) *the view from the monastery of Iviron*

Pirates, or piratical Latin Unionists, destroyed the house in 1285; but the necessary benefactor was always found, none outdoing the sixteenth-century Moldo-Wallachian princes and nobles. Eighteenth-century Rumanian hospodars came forward, and a period of rebuilding took place about 1784. Following a destructive fire in 1807, the monk and ex-bishop Philotheos built the new church with personal funds, aided by collections; at which time the inmates appear to have been Serbs and Bulgars.

Before going in, I went down to the beach to two Russian monks, who had made a boat fast to a yellow rock beyond the monastery, and were on their knees filling a row of water-jars at a spring oozing through the seashore pebbles. The younger, tall, strong, graceful, wore a long, silky chestnut beard, and had been a schoolmaster in Tsarist Russia, though his life was now passed in the boat he fished from. He shared it with a stolid, letterless partner. So changed was his life that he could seldom have opened a book, and his partner was not able to read. The Bolshevik hurricane had blown them both to the Mountain. The peasant partner stood on the rock of a stubborn belief in God; but the younger man's feeling for God occasionally flashed from him like a sword-blade turning in the sun. Both wore their hair to the shoulders under soft chimney-pot hats, and their dress was identical, with black belted shirts falling loose outside their trousers to their high, baggy Russian boots.

A trickle of water oozed from the shingle, though a decayed stone coping had originally stopped the spring from silting up. The mildly purgative water caused the neighbouring patch of sea to be known as the "bitter waters", and was credited with blood-cleansing properties.

The south-east column of Xenophontos' church supports an ikon of St. George. The monks claim the gash appearing in the saint's chin was caused by ikonoclasts attempting to split the picture, after flames had recoiled from destroying it. Blood flowed from the wound at the time. The ikon was tossed into the sea or, according to some, the criminals fled in terror of the blood and a pious man threw the picture into the sea, to be out of reach of further insults. What nobody disputes is that wind and wave helped it; currents lifted it forward; directing winds blew it, until league after league had been covered, and the Holy

Mountain reached, where it was beached beside this large yellow rock. The medicinal spring immediately gushed up where the painting drifted ashore.

"You do go off with something in the end?" I asked.

"In the end," the schoolmaster laughed, getting up off his knees; "otherwise we wouldn't be given these jars to fill every few days."

"It's surprising nobody from the monastery cleans the spring out occasionally."

"The Greeks don't seem to use it. It's we Russians who apparently need drenching."

His partner pressed the trickle from the sand into a mug, and emptied the mug into the water-pot. He straightened up into a monument of a man, with dreamy blue eyes that remained a memory when his size was forgotten.

I sampled the water, which was stale and flat. Their boat, which rocked a few yards away, reeked with drying octopuses, folded along the spears set fore and aft in wooden crotches. The monks used octopus meat as freely as the peasants. Not counting as a fish, it can be eaten during fasts.

Octopuses go into shallow water morning and evening to feed. The fisherman poles his boat forward, sprinkling sand that has been soaked in oil from the bows to give the water a silky surface which shows up the sea-bed. The pallid octopus may be cruising for a meal, or showing a tentacle tip at a rock hole. The boatman dangles a lump of fish in front of the hole, and the octopus shoots out of hiding, resembling an open, handleless umbrella. The fisher, poised in the bows, calculates refraction, launches the spear, and drives three prongs into those leathery vitals, twisting and heaving an eight-armed mass out of a watery into an airy world; a writhing lump which has to be wrenched inside out to be quieted.

"Are you staying overnight at Xenophontos?" the schoolmaster asked.

"Yes. I've just arrived, and came here before going in."

"I'll row along the coast after vespers, then I can admire their ikons again."

"Yes, the small ikons in their choirs are one of the best collections on the Mountain."

"When the light's right those old golds, clarets, clear blues, glorious old colours immediately burn up into life!"

"Wonderful! Like fires, or should the word be jewels?"

His face glowed with artistic pleasure. He was one of the few individuals on the Mountain capable of approaching an ikon as a work of art. He had no praise for his countrymen's ornate silver-work; it was the severity and discipline of the Byzantine tradition which drew him. His appreciation disturbed him, as an ikon should be the medium of veneration of a saint to a monk—nothing more. A fine feeling for art belonged to the world, and was unbecoming to one who had left it.

I turned away to go to the monastery. The keep, the oldest portion of the range of buildings, had been raised by the naval chief of the Byzantine Empire, Stephen the Eunuch, who had rebuilt the monastery by 1083, using personal funds and gifts from his master, Nikephoros Botaniates. He was later to take the vows here, and lived out his remaining days under the name of Simeon, using the tower's still existent chapel of St. Stephen, and occupying a cell beside it.

The court took in the old and new churches, and the approach led round water, through a frescoed passage joining the church of St. George to the refectory, a chamber of old murals.

This small church has been arrestingly decorated about 1546, it was claimed by the famous master, Theophanes of Crete. Nineteen years earlier the interior had been covered by another hand, earlier than El Greco's but directed by a similar feeling. He was apparently an obscure painter whose name, Antonios, is all that is known of him. Time and restoration have done a good deal of damage. The nave's south-east corner contained the chapel of St. Dimitrios, existent before the monastery, and its south-west corner a chapel of Lazaros. Both chapels are worth examination. The flow of water in the court was increased by a stream running under the eleventh-century pavement, and useful for washing it.

After the monastery grew the church was too small, and the new katholikon of St. George was built early in the nineteenth century. Two fine old doors open the way into a lofty nave, unfrescoed but full of small, choice ikons. These minor works, crowded in the choirs, are examples of a successful manipulation of the traditional strictures of the School.

The fetters imposed by rule seem to have helped the moderate artist to produce his best, as moderate poets can sometimes be helped towards success by imprisonment in a strict poetic form.

This is the church of the two important mosaics of St. George and St. Dimitrios, placed by some expert opinion in the eleventh century, and by none later than the fourteenth. These large mosaics were made to decorate a rich man's walls, as pictures adorn walls to-day, and the artist aimed at making his marble effective at a distance; building up the face minutely, suggesting the raiment more coarsely, and employing a yet broader treatment of the background.

The two ikons bringing pilgrims to these doors are the St. George of the miraculous spring, on the south-east column, and the Virgin-of-Guidance against the north-east column. The tale of the latter ikon's miraculous transference twice, together with the church column, from Vatopedi to this place in 1730 must amaze the most pious.

Behind the grey and gilt screen is that arresting Virgin and Child with cheek laid against cheek, a fiercely fond mother. Reliquaries hold a drop of John the Baptist's blood, and a fragment of the First Martyr's head.

I expected the monastery to be dead at this hour, and when I walked in there was only a single monk in the court, near two cypresses he had planted in front of the new church as a novice. Years of monastic life had turned a youth into a large slow man who, as a monk of the Great Habit, was vowed to numerous daily protestations in his cell, to stricter fasting, and a more pronounced silence than his fellows, exercises he took devoutly, for he was sincere. The scapular of the Angelic Habit was usually to be seen on a nail in his cell, though he wore it on certain occasions, and would be robed in it at death; a sombre garment, embroidered with a cross, under the base of which grinned a skull, supported by lance and spear of the Passion.

He led me over to a garden plot under the battlements to give me a rose, and from there I went on to the guest quarters, passing under a cloud of nesting martins. I felt none too sure of my welcome by the paunchy guestmaster, Pankratios, for he smoked in his dingy kitchen at this hour. When he saw me in the doorway he did come to meet me, his slippers slapping the flags, his steel-rimmed glasses giving an air of hostility rather than welcome.

"What a time to arrive!" he grumbled.

"I've walked from Docheiariou."

"What did they send you off with?"

"Coffee and raki."

"Leaving me to find your beans. Was man put on earth to work all day? In the Garden of Eden he had no work beyond naming the animals."

"And how long was he there, Elder? I got a little late through going down to the 'bitter waters' to talk to the Russians."

"What do you want with the Russians?"

"I've friends among them. A people of rich nature. Earthly angels, with a wing-tip sometimes in heaven, and the other occasionally in hell."

"Ah-a, may the Virgin never forget the Greeks here as she has forgotten the Russians. There was a time when the sea off Panteleimon was thick with ships; you could have walked ashore on them. And the pilgrims numbered the hairs on my legs. The Russians tried climbing high," Pankratios started chuckling, "but in the end they had to boil Bessarion."

"An old, old fairy-tale."

"In the end Bessarion was boiled! That Russian intriguer who tried using Russian wealth to corrupt us into selling our monasteries, so that they could get more votes on the Assembly. Bessarion came to the end of his days, and his brother monks buried him. And when it was time for him to go into the charnel-house three years afterwards, not a hair of his had decayed. Nor after a second three years; nor a third three. So they boiled him to clean his bones!"

"A fairy-tale, Father."

"There were those to see. And to tell!" And Pankratios hooted at his own wit, as he poured water into the coffee-pot.

7

St. Panteleimon or Russiko: the Coenobitic Monastery of the Russians

Port of Daphne

Xeropotamou: the Idiorrhythmic Monastery of the Dry Stream

Koutloumousiou: the Coenobitic Monastery of Koutloumoush

I HAD THE GOOD luck in the morning to be picked up by a passing sailing-boat bound for Russiko. A powerful, ragged, mottle-faced boatman, every inch of six foot three and always sailing up and down the coast, made a careless catch at the rucksack, pulled me aboard after it, and settled me aft on a square of bright carpet, next to a pedlar nursing his showcases. He then laid a course for the glittering Russian monastery, and the last air died. He stood up amidships, and grinned foolishly as he gaped round the horizon.

"Down with the sail, Marko," I suggested, after a minute. "Out with the oars."

"I asked for wind," he roared back. "But can you always make God hear?" He pulled out two clumsy sweeps and, standing to row in the local fashion, face for'ard, began pushing us across the flat sea to the monastery.

He had the Greek boatman's virtue of rowing all day on a handful of olives and a wedge of black bread. He could load timber into a caïque like a young man. When there was no other work he speared octopus morning and evening, and argued the rest of the day in the tavern until gathered home by a masterful wife. He liked best to sail me round the coast, on trips that might last a month. He pitched my tent for me, and caught and cooked supper while I went to a monastery.

The pedlar was a homeless bachelor, who had been catering for the local villages for years. He would sit for a day or two under a leafy tree selling stale sweets to gluttonous children, and highly-coloured religious prints.

As I settled aft I nearly put my hand on a bunch of Flowers-of-the-Virgin, a plant hawked round the villages to sell to women in childbirth, and said to turn green as a warning of the infant's arrival.

"I'm so sorry," I said.

He agreed no damage had been done, and tried to sell me a three-volume German theological work, published half a century ago in Leipzig. A monk had exchanged it for a few pencils. The weight of a single volume caused me to refuse.

The water round us was flat as a floor, but a breeze would come out of the south-east before midday; strong, generous, persistent as a trade wind, adding knots to the run home. In the meantime Marko stood up in his rags, falling forward on the sweeps with the regularity of a lullaby. Finally he poled the boat round the breakwater at Russiko, and tied her up, for he agreed to wait until I wanted to move on.

I left him filling a water-jar under the ikon of Christ's Baptism. The great house spread up from shore to the forested slopes behind. Walls, lichened roofs, green cupolas, and the golden crosses of more than thirty churches and chapels. This largest of the monasteries had sheltered fifteen hundred monks at the turn of the century; employed numerous labourers; annually offered hospitality to many scores of pilgrims; but now a handful of old men gossiped on the balconies in the evening, for novices ceased to arrive after the Bolshevik revolution of 1917.

There was activity round a three-masted timber-ship when I arrived. A grand caique, with a cross at each truck. It lay most of the year off Drenia Isles, with the crew of monks at their offices in the chapel on board. It was now being loaded with wood for Salonika, and muleteers strode behind mules which stepped as carefully as cats under heavy lengths of timber.

I edged through the moving traffic of mules and men, and disturbed a hardy little fisherman who was passing over half a dozen cigarette papers to a muleteer. Tobacco leaf from the fields was dried under Government seal, and possession of cigarette papers illegal. He felt an explanation was due. Weather had wrinkled this old acquaintance to the shoulders. He worked me into a corner and began shouting in a whisper, his lips to my chest, and a bare foot scooping backwards at the sand.

"It was this way. Last night the gendarmes heard of cigarette papers—a nice little wad—to be found in a hut near Kapso-kalyvia. Two lads were sent to see about it, the redheaded one, and the redfaced one; one thick in the skull, and the other thicker, for when did God make all the fingers of a hand the same length? They hailed me as I came ashore from my night-lines, and made me sail them up the coast. Redface was to stay outside the hut in case of an escape through the window, while Redhead went inside. It was just such a starry night as a king might have chosen to look through the telescope.

"The kelliote guessed Redhead would search, and sent the cigarette papers out of the window in his raso. It wasn't Redface, it was I who saw them roll out of the raso into a bush. Redhead and Redface turned the hut upside down, and wanted to know why the kelliote had thrown his raso out of the window. But it was a case of poverty marrying poverty with their brains. I rowed them down to my lines, left them to walk home, and thought there'd be no harm going back to the hut. There was the kelliote calling on St. Minas to find the packet for him. While he was in the chapel lighting a candle to him, I lifted the packet out of the bush, and left that part of the Mountain till the moon gets small enough to make night-fishing worth while."

His face was the hue of the pounded pine-chips they use for dyeing their nets, and he smelt like a beach. I left him still saying good-bye and made my way uphill.

This great place, admired by those liking size and neo-Byzantine architecture, holds nothing for the antiquarian, having grown up in less than a century beside an empty shore. Russians have always been connected with the Mountain, and early founded a monastery of the Falling-Asleep-of-the-Virgin, to abandon it for the monastery of the Woodcutter, near the site of Bogoroditsa, which was given by the Protos in or before 1143. Twenty years later they moved to another monastery, burned about 1313, and at a date thought to be 1765, to the present site.

A steep path behind Russiko leads over lonely country to Karyes, and in the better part of an hour reaches the large church dedicated to St. Barbara and St. Catherine, below a secluded lake. The building is deserted, the door locked. The Russian monastery is thought once to have stood here on the gradual march from Bogoroditsa to where it now rises on the sea shore.

From the fourteenth century the house seems to have been dedicated to St. Panteleimon, a fourth-century martyr, a physician, and since patron of medical men. Byzantine emperors helped the restoration after a fourteenth-century fire, and Serbian sovereigns continued to be benefactors after the fall of Constantinople; for the monastery has had periods of Russian, Serbian and Greek direction. It was closed in 1582, was in decay throughout the next century, was again closed, and continued in destitution until the 1821 revolution of the Greeks against their Turkish masters. The oldest of the present buildings date back to about this time, when the monastery received protection from the powerful Kallimachis family, Phanariote hospodars. Russian monks, who had settled in with the Greeks after the rising, paid off its debts in 1839, and in 1875 elected the first abbot of Russian nationality.

The election was followed by a period of astonishing expansion partly accounted for by political backing from a Russian Government willing to exploit national piety to obtain a foothold in northern Greece. Monks from all ends of Russia were sent to the Holy Mountain, backed by funds to maintain them and raise the imposing churches, chapels and buildings nearly empty to-day. Though persuasion, bribery and intrigue failed to elevate more than this one house of St. Panteleimon to monastic rank, and provide the Russians with more than one voice on the Karyes Assembly, the sketes of St. Andrew and Prophet Elijah outgrew many of the Greek monasteries, while colonies of Russian kelliotes and hermits settled round the Mountain end. At the turn of the century two thousand Slavs occupied the Mountain with three thousand Greeks. But the Bolshevik revolution of 1917 cut off the flow of Russian novices at source, and the Greeks were not to forget how nearly they were drowned in a foreign flood.

The Greek hostility to the Russian is understandable. When, in 988, the Russian people officially embraced the Eastern Orthodox Church, a giant came into being beside a man of average stature. The Russians greatly outnumbered the Greeks; they outgrew them in political importance, and outstripped them in wealth. They were also a people with a feeling for God.

Monks were recruited so carelessly after 1875 that criminals, glad to leave home for a less-policed country, took the habit here. This element strengthened a mutiny which was not controlled until scores of them had been removed on a Russian cruiser and sent back to their villages.

Antony Boulatovitch, an ex-officer of hussars in the skete of St. Andrew, conceived the idea that divinity was attached to the name of Jesus, as a name of God incarnate. Faction war broke out over the question; monk stoned monk; father bludgeoned father in the surrounding woods; and when the abbot was defied, and strife continued spreading, the cruiser steamed up. But that was in Tsarist days, and the calm of desuetude has since descended on this sad house.

The road led up ramps past a fountain into the big outer court. The charnel-house stood in isolation, and the numbered skulls of the dead lay tidily on shelves, other bones finding a place in racks. The dead were remembered, and an angular monk was reading out names in a huge tortured voice, as the brevity of earthly life was brought home to him in that company. His body rolled, his face worked, the vast audience of skulls grinned.

A gateway to the left led to the monastery proper, between stone and brickwork curtained by shrubs and creepers. The monks shambling through the gate in high black boots were the most rustic on the Mountain, and dated all history before the 1914 world war. The youngest had turned grey, the others white; and poverty kept these ageing men out at work in the fields as if they were still youthful peasants. As men died, others were drawn in from the outposts of Chromitsa, Thebais and Bogoroditsa or the Mother-of-God. But this did not stop the corridors of cells from emptying and the cultivated lands returning to nature.

The church of St. Panteleimon (feast July 27) is in an inner court, together with an enormous frescoed refectory. The interior of the big church is splendid in an untamed style. Behind church and refectory, cells, chapels, reception-rooms and a campanile rose in banks. The church had been built between 1812 and 1821, and nearly all else fifty years afterwards.

The chanting of the Russian voices during the long services was still warm and musical. As night lengthened into morning, the old singers, tiring more and more, squatted on the dark pavement of the church, and made their responses from there. Though squatting, they still seemed reaching up to God, and this proximity to the divine was the wealth remaining to them on earth.

The library preserved some illuminated Gospels dating between the eleventh and fourteenth centuries, a number of fragments in envelopes, a few Slav parchments, a few score pre-nineteenth-century Slav books on ecclesiastical matters, and there was considerable modern theological literature.

The second church of importance was a light and airy chamber on an upper storey, dedicated to St. Metrophanes, fourth-century Bishop of Byzantium, and close was the cell of Anophrios, a man of breeding, who had taken the habit after the 1917 revolution. He received foreign visitors, for he had good manners and the gift of tongues. His small whitewashed room had a bench for bed, a chair and table, and a shelf for books in several languages. I put the one in my hand among them.

"I'm returning your book," I told him; "I've a boat below and am on my way to Daphne. I've had a number of callers en route for the Mountain. But you will have had more. The tourist traffic increases every year."

"Without feeling any responsibility for sharpening the memories of men bent on forgetting the world," he answered, smiling. "A monk does better without memories. Life is a country to be advanced across, not returned over."

We spoke a few moments about the book he had lent me, and then I returned to the shore.

Marko had tied up again at Daphne in half an hour. The little port, sighted across the water, looked an inviting group of red-roofed buildings set in pine and chestnut woods; but it turned into two modest general stores, a post-office and warehouses, cheek by jowl with a humble inn, and a police station where visitors' passports were checked. The traveller entered and left through the customs shed, as a check on manuscripts and ikons leaving the Mountain. There was a church, and the innkeeper wore the habit. Boats had touched here since 1881, and the neighbouring monasteries of Xeropotamou and Simopetra divided the land. The mountain road leading to Karyes stood on end among the surrounding slopes.

By special convention with Greece, imports to the value of a thousand gold drachmae a month enter Athos duty free, and dues collected are on goods exceeding that limit, and on the imports of lay merchants. Exports are untaxed, though the hazel-nut harvest occasionally reaches three hundred tons, and the sale of forest timber is a main income of several monasteries.

I walked through the customs shed, past a group of petty officials stunned by boredom, towards some fishermen drying their nets along the shore. Two English tourists stood near the inn vine, and made part of a group completed by a leathery muleteer, four of his mules, two helpful gendarmes, the habited innkeeper and an out-at-elbows layman claiming to be an American on the strength of half-a-dozen words of English picked up on a tramp-steamer.

The monk in charge of the port, with an ecclesiastical policeman in white kilt and shoes with pompoms, overlooked from a distance.

The Englishmen had disembarked from a steamer in the dark. They did not know the local tongue, and they had settled on the tavern's wooden seats to wait for daylight. Neither Turkish coffee nor cigarettes had saved them from depression. Then the sky had lightened and uncovered the mountain road winding up to Karyes, where they must go to present themselves to the Holy Assembly. Nothing with fewer than four legs could bear the luggage up that dizzy road. A call for mules was telephoned to the nearest monastery, and until their arrival all that could be done was to sit drinking little cups of sweet Turkish coffee.

"Can I help in any way? I know this place," I said to them.

"My God, can you speak English?"

The nearest tourist was lanky and jointy, with glasses split for double vision; his companion a much stockier person. Both were already on the run. Their suitcases were roped to a mule, and the muleteer had made his first request for cigarettes. He was a tough little Epirote, and was to be found on all paths, but more often between here and Karyes. He specialized in new-comers, mounting them on his mules and pattering behind them on shoes made of strips of motor tyres.

"I see you're for Karyes," I said.

"I'm told we get our permits there."

"The Assembly's morning session is over at ten-thirty; but see you get through with the police on arrival, and you can call on the Assembly at the afternoon session. That gives you time to reach Iviron or even Vatopedi before dark."

"This ride goes right up into the sky, it seems," interrupted the taller one, contemplating the heights.

"Half-way there, anyhow. Karyes is some distance down the farther slopes, more than two hours away."

The muleteer had recognized one more fare in me, and I was ready to be carried past Xeropotamou and over the ridges to Karyes on other legs than my own.

"What's this beast like you've got for me?" I asked, eyeing an animal laying its ears back.

"Is it worse, is it better than its kind?" Petros asked. "Get up."

"I hope I get to my seat without a piece gone from my pants."

"God, who has given lice to the little birds to eat on their long journey, will see to your safety, who can read a book faster than I can peel a chestnut. Yah, yah, yah!" he shouted, bringing his stick down on the mule while I was settling. "Would you open those teeth of yours? Crooked you are as the mother you came out of. Haven't I seen you nip a kind old monk? Yah! Such a kind old man. One of those who can't shake a bed-bug out of his blanket without looking down to see if it's broken a leg."

We strung forward, head to tail, turning from the shore near Xeropotamou's arsenal. We bowed over sawing mule-heads while the animals used their powerful quarters to lift us up the slope. The two travellers stopped asking questions to hold on, finding hands more useful than unpractised thighs. The great gorge was covered with macchie, and the last silver thread of the dry river fell seawards through it. The wild scene was cheerful with spring. In half an hour we were on a high plateau outside Xeropotamou. Monks had cleared this open space from the surrounding savagery a thousand years previously, and it offered seating to gossiping fathers and exhausted travellers. The afternoon wind was raising the sea far below us, and blue water rolled landwards out of the horizon, rank after rank of white-crested waves. Wherever an olive-grove stood on the leagues of slopes, the wind rocked it, turned it from grey-green to silver.

"The sightseer should begin his work here," I said pitilessly. "One of the oldest houses, tenth-century, and claiming a false fifth-century foundation. The monks are rather critical of a hurried visit, and think their house neglected."

"We'd best go on," said the lanky one, shifting a camera from the small of his back; "one can see it's extraordinarily interesting, but one must go canny to survive. I'm for getting our permits."

The idiorrhythmic monastery we were passing claims to have been founded in A.D. 424; but the supporting documents have been proven forgeries, executed in claim of the neighbouring lands. Nevertheless it is an early foundation. Remoteness on a height has not saved it from raiders. Arabs destroyed it early in its history, but it found restorers. In the thirteenth century it was partially shaken down by an earthquake, and Andronikos II Palaeologos came forward with help. A century later it owned land as far as the typikon skete of St. Anne, and was an important house in the typikon of 1394; but it again declined early in the sixteenth century, and gave up its fifth rank to Dionysiou. Pirates twice burned it; but it was reconstructed again by Sultan Selim, conqueror of Egypt, and was further rebuilt about 1600 by Alexander of Wallachia. Though it had again decayed by 1701, it is to-day looked on as well off.

The pleasing church of the Forty Martyrs of Sebaste—fourth-century Armenians whom Licinius attempted to freeze to death in a lake—was begun about 1761, and frescoed by 1783, with funds raised by Kaisariss Daponte, a monk loving this house well. An interesting fifth- or sixth-century relief of St. Dimitrios, said to have been removed from St. Sophia in Constantinople, has been built into the exo-narthex, and an unusual late-eighteenth-century clock-tower stands in the court.

Six silver lamps burn before the screen ikon of the Forty Martyrs, a memorial to Sultan Selim to whom the Forty appeared in vision. They advised him to restore the monastery lately burned down by pirates; and in return they would help him in his Arab wars. He restored the building and remitted taxes due, and supplied oil for the ikon. His successors continued to do this for a long time.

A legend lingers that from the tenth century a mushroom invariably sprouted under the altar at the feast of the Forty. It enlarged until it bore branches loaded with forty apples honouring the martyrs. It grew until the altar was overshadowed. However, after the monastery received the envoys of Michael VIII, who introduced the Latin rite, an earthquake threw the church on top of its priests, and the giant mushroom appeared no more.

The present church possesses the largest piece of the True Cross on the Mountain. This impressive fragment, set in gold and precious stones, is a foot in length and lies in a silver-gilt reliquary. Three lesser pieces are sent out occasionally to villages to stop outbreaks of sickness; but the great fragment no longer leaves the Mountain.

"Should either of you be bitten by a viper," I said, "the best place is here, for a treasure inside is an eleventh- or twelfth-century green ophite silver-mounted patera, some inches across, a gem of art, carved in high relief with figures of Virgin and Child surrounded by angels and apostles. The monks know it as Pulcheria's cup, and claim it to be the gift of fifth-century Pulcheria, sister of Theodosios the Little, though no monastery then existed on the Mountain. It may date back to another Pulcheria, sister of Romanos III, who reigned in the eleventh century. Water poured into it is said to boil within twenty-four hours, and anyone poisoned or snake-bitten recovers after drinking it."

"Should they live while the water's coming to the boil," said the lanky one.

"I am told the monks keep prepared water on hand."

We strung on up through chestnut forest.

"Where did you get that limp, Petros?".

"Wasn't I riding down this road last month when a stone got under the mule's shoe?"

"It's not often a mule comes down."

"It didn't that time," he defended it quickly, "but you see I was drunk and fell off. But one of my abbots fell off it once. And that good man had been all night at his prayers. God is careless sometimes."

The track reached meadowland at the top of the pass, and was level for a few minutes before falling over steep forested ledges. At last the straggling capital of Karyes opened out on slopes half-way to the other sea; a village of churches, chapels and brilliant green gardens.

"Charming! But surely we'll seem very unusual to them?" said the stocky one. "Are they used to visitors?"

"More arrive every year."

"Foreigners? Our sort?"

"Foreigners and Greeks."

"Charming, charming," said the lanky one, giving what attention he could spare from his mule to Karyes.

"It's not the same close up," I warned him. "However, it's the capital, and anything looks like a capital when you come on it out of these trees and bushes. That is the outstanding feature of this land. Go a quarter of a mile from any of the monasteries and you find yourself in a country unaltered from the days when men came here in the ninth century. The sea's generally without a sail. It must help the monks to feel secure from the outside world."

"From people like us?" suggested the stocky one.

"You'll find monks ready enough to help a visitor when they know what he wants; but most foreign sightseers mean very little to them.

Languageless tourists can't penetrate into the spirit of the place more than to admire the scenery, architecture and treasure."

"If the traditional hospitality belongs to the era of odd pilgrims and travellers, it must have grown into a heavy tax lately?"

"Exactly, specially on houses easily reached from Karyes, such as Koutloumousiou, Iviron, and Vatopedi. But there are unvisited districts. Though you won't starve anywhere, you may not come across food you understand; and when men are given cold beans in oil at three successive monasteries, they return in flight to the world. But the loss is theirs."

"Can you give us tips about manners, while there's time?"

"Some monasteries allow smoking. Others don't. Never smoke in the court because it holds the church. Fold your hands in front of you during a service, and don't cross your legs in a stall. The monks are full of good will."

Having bent to the ears of the mules, we now lay back towards their tails, and so made Karyes. No arrivals in the centuries of that womanless and childless village's history can have entered it other than exhausted. I told my companions to dismount at the entrance to the main street, for nobody may ride along it. Petros undertook to clear them with the police in time for the Assembly's afternoon session. Then I turned towards Koutloumousiou, ten minutes away.

The lane wandered downhill, skirting one of the hazel-woods which gave the name Karyes (Hazels) to the capital. Covert was so thick on the hamlet's edge that the year before a jackal bounded up from my feet. Koutloumousiou was in the throes of the siesta, and I became doubtful of my tact in waking the place up, so I halted to fan myself beside a stile.

Koutloumousiou makes no claim to an early foundation, but will soon have seen seven centuries. The foundation is credited to a converted Turkish prince, son of Azzedin II Koutloumous and a Christian mother, who was baptized Konstantine and became an Athonite monk in the latter half of the thirteenth century, dying in 1268. Possibly the monastery was founded on an earlier one, as the name is said to appear in a tenth-century document. The tower was built early in the sixteenth century, and the imposing church of the Transfiguration (festival August 6) a few years later. Wallachian voivodes gave considerable help about this time; but a fire in the eighteenth century and two during the nineteenth have left little that is two hundred years old. The north chapel is that age.

The church murals date about 1540.

The south-east pillar supports an ikon of the dedication, the Transfiguration, and on the north-east pillar is the forbidding ikon of the Dreadful Presentation, a rich glow of reds and blues on a golden ground. This picture came from a Cretan monastery belonging to Koutloumousiou. When fire destroyed that house the ikon escaped destruction, defied the flames, and was brought to Athos. It is visited on Easter Monday by the Axion Estin ikon, borne in procession from the Protaton church, and on Easter Tuesday this ikon returns the visit. Two other ikons call for notice, a St. Nicholas by the bishop's throne, and an ikon on the opposite pillar; but the church's interior is regrettably dark.

This house has less history than others. There are those who claim it suffered from the soldiers of Michael VIII, which again suggests an earlier foundation; that it absorbed Philadelphou about 1334 or 1344, and Alypiou in 1428. The tale is told of an abbot who burned it down to rid it of wealth's temptations, winning the monks the reward of a miraculous mist, which closed round a Turkish raiding party who came after ruining Iviron. They were guided by a miserable monk whom they had captured. Mist continued to spread, and Koutloumousiou stayed undiscovered, though the raiders must have been close to the gates at one time, for the monk who guided them was found hanged to a mulberry tree in the neighbourhood in the morning.

In the seventeen sixties a Patriarch of Alexandria who spent his youth in the monastery retired here in old age as a simple monk, Matthew.

I was not alone by the stile, a priest in a ringed hat sat by the fountain nursing his possessions in a hand-woven bag.

"Have you walked from Iviron, Father?"

"I have. This land has sun and distance. Sun, hills and distance." He sighed. A light-eyed beggar joined us. He was disfigured by pockmarks and a knife-wound; but had a mouthful of white teeth. His story was of lost jobs, a lost wife, lost children, lost health, and a lost reputation. Then he dropped professionalism for general conversation.

"Ha," he finished up his story, "the wolf ages and gets white hairs; but neither changes his opinion nor his teeth. My eyes have been my only asset—never turn away a light-eyed beggar!"

The priest was damping his beard at the fountain when a spectacled, lightly-bearded monk from a kelli beyond St. Anne's ambled up on a strong mule. He looked us over shrewdly from his high seat, then lowered himself from the wooden saddle with a certain tenderness.

"Have you come from outside?" he asked the priest.

"I have."

The kelliote turned to me:

"You were up behind Dionysiou the other day?"

"Wearing a pair of shoes out trying to reach the saint's cave."

"Only vipers are up there now."

"A monk, Antonios, used to look after mules there. Just under the peak with the cave. I didn't find him this time."

"He's dead."

"I'm sorry."

"God carries out what He wishes. Did you get into the cave?"

"It's no longer possible. It's destroyed. I met with the adders, and there are lovely chestnut woods."

"An abbot might gather his firewood in them," observed the beggar, suggesting he knew them.

"I was up there once," I continued; "I don't remember the month, but it was as hot as to-day. Half of the path had been turned blue by a flower that seems unknown to science. The stalk was eighteen or more inches long, and stems hung over like the spray of a fountain, with bells the size of egg-cups at the end. Only Klement, the herbalist, seems to know it, and he tells me it grows there and at St. Paul's twice a year, immediately after rain."

"Flowers grow on the Mountain," the kelliote agreed, "but there's nothing to tempt anyone up there. A single chapel, and the doors of that only opened once a year. But we heard you found a lost priest up there. Not one of those who waters a village with his good deeds."

"I ran into him on the path behind Dionysiou, and I put him on his way; but it's a steep road."

"Even for the sober, you mean?" said the kelliote. "There are priests who lose their way, and some of them find the Holy Mountain. One came to Philotheou the other day. 'Have you no luggage at all?' the porter asked. 'It fell into the sea as I landed from the boat.' 'The Panayia will know that,' the porter replied. 'It was a fine day at the start, but came on stormy,' said the priest."

"God sometimes lies," the beggar interjected.

The kelliote ignored the beggar:

"While he stayed, that priest showed himself more ready to uncover the bottom of a glass of wine than to say a prayer before the Sweetly-Kissing-One, so they put him on a mule for Karyes; but it arrived at the konak without him."

The beggar took the bit between his teeth.

"There was a priest once, a fellow of fellows he was, who couldn't leave wine alone, nor the collection plate, until he came to die. One of those priests he was who forgets to take a lantern with him when he visits the women of his flock at night. One of his flock came across him in the next world, sunk up to his chin in mud, and vipers crawling round him. 'What's happened to you, Father? Why are you deep down in this mud? How long are you to be here?' 'For ever and ever, alas!' 'Why? Why?' 'The sins of my life have sunk me down here.' 'But if it was those sins of yours, Father, you would have sunk completely out of sight.' 'Am I not standing on my bishop's head?'"

The beggar's cackle of amusement at his story broke off on observing our mirthless faces. The kelliote looked at him squarely and remarked: "It's a long time since that story first went round."

"And time to get inside out of the heat," I suggested tactfully. We thereupon presented ourselves to the dozing porter, a cross-section of the travellers arriving at a monastery's gate, emboldened by the Mountain's inexhaustible hospitality.

8

The Capital Town of Karyes

IN KARYES I RAN into Charalambos, Dionysiou's representative on the Holy Assembly, as he rounded the post-office corner; he carried the black staff of his rank. His large face lighted up as we avoided collision, and blocked the traffic on the narrow thread of pavement. He had been my guest in the past and I must be his that night. He expected his own way and, liking him well, I accepted.

The ramshackle capital had grown up round the earliest of the Mountain's churches, the thousand-year-old Protaton, and looked bigger than it was because it rambled up and down over ravines. The main street was a lane of saddlers, monastic tailors and shoemakers, general stores and souvenir shops, spreading, with the Assembly headquarters, into suburbs of tumbledown country houses, the kellia and konaks of the twenty monasteries. The settlement made a better showing from the heights, where the pile of the Russian skete of St. Andrew at one end, and the Greek monastery of Koutloumousiou at the other, the domes and crosses of churches and chapels gleaming in gardens and vineyards, improved on reality. The sea spoken of as the Holy Sea lay an hour or so away, and nearly two thousand feet below.

Originally the village had been known as Messi, or the "Middle", from its central position; but by the end of the tenth century had acquired the name of Karyes, or the Hazels, from its nut-groves. Soon afterwards it was mentioned as the lavra of Karyes, and consisted of a number of cells under the Protos or ruling ecclesiastic. In the third typikon of 1394 it was written of as the skete of Karyes. To-day it had seventy cells inside Karyes, forty outside, and the Holy Community owned church, theological school, hotel, and cemetery.

Most shops and booths had passed into lay hands, and craftsmen from "the world" were settled permanently as shoemakers and tailors, leaving the souvenir trade to the monks. Communities of monks, living by ikon-painting and wood-carving round the end of the peninsula, sent work to this centre where tourists could see it; such humble stuff as tastelessly carved wooden spoons and salad forks, eucharistic bread-stamps, and rather intriguing wooden wine-jugs. The litter lay cheek by jowl on the counters with wooden and wire hairpins and combs for the long-haired monks, rosaries strung by wandering hermits of seeds picked up in the woods, walking-sticks straight off the trees, herbs, salves, scents and distillations, and picture postcards of the monasteries. Better and higher-priced work sometimes arrived in the form of carved and painted ikons, holding rigidly to tradition, a type of handcraft mentioned in the sixteenth century.

Such a souvenir shop was close by, with a hermit like a forest bird inside, shyly offering his work to the habited shopkeeper. A monk who had obtained the appointment of police photographer was setting up the tripod of his passport camera outside the police station.

A lay shoemaker had a pigeon-hole of a shop just beyond, and shared a bench with an assistant who stitched by jerking two ends of waxed thread in opposite directions with a powerful elbow movement. A chair to sit on and somebody to watch at work was as much as the village ever offered at this hour, and two or three idlers already filled up the shop without more intention of ordering a pair of shoes than myself. Both cobblers were ready with local gossip in exchange for outside news. I took the free chair.

The master-cobbler, an up-and-down fellow, whistling if no ecclesiastic were by and sighing the moment after, pulled his last sheet of leather off a shelf.

"This finished, and up go the shutters," he announced, guffawing mirthlessly. "Can I find a monk partner to get my leather in duty free for me? And how to pay duty on leather and charge the same as duty-free cobblers? Even holy men know the difference between good and bad bargains."

He was sighing again as a monk, bearing the furled umbrella carried on outings, went by with a wiry step. One of the gossipers, in muleteer's homespun, shot to his feet, and went in pursuit.

"There's the sort of partner to be in with," the cobbler remarked, with a final hoot, watching master and man disappear to the waiting mule. "That's Pavlos of . . ." and he named a distant kelli, "in on business. Before his wine goes away you see five barrels, four of wine and one of water. And if you're back in half an hour you'll see five barrels of wine in the same barrels, Pavlos having duplicated the first miracle of the Gospels, and then marked those barrels with red crosses to show they've been blessed.

"Who's having a day's change down here is Gabriel from up there," he went on, stabbing at a kelli on the heights with his awl. "Went by five minutes ago, though not once a month you see him round this way."

"Why should you?" the assistant asked.

"Why? why?" the cobbler exclaimed, opening his hand in the air. "Have you called at that paradise up there?" he demanded, swinging round on me. "There are four of them, and old Gabriel's their elder. What water! What air! What trees! And Gabriel full of money. One runs about for the rest, one gardens, one hunts. They leave Gabriel to sit all day on his veranda watching us here, where a mule can't sneeze without him knowing. What can't happen to a man full of money!"

He ran to the door to hail a handsome, foolish youth loitering by. He had won an hour's notoriety by claiming to have been called by nereids, tall, sweetly singing, golden-haired women with floating veils who are said to be encountered at the opposite hours of midday and midnight. In certain moods they look for a bridegroom, but are untrustworthy unless caught by the veil, whereupon they become obedient. But should she steal the veil again she vanishes, nor may she be sent to the well for water, for then surely will she find freedom. Marriages between villagers and nereids are known by hearsay, though generally the nereid turns out to be a goldenhaired Swede or Norwegian.

"I hear you've been back to your village?" the cobbler called. "Have you had more trouble?"

The youth signalled "no" by slowly raising his cleft chin skywards. The cobbler helped him past the shop with a thump between the shoulders, then he leapt back to his last and brought his hammer on a boot heel, lamenting: "Another lost five minutes!"

He had not evened up the heel before another worthwhile spectacle had him at the door again. Two thieves had been taken on the Mountain, which led to the arrest of a couple of youths from Prosphori as receivers. The regulation was that thieves and receivers must be taken to the scene of their activities before serving sentence, and appear publicly with the stolen articles.

This warning spectacle now drifted past the shop door. The prisoners meandered between gendarmes down the middle of the road, handcuffed in pairs, decorated with watches, clocks, blankets, lengths of cloth, while a bored mule followed under piles of blankets and a carpet. One of the receivers grasped a cross, as if blessing the people who watched. His partner was full of bravado. But he with the cross hung his head. The out-of-step procession wandered away down the street, the mule yawning.

The cobbler bounded back to his last, exclaiming:

"How they're eating stick for their three meals a day!"

Finally he shot off the bench to welcome an elderly Russian monk who came to try on a pair of boots. These went on, and became fixtures; but the monk was an agreeable old man, and blamed his vanity for not having insisted on a roomier measure. The boots were still being stretched when we glanced at our watches and decided the morning must be gone. Mine, set by the "world", stood at eleven-thirty; an Iviron monk, timing from sunrise, showed six-thirty; his companion from Xeropotamou, reckoning from sunset, had three-thirty. The cobbler's watch had stopped. The common interpretation was, it was time to break up the meeting. The cobbler's hoot followed me half-way down the street.

The street ran on for a hundred yards, to end at Assembly headquarters, and then turn into a lane leading towards St. Andrew's Skete. I turned into an eating-house. Everyone sooner or later passed the window of its dining-room; but when I sat down shops were shutting for the siesta and would not open until after vespers, and the road, which had been full of striding and pacing monks, had hardly a human being left on it. Almost the last man abroad was the Mountain's senior monk, the protepistates, handling his black staff, and trailing a full-bearded kilted guard at his heels.

The bare dining-room was full of munching labourers, and monks entertaining relations from the world. Talk drowned the clatter of cutlery. The Greek diner found enough in a little red wine, or a thumbnail glass of raki, to magnify a saucer of salted herrings and another of salted cucumbers into a repast, capable of being lengthened indefinitely by optimistic talk. A waiter moved between the tables calling, "Command me!" but nothing of account was ordered, except a bottle of beer for me to garnish the beans.

Father Athanasios, whose dental chair had an unparalleled view of the Mountain, went gliding past the window. The amiable old man pinned his beard into his knot of hair before bending to fill a cavity. He had come to the Mountain at a time when they stood a comb in a man's whiskers to see if he was old enough. If the comb fell out the novice was not accepted until time had stiffened his hairs. There was an absence of terror-striking instruments in his surgery; he kept them in an old chocolate-box.

My hand-wave brought him to the window:

"That tooth didn't worry you?"

"Not a twinge, Father. Won't you join me in a coffee?" But he was in a hurry and dipped away down the street.

A gendarme made his way towards the landlord washing glasses.

"That's the new lad," observed my next-door neighbour to a companion. "Seems the right kind." But the old man he had jogged screwed both eyes at the gendarme's back and observed:

"There are white dogs in this world, and there are black dogs. Both are dogs."

All the world would fall asleep for two hours, and so I could not call on the Holy Assembly until after vespers. I turned into the sun-stricken street, the last of the diners, as the waiter was slapping up the wine-stains from the tables. Crushed with heat I made my way to the first tree that offered its shade.

On the way to the Protaton Church for vespers I passed an eighteenth-century bell-tower, which held a small library of forty-odd vellum manuscripts dating from the thirteenth century, and a few early books. An historic document was the Mountain's earliest typikon or charter, known as the Tragos, or Billygoat, dating from the end of the tenth century. The early hermits had sent the Protos, accompanied by Paul of Xeropotamou, to complain to the emperor, John Tzimiskes, of the modernizing activities of Athanasios of the Great Lavra, and the emperor delegated Euthymios of the Studium to draw up a constitution.

The name of the church is derived from the Protos, ruler, of the community, until the office ceased half-way through the seventeenth century. It is the oldest church on the Mountain, a tenth-century renewal of an older building. Yet its destruction is spoken of by the creatures of Michael VIII Palaeologos, and two tombs of murdered monks are pointed out near the door. It was certainly rebuilt by John Bogdan, voivode of Moldavia, in 1508, and with its flat wooden ceiling and absence of a central dome on pillars is unlike other churches on Athos.

I stared from a stall into distances palely lighted by a shaft from a window. Though the light was frail, it brought out the clarets, ochres, and cold sea-greens of the ikons it fell across and, as it moved, uncovered new stores of wealth on the way. The church has exceptional murals of the Macedonian School, showing certain pre-fourteenth-century tendencies, though partially attributed to the sixteenth-century Emanuel Panselinos of Salonika, the legend of whose fame and influence has survived nearly all, and perhaps all, his work.

The capital's other important murals belong to the chapel of John the Baptist, and unfortunately have been restored.

Byzantine art seems to have crept out of the catacombs into the light of imperial favour about the time of Christianity's official recognition. It was a plant of three flowerings, breaking open into full beauty in the fourth and fifth centuries, and at its richest in the sixth under Justinian. A second flowering followed during the tenth to twelfth centuries, after the long ikonoclastic struggle led into that age of prosperity and luxury. Then rose that school known as "Macedonian" of which a few remains are recorded on the Mountain. It was remarkable for powerful treatment of rich colour disciplined within the framework of austere design. Byzantium, as gateway between east and west, was susceptible to the artistic influences of both points of the compass, and, presented with Greek idealism and Oriental realism, moved towards and presently accepted the former.

Byzantine decoration was usually expressed through the medium of mosaic work until the twelfth century; but on the growing impoverishment of the Empire, patron and artist acquiesced in the cheaper medium of the fresco.

The final flowering was in those centuries of the Empire's greatest trial, the fifteenth and sixteenth, when the scattered learned gathered at Constantinople and increased the pace of the Renaissance. The sixteenth century was the copious period of Athonite painting.

The Cretan School had arisen, bright with the old qualities of faithful idealism and strong treatment of colour, and its master, Theophanes of Crete, stood out against the tendencies towards orientalism and the amiabilities of Italy, which had entered the Macedonian School. The outstanding exponent of this betrayal of tradition was the mysterious Panselinos, whose only unquestioned work (and some people doubt even this) remains in the Protaton.

I faced the wide screen, behind which several imposing ikons of large size looked down into the beam; among them the Axion Estin ikon, moved annually into the nave during Easter week, in anticipation of the ceremonial visit to Koutloumousiou. The imposing procession is set in motion on Easter Monday after the Liturgy, led by a monk with semantron, a priest with cross and basil, banner-bearing monks and carriers of candles in man-high candlesticks. The police appoint themselves standard-bearers of the national flag, and these majestically-pacing people are the spray before a wave of robed ecclesiastics and black-habited monks, pressing down the narrow confined street, bearing the Axion Estin ikon exposed under an ornamental umbrella, flanked by guards, rifle on shoulder. The procession halts at stations for offerings of eggs, bread and cheese, and white and red wine.

At the bottom of a deep valley behind St. Andrew's lies Pantokratoros' kelli of the Falling-Asleep-of-the-Virgin, and there on June 11, A.D. 980, during the reign of Basil II, the junior was alone during his elder's absence at matins in the Protaton. The youth was on the point of reading his office when a stranger arrived and agreed to read it with him. On coming to the Ninth Ode, composed by the eighth-century monk Kosmas Maioumas, the stranger prefaced it by the chant: "Worthy it is

(Axion Estin) to magnify thee, Mother of God", and instructed the junior always to preface the ode thus. When the untutored youth proved unable to remember the phrase after three repetitions, the stranger asked for writing materials and, finding these lacked in the primitive place, had a stone brought him and wrote the words with a finger; for the visitor was no other than the Archangel Gabriel. During this glorious office, the archangel stood on the right of the tiny chapel, facing the junior on the left, and so great was the pleasure of the ikon of the Virgin on the screen, in whose praise the ode had been amended, that it miraculously changed places with the ikon of Christ, and became attached to the right of the screen doors, the Christ shifting to the left. The obscure chapel is the only building on Athos where the Virgin is to be found on the right of the screen doors and Christ in the lowlier position.

The elder on his return heard the youth chanting the canticle, and advised Karyes of the miracle. The stone inscribed by the archangel was carried there, and later forwarded to Constantinople, while the ikon before which the archangel had chanted "Worthy it is" was placed in the Protaton.

Behind the screen in the Protaton was a second ikon of Christ as Pantokrator, known as the Answer-in-place-of-Another, since a heedless priest loitered over his office, though begged to be speedy by an aged monk who was weak from fasting and wanted to communicate. Christ took pity, though the priest did not, and this ikon ordered speed three times for the fainting monk's sake.

I stood in my stall through vespers. The holy door opened to reveal the priest beside the altar with the thurible, and the deacon with the taper. The two moved forward to cense the church, the deacon leading censed all in turn in allusion to the first amazing motion of the Holy Spirit over the face of the waters. Then the holy door closed in awful remembrance of the shutting of Eden's gates. Out of sight in the sanctuary the uncovered priest recited the seven prayers of light, in token of miserable Adam's repentance. Stage by stage, the service continued to its appointed end.

It was over in an hour and I free to go to the Holy Community's headquarters. The morning session had drawn leading monks from all over the Mountain to join the Twenty, and I penetrated below stairs for news and caught the ecclesiastical police in a moment of relaxation. The nearest pulled himself up in the middle of an anecdote, his bearded face became a formal mask, and he assured me that business was over and the meeting socially inclined.

Up I went to a room where the monastic representatives occupied allotted seats to transact business and receive visitors with credentials. Monks stood, walked about, relaxed over coffee. A few still sat over business at side tables.

This ruling council crystallized into its present form in 1810, and is composed of a single representative (proestaminos) from each of the twenty monasteries, and meets at the Protaton on Mondays, Wednesdays, and Fridays, in stalls assigned to the representatives in accordance with a ranking beginning with Lavra and ending with Kastamonitou.

Representatives are elected at their monasteries on January 1, and set out for the monastic residencies at Karyes, where they remain until returning to their monasteries a few days before Christmas. The Holy Community acts as a tribunal of first instance in intermonastic disputes, with the Patriarch in Constantinople as a final court of appeal, and as a court of appeal for plaintiffs dissatisfied with judgements given against them by monasteries acting as a court of first importance.

On the other weekdays the business of the Holy Community is transacted by a separate committee of four overseers (epistatae), elected yearly on June 1 from groups of four monasteries taken in rotation. Thus all monasteries are represented on this committee in the course of five years. The committee includes one member of an important house, who takes the title "protepistates", and fills the presidential seat.

This "epistasia"—the executive arm of the Holy Community—sees to street cleaning, price fixing, and public behaviour generally. No lay voice stays lifted in song should an overseer be in the neighbourhood, nor does the smoker solace himself in the forbidden place, nor the card-player allow himself to be seen. No meat hangs in the market on Wednesdays or Fridays; no shop stays open during vespers, nor on Sundays, nor on festivals. The "epistasia" receive the communal correspondence, and handle the common purse.

A number of men looked administrators. Humbler monks had voted them into office, and a charge is often brought against the elders by the lowlier of acting too proudly after election. The idiorrhythmic houses are especially accused of allowing privilege to pass into the hands of a few. The cylindrical hats and sweeping habits magnified an average stature; but tall men were present and others were impressively corpulent. The long hair worn by all was pinned up under the chimney pot hats, and an unscissored beard spread down from every chin. Through this socially inclined company moved the blackjacketed and white-kilted police, bearded too, with salvers set with coffee-cups and water-glasses.

The civil governor and his secretary were two laymen present, and the former stepped up within a few minutes of my arrival to press my shoulder meaningly; for this wistful official was temperamentally a man about town who lived out a perpetual Sunday in his capital, where semantrons everlastingly called him to services he did not wish to attend. He would absent himself in the woods, to shoot, against public opinion; or descended on a remote monastery, hoping to benefit by a change of scene. But the rapping broke out in the court, day and night, wherever he was. Occasionally he was able to fly from the Mountain, and then he appeared in city teashops where his incredible fate was forgotten.

In 1924 Greek Government representatives met with members of the Athonite community to formulate a new constitution. This recognized all the Mountain's monks as Greek subjects, left ecclesiastical justice to the discretion of the Holy Community and monastic authorities, and brought penal cases before the civil courts in Salonika. A governor was appointed by the Greek Foreign Office to see the Holy Community's decisions were carried out, provided they did not run counter to the Constitution.

Euthymios, representative of a shoreside monastery, pressed forward to shake hands.

"This is kinder weather," he chuckled, referring to a previous winter's invasion of our premises by a boundary commission of the governor and half-a-dozen elders with their attendants and mules. "What weather we had with you! Was there a day without a snowstorm? But look at it now.

PLATE II   *An old fountain, Iviron Monastery*

PLATE 12   *Kastamonitou Monastery in winter; and* (below) *Xenophontos Monastery*

We lose a thing out of our left hand sometimes only to find it back in the right."

"Your cairn seems to have taken in several yards of the village soil, and left us less of the world than ever. The women complain."

"They'll still step over the wall if they think no one is looking," he chuckled. "It was nearly impossible to find the true boundary marks under the snow."

I pressed deeper into the gowns. The hum of friends making the most of friends before roads cut them off again recalled a successful tea-party. I was signalled to over intervening shoulders, and smiled back into the unseamed, sanguine face of Meletios, once secretary-general here, and now Vatopedi's secretary. We settled at a table out of the way and took jam and coffee from a servant. Meletios was lame, but he was a man of manners and delicate attention, who had the month before sent me fifteen okes of wine and a back-scratcher, which was a hermit's masterpiece, in exchange for a canary. The back-scratcher's handle was carved in the engaging conception of a snake displaying a line of swallowed victims in its stomach. Vatopedi's secretary now asked on his committee's behalf for a few dozen gambuzia fish from our tank, to introduce to marshy country near his monastery. The gambuzia feed largely on mosquito larvae. We arranged then and there that he should visit me and get them.

Meletios was writing a book on his monastery's treasures. He wrote in a florid French rather than in his native Greek, which he knew a great deal better. When I saw the manuscript it had advanced no farther than a graceful dedication to the King of the Hellenes. Inasmuch as there was the same elegance of handwriting as in the turned French sentences, for Meletios could do nothing inelegantly, the three or four pages in being were a pleasure to turn over.

"How's the book?" I asked, having settled about the fish.

"Our monastery's a thousand years old," he replied pensively, "so a thousand days should not be too many to give up to a book on it." He passed a hand down his burnished beard, and continued to coo: "I'm setting aside a hundred thousand, two hundred thousand drachmas, and in ten years' time, when fully middle-aged and able to weigh the world, I shall ask for a year's leave to visit foreign countries. Then I shall return to the Mountain for good. I shall have seen the world and be satisfied in a way I am not yet."

He sighed in the same gentle fashion, and his large sentimental eyes liquefied at the size of the adventure. I turned the talk down a less disquieting avenue by asking after the canary.

"Why have you never been to see him?" he asked reproachfully. "He has a cage to himself in the window. Come and see us. I've potted a gardenia for you."

"Have you tamed him like the other?"

Meletios' face travelled ceiling-wards in negation:

"He has another nature to my first bird."

One of the Mountain's sensations was to be present when Meletios cheeped his original bird along his brown beard as far as his full red lips, against which it laid a yellow beak.

We had arrived at the coffee-dregs when disturbed by Charalambos of Dionysiou advancing down an opening channel of monks, black staff in hand. He came to suggest that as he expected to be late I should go on to the konak ahead of him. I told him that I meant to leave early in the morning for Pantokratoros, then I departed with a new permit in my pocket.

The konak was a decaying wooden house near trees gilded by evening. The pyramid of the Holy Mountain presented its unclimbable face, and rose treeless to its apex. It reigned at the end of leagues of forest and meadowland. The Holy Sea spread as far as eyesight reached, and in the garden round the house, birds entered into full evening song. Five habited labourers dug the glinting meadow, and two students from the Theological School, who served in the house, hurried out to invite me inside.

They were gay, polite youths of eighteen or so, with heavy uncut hair lying on their shoulders, and half-sprouted beards. They took me to a chair on the flat roof to enjoy the view of the Mountain, and after serving me with coffee and jam, left me with a jar of chilled water in reach.

Gardeners worked below. An octogenarian in a monastic bonnet tottered up and down, irrigating vegetables, leading a stream through channels and talking aloud to it. I raised my feet to a rail and my eyes to the coloured peak. Into every marble corrie, into every harsh ravine passed a golden light, which turned to the roses and amethyst of evening.

The burning out of a day could not be better passed than in watching men guide water over parched earth.

It was dusk when Charalambos came along the passage calling for cold water, a bottle of raki, and a plate of raw beans, which we sat over for the next hour.

"I've been watching the peak colour," I said.

"There's no view like this at Dionysiou! And I meet people here. Some representatives are unhappy leaving their monasteries for Karyes, but helping to govern the Mountain satisfies me." His eyes flashed.

"You prefer work to prayers?"

"God uses both types," he answered. "As a youth I wondered where the place could be which gave an opportunity for both lives. It was here."

"Did you have misgivings at first?"

Charalambos nodded.

"I was not useful for much. I had hours given me for reflection without knowing how to reflect. I've fallen asleep in church. Young men are more afraid of a vigil than the old are. How the peak glows! I've heard it suggested that this was the 'exceeding high mountain' of our Lord's third temptation in the wilderness. But I don't know. One can see a great distance from the summit; but hardly all the 'kingdoms of the world, and the glory of them'. Most men agree the mountain is in Palestine, but do I know?"

"It rises over Jericho, looking across that waste they call the Ghor. Where the brood-camels graze on thorn, towards the swelling of the Jordan."

"Then it isn't our mountain. But the Virgin has trodden here. It should be enough." But his sigh suggested that, like most monks, he would have liked to believe that it was the Mount of Temptation too.

He called down to the old man to go inside; but the dodderer, privileged by age, did not notice him.

"Don't you hear, old man?"

"The water's to run a little yet," the old man quavered. "It'll be running some minutes after you turn it off."

"Do I know less about my work that I did?"

"I meant nothing, old man. The stones a shepherd uses to drive his dogs off a stranger aren't intended to break bones."

The patriarch turned his back at last on the long burning landscape, crowned by the Mountain, and washed by the sliding platforms of the sea, and doddered out of sight.

Tapers and ikon lamps in the chapel saved the ikons from the darkness that shrouded them. A solitary wider round of light was thrown by the reader's larger taper across his own gaunt face and on the page of the tome he read from loudly. Compline ended the day's work. We filed into the broad passage to supper, which was laid down a long table, with various fish and salad dishes. We were served by the students from the seminary. This seminary exists to leaven the lump with a little learning, and is supported out of a tax levied on the monasteries, according to the individual wealth of the monastery. Each house is expected to supply the school with two pupils, preferably from inmates, and failing that from religiously inclined young men from the "world". It is poorly attended in spite of an excellent teaching staff.

Charalambos settled the affairs of next day over the meal. Then, the meal finished, stood up, his face flushed with the good wine we had drunk, and his eyes glowing. We all turned to the wall ikon as one. Heads inclined, hands folded. The brief thanksgiving was sonorous.

In a stride or two Charalambos had thrown open the door into the passage, and then from the passage into another room, forcing me in before him, in spite of his habit. There we sat on a divan sipping coffee, while he called for the sheets from his own bed so that I might enjoy them for the night. He alone of the company possessed this luxury, but he was ready to forgo it in observance of hospitality.

9

The Coenobitic Skete of St. Andrew

Axion Estin Kelli

The Coenobitic Skete of Prophet Elijah

Pantokratoros: the Idiorrhythmic Monastery of the Almighty

The Idiorrhythmic Monastery of Stavronikita

HUNDREDS OF BIRDS sang the day in as I set out next morning at the crack of dawn. The path ran through a grassy paddock into a lane which led to a kiosk outside the village, then through an outer court of the Russian skete of St. Andrew. The way was round the outer wall, and down a slippery track that plunged into a valley. A few people were already abroad, trying to go their several ways before the heat of the day. I could remember

St. Andrew's court full of monks and mules collecting for work at this hour; but the great house steadily emptied year after year.

This coenobitic skete is a range of buildings in the Russian style, conspicuous at a distance on account of flashing gold crosses and green domes, built round an imposing church dedicated to St. Andrew the Apostle. The monk Bessarion founded it in 1849, on the site of the ancient monastery of Xestre, and filled it with Little Russians. It is a dependency of Vatopedi. Bessarion made a gift of the ikon known as the Consolation-of-Mourners, which is said to have untied the tongue of a dumb Russian youth praying before it.

The prior, an austere man, accustomed to long nights on a throne in church, once led me down empty corridors, past disused chapels and unoccupied cells, to a locked room where the instruments of penance which had been stripped off dead monks were kept. Iron belts, iron braces, massive crosses of iron, an iron helmet taking two men to lift it on to the wearer's head. After giving a monk permission to discipline himself in this fashion, the prior shared the wearer's secret until death made it known to all. The prior's own black staff ended in a carving of two serpents entwined through the eye-sockets of a skull.

The usual skete is a settlement round a common church—the kyriakon—used on Sundays and festivals, but the monks read their daily offices in chapels attached to their cottages or kalyvas. A cottage is usually shared by three or more monks; an elder (yeron), a full monk (pater), and a novice (archarios). Cottage and grounds are held on a life tenancy bought by the inmates, who succeed one another in rank, and on the death of one pay the overlord monastery a further sum to allow admission of a new partner. The elders of a settlement choose their prior, who must be acceptable to the sovereign monastery, and must be a priest.

Several sketes of this type are on the Mountain, where the monks employ themselves at ikon-painting and wood-carving; but the Russian skete of St. Andrew, and the large Rumanian skete behind Lavra dedicated to the Forerunner, are run on monastic lines, but have no vote on the Holy Assembly.

At a corner I passed close to a monk on his knees, who bowed to my moving legs, having probably to prostrate himself to passers for some misdemeanour, perhaps pride. The road began its steep fall, and narrowed to a track embowered in the tender foliage of chestnuts newly in leaf, and scented by flowering acacias. A stream bawled out of sight in thickets of honeysuckle, box, and laurel. The long, slippery descent called for care.

The kelli's farm-house lay at the bottom, where the stream ran out of the tangled scrub and crossed the road. A deacon, a friendly young Bulgar, stopped digging the garden to take me inside to his elder, who at once remarked on my damp face.

"Some of your roads are as hard to go down as up," I answered him.

"That's why they don't bring our ikon down here any longer at Easter," he answered, amused. "Now they take it to Koutloumousiou instead. Modern monks haven't the hearts and legs of the early men."

This was the Axion Estin kelli, the scene of the angelic intervention of a thousand years ago. Both elder and junior were delighted to have a visitor, for few pass that way.

"Is one of you responsible for this delicious roseleaf jam?" I asked, on being served.

"Give the credit to St. Tryphon for keeping away the caterpillars," said the elder, pleased at my appreciation. "We'd be wise to dedicate more chapels to St. Tryphon. His heart is with gardeners."

They rarely left their big, well-kept garden, and Karyes saw them seldom. The junior was due to go to Sophia on family business and meant to fly there. From being a thousand years behind the times the hour's flight would bring him right up to date.

The ramshackle building was pleasantly cool, but lost time would be paid for in the shadeless country ahead. The empty coffee-cup went back on the tray and we stood up. The elder took a key several inches long from a nail. The chapel it unlocked had absorbed the original thousand-year-old chapel of the Axion Estin miracle, which was now an apse; a space so confined that the archangel and the monk must have knelt barely a yard apart to chant the office. The original chancel doors are preserved in a wall-case. Here it was that the Virgin's ikon miraculously changed places with Christ's.

The three of us stood elbow to elbow, and a mellow wandering light kindled the clarets and greens of the ikons. The murmured recitation of the story further tranquillized us. A panel outside the chapel records it in painting.

I was soon on the path again. It ran through scrub towards the unseen sea, and soon merged into a wider path which mounted over sandstone and through cistus bushes until blue water shone in sight; then it forked, to go towards Stavronikita, and finally bent left to Pantokratoros.

Near the fork stood a shady tree, a pillar of importance now the sun was well up. A layman sat in possession, poring over envelopes and scraps of paper held to his eyes. Feeling entitled to a share of the shade, I walked up.

The man lifted a sallow, angular, unshaven face. His lap was full of postage stamps, obsolete Rumanian issues.

"Where's this haul from?" I asked, tossing my hat off and sinking beside him.

He passed over a handful of stamps, some glued to the original faded envelopes. My interest tickled him.

"I stopped collecting as a boy," I said, turning the stamps over, "and have forgotten nearly all I knew then. Some of these must be scarce."

"Most of them are," he answered, licking his lips.

"And still on the original envelopes."

"On their envelopes," he agreed. "I expected them to exist. And they did."

"Are you a collector?"

"I keep a stamp shop in Athens."

I continued turning over the stamps, which he seemed relieved to get back.

"Monks never get rid of letters," he remarked. "I went to the Rumanian skete behind Lavra for them."

"Isn't this the find of your life?"

"Those old men had kept them about their rooms for a generation. They thought them rubbish, and handed them over. I've interested you?"

He began wrapping up his spoil in a cloth, and we stood up, he taking the path I had come along, while I headed for Pantokratoros. The barren country became decorated with a violet cistus, in addition to the commoner rose and white varieties. At last the monastery came in sight, perched above the sea, and finally the falling path brought me level with the long range of buildings on a hill.

The Russian skete of Prophet Elijah, withdrawn among gardens and cypresses on a higher level, dreamed in the sunshine. This coenobian skete was founded in 1839, but completed later: however, traditionally it reached back to a Russian, Paisios, of 1753. It was privileged to elect its own prior, but was a dependant of Pantokratoros. The fine church was begun in 1881. The era of Russian pilgrimages brought countless pilgrims to revere two ikons, the Virgin on the south side, said to have wept on a February day during the Turko-Russian War when Turkish soldiers burst into the church searching for arms, and the Virgin-giving-the-Child-suck, on the screen above the holy door.

A backwater, the paddling ground of turtles, cut the path, and on the bridge's farther side stood the wellhouse connected with the Virgin-of-the-Elder. Turkish raiders sailed into the harbour, and swarmed up into the monastery's court, bent on plunder. They found the monks looking down from the upper windows of the keep, out of reach with their treasure. The robber leader hoped to draw them from their security by breaking into the church. He carried out the Virgin-of-the-Elder, so called because she reproved a tardy priest and sent him hurrying to a dying elder. The robbers took it downhill to the bridge. But the monks proved more prudent than indignant and remained where they were. The Turkish captain carried the insult farther by lighting his pipe with a splinter from the ikon; but still prudence kept the monks in the keep. However, the Virgin did not overlook the insult, and the splinter flew into the Turk's eye, and blinded him. His followers threw the ikon into the well, and then sailed away.

Towards the end of his life the blind Turk was troubled by his sin. He called his relatives and sent them to inform the monks of the ikon's whereabouts. A volunteer set off, and the lost ikon was fished up from the well after seventy-five years at the bottom.

I reached the gate without encountering porter or guestmaster, went inside and leaned over a court decorated with faience work. Swallows and martins wheeled on a level with my eyes, crowding the warm, golden air with joyous winged forms. A greybeard, slithering by in slippers, suggested the guestmaster might be in the kitchen garden, and later the missing man came striding in with an armful of vegetables, a swarthy Cretan of the restless type that island can produce, men ready to spring up to new activity as soon as they sit down.

He threw open a door on to a magnificent sea-view of neighbouring Stavronikita, etched on a rocky headland against the background of the snow-ribbed Mountain; then called me into a dark kitchen where he was setting the tray.

This idiorrhythmic house of thirty-five monks claimed a fourteenth-century foundation by two nobles of the period, Alexios Stratopedarch and John the Primikerios. The church was quickly completed, and the founders lie in a mausoleum dated 1363 in the narthex, beside a monk, Jonas. The walls were strengthened in 1536, and the western cells built the following year; but the rest of the monastery is hardly two hundred years old.

The church was dedicated to the Transfiguration, and frescoed throughout in 1538. Nearly all is restored work, but the monks claim certain groups to be by Panselinos, the faces of the large figures of Christ, the Virgin and the Forerunner round the west doorway of the eso-narthex, and certain other faces on the nave's west wall. Yet the only traces of this painter recognized by lay authority, and then with reserve, are the recumbent Christ-child and another fragment on the Protaton walls.

The Virgin-of-the-Elder against the north-west pillar is disappointing. Long submergence in water caused Russian silversmiths to cover the picture in a sheet of silver and repaint the face and hands. She might have left the workshop yesterday.

The ikon's claim to power rests on wider ground than the blinding of a pirate. It caused a miraculous flow of oil at a time when there was insufficient in the monastery to anoint a sick abbot. The oil-store was then, as now, off the court above the church. A monk noticed a trickle of oil oozing from the storehouse. When the store was opened a row of empty jars were being filled by one overflowing from the other. Oil bubbled from the first jar. I was taken into this storeroom. The miraculous jar was still in place, before which the monk crossed himself as he repeated the story.

The sun was low and red, inflaming the precipitous land and nearly motionless sea. Monks gossiped in a recess in a cliff half-way to shore, and I joined them. I secured a niche besidea smiling old man telling his story. He had been a village lad when a monk from Athos came to his father's cafe, and told such entrancing stories of the Holy Mountain that the lad was tempted to run away. For a few days he hid from authority in a wine-cask, creeping out at night for food and drink. Before the week was out he was found and taken before the elders, who forbade him the Mountain until there were sufficient hairs round his chin. He returned home crestfallen, to feel his cheeks daily until enough hair had sprouted to encourage him to try again.

A taciturn man beyond him had lost wife, children, a brother and sister by plague. The completeness of the disaster turned his thoughts to the habit. Next to him was an archimandrite, crippled by war tortures, his speech thickened by paralysis. Calm shone through the fog of physical disabilities. Calamity had made the first man gloomy, but introduced the second to serenity.

Others enjoyed the sunset hour. One had shown me the library, and we had gone from there to see the notable illuminated Gospels known as John Kalivitou's, remarkable among Athonite books for an antique silver-gilt binding and chainwork back.

Isidoros, the guestmaster, owner of a boat and fishing-net, flew past me down to shore in goat-like bounds, calling me to follow. Several fishermen and monks were baiting night-lines and repairing nets. A large boat at the quay had fifty or more octopuses draped over the spears, which rested in crotches. The flesh had dried all day in the strong sun, and yesterday's catch was shrivelling. To-day's hung clammily, the suckers still dripping. Rough men sat in the waists of their boats over wicker baskets, and, baited scores of hooks on the coiled fishing-lines with lumps of tentacle. They lived on the sea, and their pickled skins looked on the point of sprouting scales.

An elderly, gap-toothed, tobacco-brown islander harangued a circle of listeners as he cut bait up.

"Ah, the technician that bonesetter was! If you broke a leg, that strong young fellow, his son, would hold you, and his father made both ends meet, and bound you up. Then you counted one day for every year you had, and at the end of that time the bone was knit, and you walked about on your leg again. Our butcher was jerked down the rocks by a big red-

and-white bullock he was trying to lead. His leg was a salad when they picked him up," his ten fingers shot out to show the splinters. "They sent for the bonesetter. He came with a newly flayed goatskin and some eggs. 'Hold him down,' he called to that powerful lad, his son. And he worked that bone back where it must go, with the butcher howling! Then the egg and goat-hair were made into a paste, and the skin stretched over the break. 'As you're forty-four years old, you can take that skin off in forty-four days,' said the bonesetter. And that leg was even better than the other!"

"Where did he learn?" I asked, introducing myself with a cigarette.

"Did he not learn from his father?" the islander demanded, sticking the cigarette behind his ear. "And that father from his father. He was out shooting one day and ran into a gendarme. 'Where's your gun licence?' asked the gendarme; for he was one of that sort. The bonesetter had none; for how could a man with five children still eating bread have a licence? So they took away his gun. In a few days that gendarme fell off a balcony, and this technician was the only man who knew how to mend his bones; but the sergeant was afraid to call him, as he had no permit to practise. But that technician goes secretly: 'Look here, sergeant, shall we do like this? If I cure your man you will give me back my gun, and if I fail you will keep it.' They agreed, and that gendarme walked about in time to get drunk on his saint's day. In twenty-four days, for he was twenty-four years old."

He finished cutting bait and thrust his great toe into the mesh of his net to keep it taut for the wooden repairing needle.

"He had twelve godsons to follow him to the grave when he died, all sea captains who could take their caïques through their anchor rings! What seamen! Well, he watered the village with his good deeds!" And he sighed gustily.

Isidoros finished coiling the nets, and ordered a boy into the bows with it. I got in aft. He pulled the boat from the shore with a violence that raised him off the thwart; but once round the rocky head of the small harbour he stood up facing the bow, and drove the boat through the silky water by throwing himself forward on the oars.

The sea passed in slow, wide heaves towards the world's rim; the encrimsoned coast soared up in cliffs and precipices, which bore aloft hermitages and chapels in astonishing places. The tower and walls of our monastery diminished on the headland; but a mile away there increased on a cliff the more fantastic Stavronikita, resembling a castle more than a home for religious men. Enough light remained for the unwrinkled water to duplicate this world upside down. We crept beetlelike in the company of half-a-dozen boats moving to favourite fishing-grounds for lowering nets and night-lines.

The boy told us that his baby sister squinted.

"Blessed crab-claws will prevent a child squinting," Isidores stated didactically, tossing his head so that the black beard went up like a scythe.

"In my island," said the boy, proud of being on conversational terms with men, "we powder dried sea-horses, and soak them in raki; what a tonic for tired men!"

We floated over a deep hole, half a mile from shore. The nearest land fell down in a cliff. Isidores raised his oars from the water and rested on them; but the boat continued gliding a few lengths before drifting to a standstill. The death of effort caused the guestmaster to fix his eyes on the boy who squatted among the night-lines near the net.

"Cease fishing in a year or two and become a monk," he ordered. "What can the sea ever give you? Your bread and hardly that. If you become a monk you'll learn to read and speak gently, even to read in church. And you receive the blessed bread at dawn and start the day clean. What's a fisherman? A ragged, empty fellow, usually far from God."

"But I'm nothing," the boy answered in wonder, "and my father a poor man."

"Wasn't I one of a large family eating bread?" Isidores demanded.

"What monastery should a poor fisher-boy go to?" the boy asked.

"That, up there," the guestmaster answered, pointing violently at Stavronikita. "There they have the ikon St. Nicholas-of-the-Oyster. The Panayia permitted fishermen as poor as you to draw it up out of the sea in their nets. An oyster was sticking to the forehead when that holy ikon came dripping from the green water."

Then monk turned into fisherman. Isidoros ordered the boy over to the oars and took charge of the net. The boy slowly poled the boat in a wide arc, stern first, through the silky darkenings of the water, timing it with

Isidoros's soundless letting down of the red net. A few gourds were left bobbing as buoys.

"It is now with God," Isidoros observed, glancing down through the blackening water, deep into which the long net had sunk, and removing responsibility for the morning's catch from his own shoulders on to those of the Maker of all men and fishes. He turned his kindled eyes and hawk-like face back to the boy, and again ordered: "To-night, when you lie down to sleep, ask God to lead you to become a monk."

Isidoros promised to lend me his boat to save the walk to Stavronikita. He was up all night with two other monks in the bakery, kneading the eight hundred weekly loaves, and still had the baking to do in the morning. The bakery was an airy, twilit chamber at the top of a court, and when I looked in for news the ashes of the fired brushwood had just been raked out of the cavernous oven. Trays of risen dough were stacked ready to push in, and the three half-naked bakers in headkerchiefs had picked up the wooden shovels with handles like spearshafts. The baked loaves would be the size of a man's two fists, three hundred to last the thirty-five monks a week, and five hundred for workmen, dependants and travellers.

I stayed to watch the trays manœuvred into place across the heated bricks and hear the door clamped to, releasing the bakers for a time. Isidoros immediately plunged off to his kitchen, flicking sweat away with both hands as he galloped, to make sure I left with a cup of coffee inside me. He plunged ahead from the kitchen to the shore, and pounced on the boy coiling night-lines, but boatless, someone having borrowed it. This brought him up short on the shingle, tugging his beard. But he was no man to stay at a loss.

"If mine's gone you shall have another," he vowed, and sent me off in a tub rowed by two small brothers, who pulled me across in thirty or forty minutes. A threatening sky darkened the sea, and disembowelled octopuses were doubled so closely along the spears that there was little room for a view. The stench was awful.

We stood rather towards land, under the sombre cliffs, and passed close to the Rock of the Dead Man, where a caïque skipper once put ashore the corpse of a passenger who had died on board. Monks say the cliffs above rolled down rocks over the body. A cross and primitive stone chapel mark the place; but the boys could not be persuaded to beach the boat when I wanted to go closer, but declared it holy and forbidden ground.

By seven-thirty I picked a way across the rocks below Stavronikita to shore. A man loitering there turned into the jobless tailor from Docheiariou, still toying with his amber beads.

"We've done some walking since last meeting," I said as I eyed the climb to the monastery.

"I'm looking for a boat to Iviron," was his answer as he stared at the one that had brought me.

"It isn't mine. The boys were lent me by their fisher father, who expects them back."

The tailor's eyes became pits of cynicism.

"What are those boys doing here?"

"Fishing with their father."

"Never any women on the Mountain, and never any boys," he sneered. "Are ten years never? What about that girl a monk kept at one of the monasteries for ten years?"

"An out-of-date story."

"Not so out-of-date as to be forgotten. He slipped her in at eight years old, and kept her dressed as a boy until she was a fine young woman of eighteen. Said she was his orphaned niece when found out."

"A girl couldn't be hidden for a week. What of this rain that's about to come down?" I jerked a thumb at the sky, which was blackening fast. "It's time we started up this hill, if we want dry skins." I moved uphill towards the monastery, and he came at my side, losing his breath little by little, but still talking.

"She's been married for years now in a village on the other shore. A deer's head's a pretty thing until it starts rotting. And those fisher-boys? If the Virgin had so much to say about beardless men, why aren't her orders carried out?"

"We'd better sprint," I said, feeling the first heavy splashes of oncoming storm.

"Too many tailors in this holy land," grumbled the tailor; "half the monasteries have their own tailors. I've been a waiter before and might find something at Daphne or Karyes in that line. What a country for hills!"

PLATE 13   *Well of the Archangels, Docheiariou Monastery*

PLATE 14 *View of Xeropotamou Monastery from above; and* (below) *the capital town of Karyes*

The monastery had an imposing ruined tower, with a castle's grim outlines from the sea; but trellising and gardens softened the buildings from the land side. Larger clouds were rolling up, and I debated doubling across the last hundred yards when voices on the other side of a wall brought to notice nearly all the monks of this small house of twenty-two men raking their hay, and hurrying it to shelter. An elder left the older monks to rake, but saw the younger men did all the roping and lifting. There was a certain amount of horseplay; but threatening rain was turning the effort into a *sauve-qui-peut* affair. They asked me to make one more, and we cleared the field in the next twenty minutes, with rain first spitting and then pouring. It ended in a deluge, but the hay safe in the barn.

The founder of this house, dedicated to the Virgin and raised on the ruins of an earlier monastery of Chariton, is said to have been a certain Nikephoros Stavronikitas, an officer of the tenth-century warrior-emperor John Tzimiskes. The property was ceded to an Abbot Gregory in 1533, while a cell of Philotheou. It was destroyed in a few years by fire, then its present restoration, or original foundation as some count it, in the name of St. Nicholas was obtained from the Patriarch Jeremias II. It has been burnt out several times, and misfortunes have more than once reduced it to debt.

The small church fills up the restricted court oppressively. The dedication is to St. Nicholas the Wonder-worker of Nicaea (feast December 6), and the murals date as early as 1546, about the period of the raising of the church. The refectory was frescoed in 1770 and the synodikon in 1810. St. Anne's left hand set in filigree and enamel is enshrined in the church; but far more famous is the ikon of St. Nicholas-of-the-Oyster, an eleventh-, twelfth- or even thirteenth-century mosaic, drawn up out of the sea in a fishing-net in 1589, with an oyster embedded in the saint's forehead. The pious consider the split where the oyster was wedged the work of an ikonoclast, said to have struck the picture before tossing it into the sea. One of the shells is venerated with the relics, the other having been sent to Russia long ago. The ikon, set in silver-gilt, is behind a sliding panel on the south-east pillar.

Incomparable sea-views from the upper storeys counterbalance the court's spacelessness, and I waited for the guestmaster's tray leaning from a window. The storm had rained itself out, the sky now shone. A novice sprouting a promising beard, a cheerful, burly fellow, joined me at the window. He said he was leaving the monastery in the morning to arrange some family business before taking his vows. He would go by mule to Karyes.

Poverty was in the very joints of this house, and I asked the novice why he had chosen it. He said the elderly monks were doubly welcoming to a young man; but as he answered he looked at the marble Mountain, to which the stormy light had given purple loins, and I wondered if this villager had an intimation of the reward offered by a perpetual view of a peak everlastingly pointing at the sky.

We hung over the high sill, watching the rocks and swaying water; watching storm travel away and sky and sea brighten. He talked of his journey. He must walk two hundred miles unless he sold a watch. He pulled out the watch for my opinion.

"It doesn't go."

"It has no big hand," he admitted.

It passed through my mind that all things might be possible to the Virgin; but a human instrument would be required for the realization of such a miracle as the sale of that watch. I was returning to Karyes in the morning. An uphill climb. The novice would have a mule to offer and, by hiring it, I could become to a limited extent the Virgin's instrument. I could become completely that instrument by grossly over-paying. Well, the Virgin's mercy was widely recognized, and she might not call upon a human being to act in solo capacity. That the future would disclose.

10

Vatopedi: the Idiorrhythmic Monastery of the Bramble Field, or the Boy and the Bramble Bush

CLOUDS OF BUTTERFLIES fluttered on to the scene in early June, and villagers cut their crops. Women tramped home from the threshing-floors as tired as men. The sea mirrored the overhanging coast during the long, calm mornings until the wind rose to toss it through the afternoon and blow the dust from the big winnowing sieves in clouds.

At the end of June, Meletios appeared in Prosphori for the larvae-eating fish. He was an agreeable guest. He sat clad in a black silk habit, or else in orange silk pyjamas worn for the siesta. He persuaded me to return with him one afternoon as a cool breeze blew through my room, but within a few hours the cool weather changed, and we then grasped the appalling fact that those fish had to be carried over the Mountain's backbone down to the farther coast with a thermometer in the nineties.

We started at dawn with a heavy tin of fish and a disused typewriter, which Meletios had borrowed to type his French manuscript. The few minutes that the post-boat touched in at the jetty was an event in the village day. Men, women and children jostled on each other's heels: the men with their tools and hand-woven bags ready to travel to some job at a monastery, women and children with bags of provisions, or laboriously written letters, for husbands or fathers already there. The vivacity of a Greek crowd swept the jetty. Voices rose. People gesticulated. The small pushed into the front between the large.

Requests were shouted, promises bawled back, as the boat was pushed skilfully into the open sea.

The civil governor was returning from a flight to the "world". His face under a felt hat turned towards us wistfully from where he balanced on twelve inches of cushionless board.

Gossip lifted his melancholy as far as the Russian frontier house of the womanless country he helped to govern, then he tilted his hat over his face and slumped down. The capture of a fish on the trolling line livened him, for he was first and last a sportsman; but after directing the removal of a spiny fin from the sea he arranged himself on the bottom of the boat, with a sack for a pillow. Meletios, who wore his own dignity to the last thread, frowned on this surrender to mood.

The boat ran steadily for the best part of two hours over the silky sea, breaking a mirror that reflected every line and shadow of the coast. Zographou's arsenal took form in the haze soon after the Three Brethren Rocks, and we assembled the baggage. Meletios drew up his cassock and poised a city shoe over the void, and this foot came down on the cement jetty; but I stayed on board long enough to swing over the fish tin and the typewriter before the leap. Sun had turned the cement into a floor hot enough to teach bears to dance. Heat ended discussion over the next move. We clutched what we could and hurried to the shade of a wooden house.

Two fishermen crouched outside the building in the dust and entertained a guest to a fish-stew thickened with black bread. The guest was a clear-eyed, snowy old man, in black homespun knickerbockers and stout sandals. The sight of him miraculously soothed Meletios, for he was our man and the mules were round the corner. He withdrew from the pot wiping his fingers, with the air of one barely resigned to God's will by our appearance; and the economy of his gait in collecting the luggage suggested the privileged servant, who felt no need for overdue hurry in satisfying even so highly placed a monk as Meletios. This was the muleteer Athanasios, who had served Vatopedi forty-eight years out of his seventy on earth.

We had planned the trek on my cool, breezy balcony over raki. Now we stared reality in the face. The sun had moved higher, there were two and a half hours' riding ahead, and we were fettered by our own lassitude and Athanasios' calm. As the old man made several placid trips along the jetty, we called plaintively to a gardener to bring us cool cucumbers out of his cistern, and we munched these under a tree through the deliberate roping of the baggage-mule.

The old man criticized as he worked. Every one of the mules was past work in his opinion, and reflected on such a wealthy house as Vatopedi.

"It's the fate of both mules and men to grow old," said Meletios.

"And is there no money to buy new mules with when the old are past their work?" Athanasios retorted as he adjusted the load with a lifetime's experience.

The riding-mules were held against the mounting-stone while we straddled the gay saddle-cloths and gathered up the head-chains. Athanasios half-emptied the fish tin of water and prepared to carry it over the three-thousand-foot backbone of the Mountain by hand, and a bow-legged, brindled dog, venerable as its master, waddled out of the shade to take its place in the procession. Meletios settled his gown and led, I followed nose to rump, then came the sumpter mule prodded by Athanasios with the fish tin and, stomach to dust, the asthmatic dog. We left the coast and thrust uphill into the splendid timber.

It is on the rocky tracks, worked into paths by the hoofs of mule generations, that the note of this wild land sounds even more loudly than in the monasteries. Along the thready roads travelling man advances, pressed between barbarous encroaching foliage, fifty yards of path to look at ahead and fifty when he glances behind, continually aware how little the surroundings have been influenced since those swordsmen of the Absolute, the first solitaries, pushed through the bushes looking for caves to pray in. As the spidery way travels through enclosing thickets and shimmers in the fierce heat thrown off rock faces, there increases a hope that round this approaching bend, or behind the rise ahead, a mystery will be revealed such as the early saints were allowed as medicine in their spiritual sicknesses.

The march ran above a mountain stream, shrunken to a chain of water-holes. Judas trees pressed us in, and arbutus. Strings of starry clematis festooned evergreen thickets of box, ilex, myrtle, and wild vine.

Butterflies ranged the path; the zebra-banded swallow-tail and orange-tip among them, swaying like flying flowers in the company of black lacewings dreaming in the air or on leaves. But certain democratic bloodsucking flies esteemed mule and human ankle equally.

It took us an hour to reach Zographou, which we counted a stage. We left the mules switching their tails under walnut trees while we climbed flights of stairs to a balcony above the tree-tops. There we trickled water, laced with raki, down our throats, and exchanged small-talk with two Bulgar monks. Conversation was in danger of foundering in the end owing to the latent hostility between Greek and foreign monks, and Meletios commented acidly on this afterwards. As we left we fell into the arms of the exiled gendarmes, who led us to their balcony for cucumbers chilled in a well. In this way we started the next stage as another pair of men, but men more than ever behind time, and having as high to ascend as we had risen. But it proved fresher in the upper country, and after the "Hand" sign was left behind, the Holy Sea spread out in view, and the Abbot's Rock came into sight off the point of shore where Esphigmenou's path ran close to the water. The rock is awash in any breeze, and the story tells how the creatures of Vekkos seized an abbot, Euthymios, and certain other monks who would not accept the Latin rite. They hanged a dozen where crosses mark the execution ground above Pantokratoros, a dozen more outside Vatopedi's walls, and Euthymios himself they rowed to this rock in a high wind, and left him to wash off and drown.

In this country of bushes where eagles sailed, and hawks brooded on dead trees, we jogged into a wandering messiah in a ragged cassock. He was a gentle madman, who was delivering his message to the fowls of the air and the herbs of the field. The Mountain is kind to the witless, who drift between the great houses, sure of gifts from the kitchen. Meletios spoke a friendly word without getting answered. Not only was he ignored by the half-wit, but the muleteer remarked:

"Leave that poor foolish fellow to himself, as our Lord intended. You can see God has kissed him."

"Since God troubles to look after him, are monks to do less?" Meletios answered, "and have you heard of anyone killed by a polite word, old man?"

A few minutes later he added, "But monks should give up passing their old cloaks over to laymen. That's a harmless lad; but the Mountain holds many evil beggars in tattered cloaks and bonnets, who go the rounds of the poultry yards dressed as a nun like the fox in the fable. Who's this now?"

A young peasant clattered up on a mule. He looked quite healthy, but immediately began reciting a story which might have sounded pitiful to less weary men than ourselves. His sorrows included a burning up with malaria, and a conviction he would never beget children if it went on. This was related at a half shout to Meletios, who suggested that he gave the old man a rest by taking the fish tin from him.

"God will repay you for this," the ancient muleteer asserted with conviction, handing over the tin. "What is your malaria? What indeed is man?"

I dusted my lips with a soiled finger, remarking:

"However, though your malaria may be thought by some to be nothing, I advise the drug 'atebrin' as a router of the enemy."

"How can I remember that name?" the young man wailed. "Any man can think of quinine. But I've forgotten the other already!"

"Have a care not to strike those fish against the bushes," cried Athanasios. "After all, they are God's humble creatures."

"I got this illness from God because I ate red grapes on John the Baptist's day," the peasant sighed, changing the fish tin to his other hand. "In our village you must not eat anything red or round on the day that holy saint lost his head. But it was hot, and those grapes in the garden by the road looked so cool! I got malaria the next day."

Meletios made no comment, he was too busy extracting a fly from his eye; but Athanasios said:

"The world never learns. My nephew, my dead brother's son, got scarlet fever after cutting a water-melon horizontally on the Forerunner's day. Several had it in the village; but he got it the day after eating that round, red fruit. People are careless."

The peasant groaned at the thought of the world's carelessness. I comforted him by handing him a piece of paper with the word "atebrin" scrawled on it.

An hour's continuous descent brought us to the spreading gardens of the great house of Vatopedi, long in view near the sea, with the ruins of the Theological School in poetic decay above. The school was founded in 1749; quickly gained, then lost, a reputation, and was finally destroyed by fire. We rode in a drooping file, unsticking ourselves from the mules a hundred yards from the gates. Meletios carefully shook down his gown for a becoming entrance and, in the short walk to the porter's lodge, received salutes from every point of the compass, gravely returning them.

The entrance was under a baldacchino porch protected by an ikon of the Virgin. Patches of paint were shot off the holy picture's hand in 1822 by a Turkish soldier, Hussein, who according to tradition most properly hanged himself from a tree, which withered up.

Three gates once barred the entrance where to-day there are two. It is related that a Turkish soldier fashioned a handle like a dog on the gate now gone, to commemorate the death of his own bitch, struck dead when he tried to profane the monastery by leading her in. I mentioned this to Meletios, who tittered, but denied ever hearing the anecdote.

We went into a magnificent sloping court. Roofs, towers, porticoes, galleries, and poplar trees quivered in the heat, which fell back off the brick walls of the delicate pink-and-white Chapel of the Holy Belt, to which scores of martins' nests were glued. Those vaulted chambers of brick held massive jars and marble tanks, the jar of the miraculous replenishment standing near the entrance beside an ikon known as the Oil-flowing Virgin.

Though Meletios flowed forward in a melody of dignified motion, we were in flight from the heat and in no mood for sight-seeing. He sighed as he touched my elbow to start me up the rising slope, past the late-eighteenth-century Chapel of the Holy Belt to a flight of steps in the western range. They led up to the quarters of his elder, Michael, one of the Council.

A door opened while we were recovering in front of it, and a brisk junior invited us into the hall, which seemed in darkness after the sunshine. The elder himself dodged briskly in from the other end, greeting Meletios affectionately, and holding out a hand to me. He was a dark and direct Cretan, with light steps and a strong profile, wearing tidy undress completed by a neat pigtail of grey hair.

He took charge, walking us off to cool in a sitting-room with a canary chirping in each open window.

"How is it you are so late?" he asked; but never really listened to our misadventures, sung to him from the depths of a chair by Meletios, but turned his dark eyes towards a pair of cats licking each other on the floor, remarking:

"They had a long wait for the boat, and the sun did the rest. What have modern men come to?"

"Oh, for a glass of water—cold water," Meletios crooned.

At that moment the junior, Kosmas, came in with a jugful and the coffee-tray.

"Ah, Kosmas," Meletios crooned on, "what a good monk you're going to make. There's no better deed than supplying a thirsty man with cold water."

The elder belted up his skirts, and disappeared into the kitchen to look after lunch; for he did a good deal of his own housework, though highly placed. The fiery duties soon drove him to change into a white shirt and black trousers, leaving the only monkish part of him the twisted grey pigtail down his shoulders.

Meanwhile we lounged in the pleasant sitting-room. The canaries hopped, and a gardenia flourished in a tub on the balcony. There was no sign of a coenobite's bare cell, and the larger of the cats suddenly rolled over and presented itself to the smaller as a fountain of nourishment, making it patent a female of her species had found acceptance in the monastery's very heart.

We recovered enough to lunch at a table set with a cloth and napkins, waited on by Kosmas, the novice. Heat took away appetite and made water more welcome than wine. Meletios later proved his strength of character by making the effort to leave the table and lead me to his rooms, which he had given up to me. Two small rooms led into each other, the outer with a stove and a strong flow of water running into a sink under the window. The inner room was overwhelmed by a wide, comfortable bed, with sheets and counterpane of virgin white. Meletios said the King of the Hellenes had stretched his royal form along it a few months previously.

There was an up-to-date lavatory, though the little cistern did not work. To be his guest was to feel an aura of modernity. I stripped, washed and lay down to rest, trying to hide my presence from the heat by stillness.

The semantron sounding for vespers brought Meletios, large and gentle, with an invitation to appear before the Committee. We crossed to their quarters near the church by roof-passages which led round two sides of the impressive quadrangle, and gave a cat's view of the court. We came out on a gallery near the main office and reception-rooms, at the top of an outside stair which led past the Chapel of the Consolation, and then into the presence of the committee members.

Committee-men of an important house, though not always lettered, are men of personality. The elders who greeted me were used to ruling and taking decisions, and the obedience they expected and exacted was absolute.

Coffee came in while we were discussing the disposal of the fish. It was decided to turn them into a small breeding-tank until they had increased sufficiently to be put in the marshes.

One of the elders, Porphyry, had the large head and deep chest of certain fish, though his dark glancing eyes were anything but fishy.

"We got some of those fish some years ago," he said in a rumbling bass, "but there's not one sign of them to-day in the marshes."

"Once they establish themselves, Elder, they increase magically," I assured him. "The fish I brought to-day descend from some brought years ago from Italy. They were in breeding-tanks outside Salonika first and then sent to the lakes throughout Macedonia. They are teeming there now. You must have at least a metre of mud at the bottom of your tank for the winter. They hibernate, and freeze to death without mud."

"You hear that, Sebastian?" Porphyry said, to the wiry father who had taken over the fish. "Mud, at least a metre deep."

"Grow a few lilies if you can, Elder. The fish enjoy sunning themselves on lily-pads just under the water. They bear young on the lily-pads. The females produce up to a hundred at a birth each month, and bear them alive. They discharge them two at a time, like shots from a gun, curled up and motionless. They uncurl in a few minutes and start chasing the wriggling larvae at once."

All nodded appreciatively, and one whose white beard covered his black belt remarked:

"Man lives out his life without learning more than a small part of God's wonders."

"I've missed vespers," I pointed out as our coffee cups went back on the trays, "but may I look round the church if it is still open?"

Their answer was to release Meletios to look after me, and he sailed beside me down the open stair past the Chapel of Consolation. The monks are shorn there, and a mural on the south side has been called the Virgin-of-the-Consolation since a night when pirates sailed into the cove to wait for the dawn opening of the gates. As day drew near the monks returned to their cells, but one still remained at his devotions in the chapel. He was interrupted by a voice, warning him to have the walls manned by dawn, rather than the gates opened. He looked up; the painting had come to life. Child had turned to Mother, and laid a hand over her mouth to prevent the warning, saying:

"Do not mind about these sinners, Mother; let the pirates destroy them inasmuch as their wickedness is ripe."

But the Virgin ignored the tiny fingers and repeated the warning three times, while the monks streamed from their cells to gape at the miracle. Presently the picture became still, and the monks scattered to man the walls.

The granite-and-marble Church of the Annunciation has a past feeling back into the tenth century. A late-eighteenth-century refectory stood opposite, and between the buildings was a basin for blessing the holy water, dedicated to John the Baptist. An arresting bell-tower, built in 1427, rose a hundred and fourteen feet into the air, and the seventeenth- and eighteenth-century ranges of cells filled the background.

Famous decorations at the west end of the church are the group of Christ presiding at the Last Judgement, supported by the Virgin and St. John the Baptist. It is considered an eleventh-century work and is over the door leading from the outer to the inner narthex. Also to be seen are the possibly fourteenth-century mosaic panels of the Virgin and the Angel of the Annunciation.

We passed into the naos, where a sacristan was still pottering before the carved and gilded wooden screen. Sufficient light from outside mistily revealed the wealth of murals of the Macedonian School, dating from the start of the fourteenth century, though renovated during the sixteenth, in some opinion. There rose up off the pavement, carrying the weight of the dome, the admired granite monolith pillars, their brass rings winking in the prisoned light. The monks firmly believe these noble stones to have been sent from Ravenna by a fifth-century empress, Pulcheria.

Vatopedi ranks after Lavra as the Mountain's second house. Three brothers—Athanasios, Nicholas, and Antonios of Adrianople—founded it in or just after A.D. 972, if the usual claim to an earlier foundation by Constantine the Great be ignored. This earlier and impossible claim is supported by the legendary finding of Arkadios, son of Theodosios the Great, in a bramble bush. The name Vatopedi (according to etymologists), Thornbush, or Vatopaidi (as written by the monks), Thornchild, refers to this miraculous preservation of the young prince.

This tradition relates that Julian the Apostate destroyed an earlier monastery on this site, after which the place lay desolate until the fourth century. Arkadios, the son of Theodosios the Great, was sailing along the coast of Athos back to Constantinople from Italy, when a storm rose and a wave swept him off the ship. He called on the Virgin, who miraculously landed him. Theodosios was sunk in grief until his son reappeared in the capital, and imperial gratitude took the form of rebuilding the monastery.

In a second version the rescued prince is nameless, but is described as a son of Vatos on the way to his uncle Theodosios in Constantinople. As he reached the shore a voice instructed him to rebuild the ruined church, and he ordered material from Rome, including the monoliths still supporting the dome of the church. The first version is the widely accepted story on the Mountain.

Labourers clearing the ruins for the new foundations uncovered a well, peered down, and drew up an ikon of the Virgin suspended in the well-shaft with a candle burning before it. The miraculous find is to this day treasured in the church's apse, where the same light is believed still to burn unquenched, the ancient wick feeding off a lump of wax beside it. They have named the ikon the ikon of the Founders, and, for another reason, the ikon of the Sacristan. A monk once told me the well, now below the altar, feeds the stream flowing out of Arkadios' well on the shore.

The ikon became the Virgin-of-the-Sacristan after a band of Syrians descended on the monastery in the tenth century. A deacon thrust the cross of Constantine belonging to the altar and the ikon of the Founders with its lighted taper into the old well under the altar while the raiders were breaking into the church. The covering was back in place when they seized him and carried him off for sale in Crete. Nikephoros Phokas retook Crete in A.D. 961, and the liberated deacon, now a venerable old man, returned to the monastery with his tale. Monks ran and uncovered the well, and brought to light the cross, ikon, and burning candle.

The sacristan took us behind the altar to examine the ikon, on the golden covering of which a great craftsman's hammer had raised thumbnail masterpieces. The Panayia stared serenely, and the inextinguishable candle burned with a steady flame. On the holy table immediately behind us stood that tall elegant cross, sheeted in antique silver-gilt, known as the cross of Constantine.

"No man need fear for his life in the presence of it," the sacristan observed, "for we are assured no man can die in sight of it."

The historic well was below the pavement we stood on. In a cupboard was that diptych, a Christ and Virgin, affectionately called the Ninia or Dolls of Theodora, who concealed them in her apartments during her spiritual loneliness as the wife of the ikonoclast emperor, Theophilos. A court jester, Denderis, blundered into her chamber at a moment when she was kissing them.

"These are my pretty dolls, and I am so very fond of them," cried the empress; but the mischievous jester carried the story to his master, reporting:

"I have been with my mama, who has taken some pretty dolls out of her pillow." The emperor, understanding, angrily denounced Theodora as an idolatress. But she charmed away his anger.

"No, husband, it is not as you imagine. I was idly looking into the mirror with my maids, and Denderis saw our row of faces in the glass and ran off with a wild account."

One of the cupboards held portable mosaics of the Crucifixion of St. John Chrysostom, and of St. Anne and the Virgin, marvellously built up in minute marbles; and elaborate silver-gilt reliquaries preserved relics of several saints. But the great treasure of this house is that portion of the Virgin's belt given by Lazar I Hrebljanovich, who ruled Serbia in the fourteenth century, a reddish-brown ribbon of camel's hair into which the Empress Pulcheria is credited with weaving the gold thread and sewing the pearls. It is said to have been dropped by the Virgin at the Cross, and to have been rediscovered in Leo the Great's reign, being cared for in a church in Chalkoprate. In the past it has been sent abroad to stay plague; but has not been permitted outside the monastery since robbers stole it for the casket's sake. On the way to Chilandari the relic was thrown away as valueless. It fell into a bush, which it illuminated, drawing the attention of a simple shepherd, who recovered it.

The bones of the benefactors Manuel II and that John Kantakuzene who put on the monastic habit here in 1355, after his abdication, lie in a tomb in the mesonyktikon. Placidia's bones were also brought to this church where she had received a rebuke from heaven when she ignored the rule forbidding women and landed on the Mountain to inspect the church her family was building. She was even passing down the passage from the narthex to the Chapel of Dimitrios, when the ikon now known as the Antiphonitria of Placidia spoke the warning:

"Don't take one step more; for another Queen than you reigns here."

The terrified empress sank to the ground, and lay praying for pardon until led up into the gallery above, where she was allowed to look into the church before sailing away.

In this narthex of the Antiphonitria is kept the ikon known as the Virgin-who-was-Slain, together with the hand of that un-happiest of men, the deacon who would have slain her. The hand that dealt the sacrilegious blow lies in a dusty glass-topped box for pilgrims to gape at, with the bones exposed where the discoloured parchment-like skin has been ripped off by the strong teeth of Russian pilgrims endeavouring to tear the unwitherable flesh away.

A Cretan deacon of the past had the duty of cleaning the church candlesticks. This caused him to be late for meals, and the trapezaris in the refectory had no comfort to offer beyond telling him to come when the food was ready, or not at all. The deacon considered himself the injured party and in a towering rage marched up to thp ikon with his grievances. He harangued that patient picture and worked himself up until his "forever-to-become-unwitherable hand" seized the knife for scraping the candlesticks and drove it at the ikon's cheek. The picture struck him down.

Monks found a prostrate and blinded man mouthing before the ikon, from which blood was flowing. The deacon's rage cooled, and he was given time to contemplate his crime. For three years he stood in a dark cupboard opposite God's Mother, whom he would have slain. But the All-Holy-One forgives, and as grief wore his life away, she appeared to him and granted him pardon, though no forgiveness for the hand, which was not permitted to fall to dust. It still remains uncrumbled, lying in its dusty case, shrunken and unholy.

I found that Meletios, the would-be historian of his monastery, knew nothing of this story until I told it to him and showed him the hand.

He had arrears of work to make up, and left me wandering to shore, where thirty or forty fishermen were making a meal round the well of Arkadios. They had been drying their nets and were ready to row to their fishing-grounds. A monk sat by disposed for pious talk about the well always there to revive poor fishermen rowing in from the sea. Nor could he much exaggerate the value of a flow of light, cool water in an arid land.

I was promised a lobster in the morning. In the colder weather lobsters are hunted along the rocky coast by wading fishermen with flares. They retreat into deep water in the hot weather but occasionally blunder into a net. The fishermen say the lobster so dreads the octopus that its flesh dissolves in the shell at the sight of the enemy. The armour is found without the dead warrior inside.

The offerer of the uncaught lobster glared at the hot, empty sky and demanded:

"Why can't God send a few clouds into it?" which brought a rebuke from the monk, who said:

"Does God always need clouds when fishermen ask for them?"

This silenced the fisherman.

Though a fisherman's existence begins and ends in poverty, a new generation of apprentices, spawned on jewelled islands set in enamelled seas, ever come forward. They are an immortal band through their generations; but time presses a heavy thumb on each individual, and by forty these men are old and worn out, their youthful looks dried away on the salted winds.

The fisherman, still grumbling, picked up a black loaf to carry off to his boat, and before going said:

"Big monks get white bread, and small monks and fishermen black bread, though we're told all are equal in heaven. If in heaven, not on earth. Last Easter week I took fish to a monastery. It was Great Saturday, when nothing touches the lips of any fasting father from Good Friday until Easter Sunday. I went to the elders' quarters to be paid, and there they were behind locked doors, eating all they could fill themselves up with, after putting the rest of the monastery on water. And I am told God sends no clouds because I forgot to have my boat blessed! The fish stinks from the head!" and he went off addressing the pebbles before the monk had time to recover sufficiently to retort.

The pagans had a settlement where we gossiped, and one of their marbles, a fragment of a bull's head, had become the corner stone of a building. Its undamaged duplicate is to be found on the church's outer wall, and compels attention.

The fishermen put off into a shining offing sinking into remote sea.

I returned to the court as Meletios appeared, large, gentle, unsoiled, to suggest a walk of leafy charm along a path following a channelled stream. Numerous monks were in sight filling their water-pots, or picking up companions for an evening stroll. We caught up a couple of Americans and a Frenchman, who had been thrown together in the guest-rooms and were talking French. Both Americans were hatless, but the Frenchman fanned himself with a panama. Meletios hurried in pursuit of this chance to practise French, and we were presently wailing over the heat in a group.

Some monks passed us and acknowledged our bows, and Meletios, who had certainly not addressed them, whispered in Greek to me:

"There went Judas."

"And did I bow to Judas?" I asked, raising my eyebrows.

"There was meat at lunch, wasn't there?" said Meletios, plaintively, "and Barsonopios, whom you bowed to, heard from Kosmas, our junior, that meat had been eaten, and reported me to the committee."

"Ah, it's Friday!"

"But I had the meat on the table for you, and you invited me to eat," Meletios continued reproachfully.

He was speaking the truth. The meat had been put in front of us, and I found myself eating it alone. I insisted that he join me, which he did without much reluctance.

"The day of the week never crossed my Protestant mind. I asked why you weren't trying the dish quite innocently, and could so easily have done without it. You underestimate a man from the world's powers of doing without. My teeth meet in goat's meat at home about once a month, otherwise fish."

"The meat was for Saturday, but put on the table for you. And then," said Meletios accusingly, "you said I must eat some."

"Whereupon Judas betrayed you?"

"The committee asked me what I had given you for lunch. I said vegetables, for we had vegetables too."

"To find Judas had given you away over the meat. Were they angry?"

"They were annoyed."

Meletios' damp face was momentarily darkened with sulkiness, and then the sun came out again, and he and the Frenchman gradually dropped behind, leaving me with the Americans.

One had some modern Greek tacked on to ancient, and remarked, after a few yards divided the parties:

"I overheard that. The good father seemed more disturbed at being found out than over his failure to abstain."

The dusk stole through a high bank of trees. The murmuring water hurried along its channel. We looked back at Meletios. There he stood in the failing light, large and mild, beaming down on his Frenchman's neat gesticulations. He had come on a figure to admire.

"Is moral teaching a strong suit of the Eastern Orthodox Church in the Greek villages?" the American asked.

"Northern Europeans think the frigid virtues of truthfulness, justice, independence of thinking important," I said. "The warmer Southerner puts more stress on the human qualities of sympathy, mercy, devotion. The Northerner is more moral, the Southerner more religious. The trouble is that virtues seem to cancel one another out. Mercy mocks at strict justice. Truthfulness is no bedfellow for sympathy. And as the virtues mankind aims at make both poles and all the longitude and latitude of the moral globe, while the individual can never touch all points at one time, success on a large scale seems out of reach. Looking at it this way, human frailty is better understood."

"But are you answering the question whether moral teaching is a strong suit of the Eastern Church in the villages?"

"Religion is probably more accepted than morality. A good many villagers seem hardly more critical of moral lapses among their priests than among their lay neighbours. The priest only becomes a man apart from others when he enters the chancel robed."

"Are most village priests of peasant origin?"

"Many are, and rightly so; for a peasant understands the peasant way of life. The village priest is required to be a married man; but having married, may not marry a second time, nor may he rise in the priestly hierarchy. Those ambitious to hold the higher posts must remain celibate, and the better-educated men are among them."

"Village priests, surely, should lay claim to moderate education?"

"It's certainly better. The priest should be the villager who's a head taller than the others. But no more than a head taller. The village child must feel it possible to follow his footsteps."

We parted at the guesthouse steps, and I mounted the sloping court with Meletios as far as the Chapel of the Holy Belt.

A figure slipped by in the dusk, and I recognized Kon-stantine, soldier and sportsman turned monk. His bones were sparsely covered, and he looked frailer than the last time I saw him. The old campaigner makes a satisfactory type of monk, but old soldiers taking the habit never enter priesthood, which is out of reach to those who have shed blood.

Last wandering airs had expired. The coming out of stars in golden points suggested the whereabouts of domes and roofs, crosses and chimneys. I settled beside Meletios on a narrow balcony overlooking the great court concealed in a velvet darkness. At the Easter Sunday service when midnight strikes and Christ rises I had seen this court choked with jubilant monks and pilgrims, holding aloft a forest of lighted tapers in the windless night, light carving openings in the dark to reveal the flashing vestures of priests and deacons, the jewels and silks on cross, on banner, on incensor. And as the cry went up that Christ had risen every loud bell gave tongue on the startled night, every great semantron thundered.

Now profound quiet, deep darkness. I could see through invisible walls. In the library safes reposed chrysobulls signed in the imperial scarlet of Byzantium; in a glass case on a lower floor stood the dragon-handled jasper cup of the Despot Manuel Kantakuzene Palaeologos; and on a shelf of an upper storey lay that tome, so fairly written by the hand of John Kantakuzene, after he had removed an imperial crown from his brow and replaced it with a monk's bonnet. Of Vatopedi's 643 manuscripts half are on parchment. The books are many, and there are church music, rolled manuscripts of Liturgies, and much else, including Slav manuscripts.

This sleeping house was overlord of the sketes St. Andrew and St. Dimitrios.

Prosphori seemed half a world away. Not that it was more remote here than there. Here was the metropolis, there the province. As a tenant of Vatopedi I was a provincial come to town. Here the charm of quiet buildings; there the glowing flares of fishermen. Beauty that seemed not of the earth.

"God has made both places," said Meletios, reading my thoughts.

11

Iviron: the Idiorrhythmic Monastery of the Iberians or Georgians

THE KARYES—IVIRON ROAD leads downhill past Koutloumousiou, and one can reach Iviron near the seashore in an hour or so. I had the road to myself on the August afternoon I went that way, until overtaken by Christo, a young muleteer from Iviron. A hail halted me, and there he was wriggling out of a mass of packages, as he jogged up offering his mule. It would have been better to hand over the rucksack and walk on; but I mounted, passed over a cigarette in payment, and was carried on downhill.

A second cigarette lasted Christo, padding on lengths of motor tyre, to the Beggar's shrine, where a dubious-looking monk sprawled near a mule which browsed under an oak tree. The mule switched its tail, and the monk snored on his back. The shrine was raised to keep green the memory of an act of inhospitality at Iviron in the minds of indolent porters.

A beggar was sent away hungry, and trailed uphill to this spot, where the shrine now pictures Iviron's powerful ikon, the Virgin-of-the-Gate, blessing a ragged fellow. The beggar slept on this spot and dreamt the Virgin placed a gold piece in his hand so that he might tempt the indolent porter. The sleeper woke and found his hand was actually closed over a gold coin. He returned to Iviron. At the sight of gold, the porter became hopeful of finding bread, but when he went to see, was told that all the bread had turned sour. Happily the house was ruled by an abbot able to recognize a rebuke and, on the story of a gold piece coming to his ears, he sent for the coin and recognized it as a votive coin missing from the ikon, the Virgin-of-the-Gate. Ever since the loaf given away by Iviron is said to be heavier than elsewhere.

The monk stopped snoring, sat up, stood up, jumped side-ways on his mule. He told me that an old Father Gregorios was waiting to be buried at Iviron; but in monkly fashion expressed no regrets, merely observing:

"The old monk in a monastery dies among friends who have grown old with him, and if he outlives them all, he's still known to everybody. The man in the world can grow so old that he loses his friends, and dies among strangers."

The muleteer turned this over as if he had come on a new piece of evidence in favour of taking the habit. He had a talent for discovering dangers in life, and was far from easy over Gregorios' death. To me the cause had been an accumulation of years; the muleteer had other ideas. The dead monk had been rash enough to plant a walnut tree as a youth, and it had lately withered. There are villagers who believe that when a walnut tree withers the planter of it dies. Christo stamped his bandy legs, passed an arm over his hot face, and said:

"It happened to that childless man, my uncle. What riches he left for his widow to eat up! My uncle planted a walnut tree as a foolish boy. It sickened two summers ago and a neighbour, wishing him ill, told him to save the tree by pouring hot water into the roots. So my uncle did it, and that tree withered up. Then my uncle became sick, and hearing there was a sick man's money to eat, two doctors came to his bed, one shouting he was dying of this, the other of that. Until he died. But had those learned men killed him? There wasn't one in our village who didn't know it was the tree. Only old men should plant walnut trees."

The monk had listened with a dubious smile, and the sceptical toss of his head at the end tumbled his bonnet off, his hair falling in a tangle down his back.

"A barber'd give you three hundred drachmas for that hair," Christo grunted, stooping for the bonnet. "My sister's husband made her sell her hair last winter, and spent the money on a young pig, which ate everything in the house and died before Christmas. How they quarrelled for the rest of the winter! When I went in last Easter Sunday to say 'Christ has risen', Marika answered, 'Not in this house'."

The muleteer tossed the bonnet into the monk's lap, observing:

"The borrower must return the borrowed egg into the lender's lap in our village or the hen won't lay."

The monk jammed his black hat over his coil of hair, twirled the bit of his head-chain like a gaucho about to bolas an ostrich, and brought it down over the mule's withers. The beast clattered off, followed by mine. The muleteer was left to sweat and lumber, the monk calling gaily from his sideways seat:

"Have no fear. You'll get to paradise on your motor tyres."

In another twenty minutes we clopped down the cobbled hill to the doors of Iviron, a house grown up round the traditional spot where the Virgin came ashore to inform the pagan idolaters that the Mountain would henceforth be known as her garden. Clocks may stand at different hours all over the Mountain, but the siesta continues uninterrupted until vespers, when the sun is descending the sky, and ours was a merciless arrival for the porter stretched on a board in the lodge. My ill-timed appearance came from using the mule instead of dozing under the oak. I walked apologetically across the empty court, which would be deserted until the semantron populated the scene with monks arranging their veils on the way to vespers. I passed locked buildings and reached the guest-quarters. The coffee-tray came within a few minutes.

This monastery of ninety-seven monks stood on a flat place up to which the pious believe the sea was rolling when storm drove the Virgin's vessel into port. St. Athanasios, himself, approved Iviron's foundation in 980, seventeen years after the Great Lavra's. Two detached chapels stood near the church, one dedicated to the Virgin-of-the-Gate, the other to St. John the Baptist. This chapel of St. John is said to stand on the site of the monastery of St. Klementos, to which Peter the Athonite's bones were carried by the hunter at the end of the ninth century. The monastery of Klementos is believed to have stood on the site of a temple of Poseidon, said to exist on the occasion of the Virgin's visit, and drawing pagan pilgrims to the Mountain.

Tradition relates that the Virgin left her ship to come ashore, whereupon the idols broke themselves to pieces after she had converted the worshippers. An awed pagan crowd gathered on the ground now covered by the church, and listened to the Virgin addressing them from the spot where the Virgin-of-the-Gate is enshrined. She declared the Mountain to be her garden, and henceforth forbidden to other women, and she foretold that the Virgin-of-the-Gate would be enshrined on the place her feet were blessing.

Three Iberians or Georgians, John Varasvatze, his son Euthymios, and a warrior brother-in-law, John Grdzelidze or Thornic, founded Iviron. Thornic left a cell near the Lavra in 979, at the call of Basil II, when the latter's general, Bardas Phokas, had been routed by the rebel, Bardas Skleros. The warrior monk led twelve thousand Georgians to his emperor's help, and threw the rebellious general back into Persia. Bringing his personal share of booty to the Mountain at the campaign's conclusion, he helped found Iviron about 980; and the library wall still has on it the bow and a fragment of chain-mail said to have been used in the great victory.

The monks elected Thornic as first abbot, but on Euthymios succeeding him they grew mutinous over the stricter rule, and drove their second abbot to Constantinople, where he died in 1028 after falling from a horse. He was first translator of the Bible from Greek into Georgian. Later the Iberian influence declined, and the Protos Arsenios, together with the reigning Patriarch, introduced the Greek language into the monastery.

This house experienced its share of suffering. Thirteenth-century pirates raided it twice and sacked it, and it continued at low ebb, after paying the penalty of opposing Michael VIII's attempts to impose the Latin rites, until the end of the fifteenth century, when the King of Georgia was approached, and the monastery put on its feet by Georgian help, though the Greeks got rid of the Iberians and their language from the church services a century before. A hundred years later the Georgians were again approached. The seventeenth century saw a good deal of rebuilding, and in 1654 the monastery acquired the rich lands of St. Nicholas near Moscow as a gift from the Tsar Alexios, after his miraculous healing by the Iberian

Virgin, a duplicate of the Virgin-of-the-Gate. In duplicating the picture, the monks of Iviron washed the naked panel with holy water and painted exclusively on Saturdays and Sundays during vigils. The monastery has since suffered fire and earthquake, but has increased in size.

The Chapel of the Virgin-of-the-Gate stands at the north end of the court. Though some distance from the present gates, it was in the vicinity of the old, which were closed after some monks objected to mules passing close to their most important ikon. The monastery acquired the picture miraculously.

In the days of Theophilos the Ikonoclast, 829–842, this picture by St. Luke (in lay opinion one of the most ancient ikons on the Mountain, possibly dating from ikonoclastic days) was insulted in a pious widow's house by an imperial messenger. He pointed his sword at the Virgin's face, but took fright on blood spurting over him. The shocked widow hurried to the seashore with the ikon, and delivered it to the waves with the words:

"Thou who canst save us from an emperor's wrath canst save thyself from sea dangers."

The ikon made her a sign by standing on edge in the sea, and took a westerly course, floating from her sight. Seventy years passed before the dark picture appeared off the Holy Mountain, moving landwards, announced by a pillar of fire which joined ocean and cloud. The astonishing advance lasted days and nights. The amazed monks finally launched their dug-outs, paddling and steering towards the fire, to find their rowing brought them no nearer the ikon. A voice sounded, a voice not of earth:

"Only Gabriel the Georgian is of enough account to carry the picture of the All-Holy."

The monks paddled back to the Georgian house for Gabriel, to be informed he was a hermit. The rocks were searched until that shy and godly man was discovered in a cave between Xeropotamou and Russiko. They led him down to the shore and placed him in a boat. Happy change! The faster his boat moved towards the ikon, the faster the ikon moved through the sea to meet it. Ikon and boat were presently coming together at such increasing pace that the hermit, in his joy, leapt out on the water and walked over the waves with arms stretched out to gather in the great black picture. He carried it ashore on an Easter Tuesday, and it was taken in procession to the Georgian monastery nearby; for the Virgin had informed Gabriel she intended the ikon for Iviron's monks.

Where the picture was carried ashore, near the present Chapel of the Falling-asleep-of-the-Virgin, a fresh-water spring, roofed over since, gushed up from the earth. The ikon was taken into the church, only to be found near the gates in the morning. Twice more the obtuse monks carried it back to the church; twice more it returned itself to the gates. Then the Virgin appeared to Gabriel the hermit, and instructed him to build a chapel for her picture at the monastery gates or it would not remain with the monks; she added that she came to guard, not to be guarded.

Anyone arriving hungry at the monastery draws the sympathy of the Portress-of-the-Gates, which she is often called. She looks down sombrely from the chapel screen loaded with votive offerings.

The monks on one occasion failed to keep her from harm. A brass-rimmed slab of porphyry has been set under the dome in the church's rich pavement and inscribed: "I have founded her columns securely, and for all time she shall stay steady. George, the Monk, Iberian and Founder." It may be the eleventh-century abbot and builder of the church who set his seal in this way; but a different explanation is given to-day.

Centuries ago a fleet of Saracen ships appeared off the coast. The monks retreated into the keep with the Virgin-of-the-Gate and other treasure, leaving the pirates to sack the monastery, which they did without satisfying their savagery. They tried to throw the church to the ground, and sent for the ships' cables, which they wrapped round the columns supporting the dome. They heaved on those, hoping to bring all down in ruin. The monks prayed. The wind rose, thunder rolled, lightning blazed; and presently a storm of such violence lashed the bay that the robbers left their work to man the drifting ships. Those vessels were swallowed up, one by one, until only the Emir's was left after the waves subsided. That chastened man sent money to raise the monastery walls high enough to make the place unassailable. The Virgin-of-the-Gate had answered prayer.

A second man's heart changed after a raid. His picture is to be found in the chapel; St. Barbaros, a pirate who struck at the ikon with a sword, leaving a blemish on the neck, still noticeable to-day. A flow of blood from the wound caused his abject repentance. He became a Christian, took the name of Barbaras, and was ultimately rewarded for the quality of the new life by admittance into the company of saints.

The founding of the church of the Falling-asleep-of-the-Virgin (feast August 15) is popularly connected with the monastery's beginnings in the last quarter of the tenth century, though an inscription under the dome suggests the builder to have been an Abbot Gregorios, ruling for a few years in the eleventh century. Little now belongs to either date, but all is old. A splendid marble pavement of opus Alexandrinum, a wealth of murals, an early seventeenth-century gilded screen, and a masterly corona of modern Russian workmanship build up a rich and imposing interior, in which numerous ikons burn in deep colour on pillars and walls. Loveliest of the apse's treasures is the holy table's silver-gilt cross of Byzantine workmanship.

The monastery was badly burned out in the 1860s, and much dates after then. An imposing seventeenth-century arsenal rises on the seashore, and a late seventeenth-century building is the Chapel of the Virgin-of-the-Gate.

I strolled beyond the gates towards evening, taking the left-hand turn under a trellis of Georgian grapes. The way led towards some plane trees, rising from the bones of a dead river-bed entering the sea. A windless afternoon enchanted the grove. Not one of the broad leaves stirred; for hours only shadows moved. A tall monk paced this solitude. His hair was out of sight under a brushed chimney-pot hat, and his beard had been so combed as to seem trimmed by scissors. He worked a black rosary over his fingers, bead by bead. An angle of the walk brought him towards me, and we bowed gravely as we met.

He had come to this monastery because of the Virgin's association with it. Where we walked was supposed to have been sea-bottom when the Panayia's ship entered the bay. Tradition does speak of the Virgin sailing to the spot where the monastery now stands, several hundred yards inshore. The golden light of summer afternoons drew him down here to muse on his house's good fortune in being rooted in such ground. The Virgin was on her way to visit Lazaros of Bethany, and from that Lazaros we passed on to speak of the beggar Lazaros, the man of sores; and from him it was an easy progression to the lepers sheltered by this house.

Close to the main buildings, unsuspected by visitors, is Iviron's lazar-house. A gate from a lane leads to a farmyard, and the lepers' wooden cottage stands across the yard. There were eight lepers when I discovered the place, during a raid with a father on the kitchen-garden salads. I noticed a gate, asked where it led, and was told to the lepers.

The beggar Lazaros brought them to mind.

"How are your eight poor lepers?" I asked. "It's some time since I saw them."

His brown eyes clouded, and a hand passed down his burnished beard.

"There are no more eight. There are three."

"It's been so swift?"

"We share the certainty of death."

"A terrible illness!"

"They are not neglected. I've heard it takes several years from the full establishment of the disease to death; but I know nothing about such things. We'll go that way, if you like. I think callers interest our three sick men."

We strolled out of the enchanted trees, not one of those mighty fountains of leaves stirring. The golden light had poured for hours out of the brazen sky, and stilled them as completely as if they were enclosed in the silver arms of ice. We followed a lane to a gate.

"Why have you only three, Father? Don't others come now?"

"No more may come. Lepers now go to the Government station. Perhaps it's best. Our monastery did this work while there was need; but we're only simple monks. The Government station is on an island and has doctors and priests."

"This care of lepers by your house may have come down in unbroken tradition from medieval times. I've a feeling for history. One would like to think so."

"There may be those here who can say."

He opened a gate into a farmyard, and on the far side stood the wooden house with a deep balcony running its length, Turkish style. The three lepers were leaning listlessly over the balcony rail, their sores bandaged. The two monks in charge also leaned, extending the row.

We refused coffee, though there was nothing so very repellent in the hoarse, wounded voices and curdled, spotted complexions. The attendants were simple villagers, who had taken the habit. They understood how to encourage fellow villagers along the last stages of a sombre journey.

After supper I settled on a balcony facing the lisping sea. Moonlight glorified water and shore. My companion was Spiridion, a book-lover, and we leant back on chairs on a narrow floor, hung high in the air.

Iviron's is one of the important libraries, with more than a thousand Greek parchments; among them some thirty Gospels pre-dating the fifteenth century, one eighth-century copy, another remarkably fine twelfth-century copy. The chief treasure, however, was considered to be two leather-bound parchment folios of the Bible in Georgian, in the handwriting of St. Euthymios, first translator of the Bible in that language. Other Georgian books existed half a century ago, and these the monastery had been accused of allowing to disappear, because of dislike of Russian memories. Spiridion was convinced they were mislaid rather than lost and blamed slack direction in the library, where an ancient was rooted until death removed him. A foreign bibliophile had recently turned up.

"He so loved books," Spiridion exclaimed, "that he ran his hands through his hair in despair when he heard there was still no trace of the Georgian books. Prokopios, the librarian, just sat in a heap. But I remembered I had noticed books in a strange language on a shelf behind shelves. How that visitor opened his arms to them! There are others somewhere and I shall come across them!"

"They are there, or they are not there," murmured another monk. "And where are the Georgians for whom those books were written?"

The remark had punctured Spiridion, but he recovered after a moment.

"What are we monks of this Mountain of rich libraries and long history other than blind fish swimming over a sea-bed of marine wonders? What indeed!"

He sighed as we stared down on the sea in the small bay where the Virgin's ship had sailed.

12

Philotheou: the Idiorrhythmic Monastery of the Hermit of Philotheos

Karakallou: the Coenobitic Monastery of Karakallos

Provata

BEYOND IVIRON LAY A stretch of garden country known as Provata, which continued most of the way to Lavra. The monasteries of Philotheou and Karakallou stood at one edge, and on the far side it took in the remote Rumanian settlement of Lakkos. It was an international settlement of substantial kelli, with households of two or three, even five or six, Greek, Russian, Bulgar, or Rumanian monks using the chapels at the east end of their cottages in obedience to the typikon, and living off their gardens, vineyards, and groves of hazel, walnut, and chestnut trees. Much of the Mountain's hazel-nut harvest, sometimes reaching three hundred tons, came from here. There was water and a sense of man having established himself, making it an attractive country after the Mountain's harsher regions.

I went that way the following afternoon, intending to go to Karakallou for the night. Mules were striking their shod feet on the cobbles outside the great gates as I left, and a short, aggressive father rated the muleteers for dawdling. They gave back some of what they got in the Greek fashion, but moved more spryly. A left-hand turn led me into the plane trees, then to the top of a low cliff above the chapel of the Annunciation and the well that bubbled up in joy at the coming of the Virgin-of-the-Gate.

A path clung to the coast for some time, though trees and banks now and then shut away the sea. Further on the way skirted the picturesque tower and buildings of Mylopotamou, in a garden and vineyard monks claim St. Athanasios planted. The track developed into a lane and the lane forked, branching towards Lavra, in addition to turning uphill and inland.

I went uphill. A contractor's clerk was in sight, measuring lengths of timber stacked for export. He was an exact and anxious person, and his measurement disagreeably less than the claims of a couple of wood-cutters. Argument was loudening when the bushes opened before the advance of a cavalcade of a dignified monastic representative on a broad mule spread with a gay saddle-cloth, a cudgel-bearing muleteer pattering behind, the great man's spiritual son perched sideways on a second handsome animal bearing his own and his elder's umbrellas, a baggage-mule following muzzle to rump, and a second muleteer striding behind all with a switch.

The train moved into earshot just as the taller of the woodcutters suddenly bawled at the clerk:

"We've done that tally, and that tally won't be proved wrong before God dies!" and his irritated mate bawled louder:

"If the Virgin was to reappear on this bit of coast again, it would be to send you ahead of your time where liars can expect to find themselves after Judgment Day."

The monastic representative pulled up, causing the muleteer behind to skip sideways. The junior's mule came close to collision, and the third beast threw its long ears back. The line halted from end to end. The leading monk oriented himself in his seat, drew his brows together, and delivered himself to the offending wood-cutters.

"If a workman comes to our Holy Athos," he warned, with a deepening threat in each sentence, "he shall speak becomingly, as we expect speech here. Or he can return to the world. I shall remember you and, if complaints reach me in Karyes, you'll find yourselves called there."

PLATE 15   *Vatopedi's clock tower*

PLATE 16   *Stavronikita has one of the finest views of the Mountain; and (below)*
Philotheou's church

His eyes blazed across the waste at the startled woodcutters, a black island of rightness in the crimson-and-green sea of saddle-cloth. In his good time he restarted the mule.

The cudgel-bearing muleteer had been frozen into something like a stand-to-attention; but as his master pulled the mule round, and punched its ribs with the heels of his city shoes, the man's eye closed discreetly at his fellow servant. In a matter of moments the train had moved out of sight into bushes, travelling towards Iviron.

I mounted inland, where the slated roofs and cupolaed chapels of farm-houses shared the slanting afternoon sunlight with chestnut and walnut trees. In an hour Philotheou's walls stood up in vineyards and gardens, by which time I was two or three miles inland and a thousand feet above sea, near the site of pagan Episcopion. The house, which lacks distinction, claims a tenth-century foundation by Philotheos, a hermit contemporary of Athanasios. Nikephoros Botaniates, who exchanged imperial robes for the monastic habit in 1081, seems to have restored the building and donated several relics. Another tradition connects the foundation with the eleventh-century monks Philotheos, Dionysios, and Arsenios, and yet a third with the fourteenth-century patriarch, Philotheos. At one time a St. Dionysios of Olympus was abbot, but fled when his Bulgar monks threatened to kill him. Several fourteenth-century chrysobulls have survived, together with documents concerning a restoration by Georgian princes about 1540. The buildings, except church and refectory, both possibly frescoed in the 1540 restoration, were fireswept in 1871, and nearly everything dates after that disastrous year.

The church of the Annunciation (patronal feast March 25) was built between 1747 and 1765, and has on the north-east pillar the ikon known as the Sweetly-Kissing-One, an impressively executed work of the Virgin kissing the Child relaxed in her arms. Monks declare it to be one of St. Luke's seventy paintings and relate that Viktoria, the pious wife of a senator, Patrikios, possessed it in Theophilos' day, and gave it to the sea's custody when imperial agents arrived to destroy it by fire. The waves carried it upright to the anchorage below Philotheou, where it was drawn out of the water and taken to the monastery. The well, that bubbled up on the picture touching shore, lies beside the arsenal.

The monks venerate the Sweetly-Kissing-One beside her well every Easter Monday, and watch against irreverence; for some fourteenth-century Bulgar monks so grossly over-ate and drank at one celebration that when they rose from their slumbers they found the angry ikon too heavy to lift, nor did she allow herself to be moved until they repented.

In 1801 a robber fled in a boat with one of her votive coins, but in spite of a favourable wind, the keel of the boat remained rooted in the same fathom-lengths of sea. Some observant monks boarded the paralysed craft and made the thief restore his booty. Since he was penitent, and that ikon the Sweetly-Kissing-One, he was pardoned, and afterwards converted.

She ordered an over-anxious sacristan never to address her with prayer concerning the house's poverty, for she would see that nothing necessary lacked. A pilgrim going to feed his horse by night fell from a third-floor window. He called on her in the air, and stood up unhurt. A boatload of Easter pilgrims would have gone on the rocks in a storm had she not taken the tiller and piloted the ship to port.

There is a similarity in the histories of the ikons of neighbouring monasteries: such as the ass carrying the ikon and dropping dead at Chilandari and Zographou; ikons arriving over sea standing on edge: Iviron and Philotheou; ikons missing from church and returning to places of their own choice. Ikons punishing; ikons saving; but one cannot separate the histories of the monasteries from the histories of the famous ikons, and I have never met a monk who had not the most profound belief in those stories.

I passed the monastery as the monks were using their pulleys for drawing up water-pots and baskets of vegetables to the high windows. It was a lively minute in the evening, and they gossiped cheerfully from window to window, and down to the distant ground.

The easy road to Karakallou wound through a chestnut plantation full of the long shadows of late afternoon. It would have been attractive to loiter, but there was the threat of Karakallou's gates shutting. Near the farther end of the plantation a gendarme, with unhooked collar and rifle at the easy, swung round the bank, walking hard; a man with a single stripe, and very hot. His expression brightened at sight of me.

"Is there such a thing in your pocket as one little match?" he called.

"And the cigarette too, if that's missing."

He had his own cigarettes, which was the reason for his hand trembling for a match. Two or three draws calmed him.

"I even ran away matchless," he exclaimed, sliding the rifle to the ground. "That menagerie of beards I've just left laughed at me."

"You're speaking of Karakallou's fathers?"

"If the monks didn't, their labourers did. What can't happen to a man living long enough in this land of saints?"

"What's happened?"

He refilled his lungs with smoke and expelled it, ring by ring, sighing with content.

"Erissos let Karyes know that the Athens police are looking for a man passing here as a labourer. We found he went this way. But all the monks could say yesterday was they had no stranger inside the monastery, and gave me a list of the outside labourers. You know monks, how they blink like owls and leave you to guess if it's slyness or lack of wits. I went to the labourers' cottage, but their mouths were black with the usual lies, and they had me walking up and down hill till the soles began to walk off my boots."

"What had your wanted man done?"

The gendarme dealt an imaginary pack of cards in the air, eloquently.

"A card-sharper? He'll have a lean time among Karakallou's labourers, surely?"

"The Mountain's the place for him for a week or two; for who'd look for a card king here? And he'll get an occasional game from a rich monk."

The gendarme whistled out of the fullness of his knowledge of wealthy monks, jerked his tunic expressively, glanced at the shadows, and tucked the rifle under an armpit like a sporting gun.

"Yes," I agreed, following his thought, "gates close at sunset, and we'll spend a night under the stars if we go on standing here."

Most visitors never come across Karakallou. It lies three miles inland, off the beaten track; but there is no friendlier house, nor kindlier ruler than the aged Abbot Hilarion, physically withering but the springs of his heart showing no signs of drying up.

I was soon clear of the wood, and in sight of the small monastery's notable tower at sundown. There is documentary evidence (or at least a seal) of the house's connection with a noble called Karakallos, alive about 1070, and other evidence of an abbot ruling in 1087. Actually the monkish love of antiquity, unchecked by any historic sense, has tempted the fathers to claim the Roman emperor Caracalla as founder, and to include his portrait among the murals.

The monastery may be of ancient foundation, but it was to be devastated in the thirteenth century, after which Andronikos II assured its existence. It seems to have been re-founded in the first half of the sixteenth century by Petros Rares, Hospodar of Moldavia, in circumstances giving it a claim to romance. The Hospodar ordered his Firstswordsman, an important military officer, also named Petros, to raise a monastery on the Holy Mountain to the Virgin's glory, and supplied him with treasure to pay for it. But the Firstswordsman misused the funds, and in 1534 could only build the modest tower and court which still stand by the seashore. The shabby piece of work was reported to the Hospodar, who ordered his death. Now the desperate general offered to return to Athos and build a monastery at his own expense in exchange for his life, and the Hospodar agreed. The Firstswordsman then built the fine church and older portions of the present monastery, beginning the work about 1535, and satisfied his master sufficiently to be received back with honour.

Time is an emollient. Neither ruler nor subject could forget the house that had saddened their fives, and eventually both decided to be shorn there. Both had shared the name Petros in the world, both shared Pachomios in religion. They retired to Karakallou and there spent the rest of their lives. A kelli, named after the general, his cell in life, is some twenty minutes' walk from the monastery.

The following afternoon found me talking to the venerable Abbot Hilarion on a wooden balcony above the court, while a monk named Luke turned over a sea of drying tomatoes. We were on a level with the church roof, and overlooked the buildings. Swallows dipped through the air, a cat rolled over lethargically on the distant pavement, and archways led to oil-mill, wine-press, and bakery. We talked out the siesta, waiting for vespers, until several old men shuffled from their cells to a gallery to turn their calico underwear and clumsy woollen socks in the sun.

A score of reasons had caused the monks in sight and the neighbouring kelliotes to take the habit. Some had come after a disappointment; some to shelter from the boisterous winds they found blowing; others were attracted by certain likenesses to a men's club offered by the monastic life, a club leading into an old men's home. The kelliotes came wishing to farm, but to farm in a religious atmosphere. Life was sheltered and regular; but the day's portion of work had to be carried out. Sleep was broken by night services. The restricted diet, abstinences, and fasts ultimately resulted in anaemia. The common factor in the attraction was a feeling for God. Luxury could have drawn nobody to the Mountain. The elder of an idiorrhythmic monastery followed the equable life of a bachelor of very modest means, restricted of all amusements. Farmers received no advantages not equally obtainable in the outside world. There was very little good soil; a sum of money must be paid for a share in the cottage and land. Obedience must be given to an elder until death turned junior into elder. That final half-hour of a laborious day when cloak and veil were put on over working clothes and the regulation office was performed before the ikons had to suffice for the worldling's hour of relaxation.

There might be truth in the hostile criticism that the intellectual taking the habit had become a rarity, that most monks were of elementary education and many were illiterate; but had simple men fewer claims to religious association than those with letters? Had the heart fewer rights than the mind? Generally the farming monk was scratching a living off soilvalueless to the peasant. Then what harm was he doing? The disappointed man arriving from the world took up no more room than before, and found himself nearer adjustment.

Hilarion settled by me to chat while waiting for vespers. Age had weakened his powers; nevertheless he remained an example of how to live and die on the Mountain. Through the long years of his rule, uprightness, piety, and kindness had been recognized as his attributes far beyond the small monastery. A deputy now took most of his duties, and he was left free to potter about on the business of doing a few more kindnesses while there was time.

Feeling the sun reaching to the bones, he stayed on gratefully. He was tickled by my reminder of our original midnight meeting on the Mountain's summit. He harked back to it, insisting on the kneeling, tomato-splitting Luke sharing and commenting on our reminiscences.

"That long, rough way up," he chuckled. "The young man does it without much trouble. Not to be done by me again."

Ten years had passed since that particular vigil, leading into the Feast of the Transfiguration, August 6 by the Mountain dating, and August 19 by the outside world, when the topmost rocks of the peak, more than six and a half thousand feet towards the sky, had been clambered over by the heavy shoes of scores of jubilant monks.

The pilgrimage had moved up the slopes by daylight, a holiday crowd in black, added to by servants leading mules with food and wine for the feast. Pious chanting had lightened the climb round from Lavra, lasting throughout a blazing summer's day. Mules and servants had halted at the hut of the Panayia, a thousand feet under the summit, and the monks faced the final rocky stretch alone by evening light.

I climbed by myself, an hour behind the others, finishing a good last and arriving at the hut in the dark. A muleteer, running inside with a handful of firewood, tempted me to follow him in. He was a big, clumsy creature in homespun breeches, a dark homespun shirt, and a monk's black hat hanging off the back of his head like a falling chimney, and owed some of his personality to the wine lately run down his throat. The face was familiar, and I remembered I had seen him last in the full beard, black jacket, white shirt, romantic kilt, and pom-pommed slippers slanting skywards at the toes of an ecclesiastical policeman. But he had fallen from grace to become muleteer. There had been a whisper that one of these police had been degraded for looking away while some petty treasures were smuggled into the world.

Stars crowned by stars, constellations by golden constellations; true earth a mile below; here, tossed half-way to heaven, rocks and larch trees. Mules corralled near the hut stamped with cold; yet I had plodded up out of a furnace. Inside the hut a wave of heat and a roar of voices ended winged speculation. A taper or two, and a leaping fire fed with logs nobody present was paying for, lighted the grimy room, into which a dozen had gathered: muleteers, labourers and monks of little consequence, talking one another down, for someone had assumed the responsibility of broaching the wine. A pitcher and mugs stood on the floor. The masters of these men had stumbled up the final thousand feet to their vigil, and dark had come on and marooned them safely out of harm's way.

I found a mug in my hand, a bandy-legged person filling it; somebody wearing the habit slid forward with more agility than piety with grapes, and black bread came down off the shelf. A flushed guest in the shadow of a rafter unlocked his jaws from a wedge of bread and observed:

"The wolf feeds in winter so as to be strong enough to sit in the summer."

A row of short tables had been pushed together in a second room to form a single long one for the breaking of the fast after dawn, and the same agile waiter in the habit who gave me the grapes scuttled towards the tables with an armful of plates. In dodging an attempt at capture by the debearded policeman he stubbed a toe on a log and, just saving his load, limped to a corner. His friend suggested:

"Say what you want to, Theophilos, and I'll wash your mouth out afterwards with lavender water."

The damaged monk, who had probably not reached the second grade by taking the vows, continued feeling himself resentfully.

The fire leapt and a beam of light revealed a sturdy peasant, with feet at right angles, standing in deep shadow. He was president of a neighbouring village, an individual a little larger than his fellow villagers, being able to drink a little deeper without ill consequences, eat a little more heavily, and shout a little louder than his neighbours.

"Comb your beard, and you'll see better next time," he said to the suffering monk.

The monk demanded from the log:

"Wasn't it you who told our abbot such a tale of woe last winter that he loaded your mule with four sacks of flour for the villagers? And after the mules passed your own door there was a single sack on each animal?"

"Isn't he the father of two girls?" the debearded policeman shouted boisterously, "and where will two undowered girls find good husbands?"

"Didn't his uncle eat the money collected for the village fountain," continued the monk," and didn't his own grandfather eat half the church in building it?"

The president stared imperturbably.

"Get up," the policeman urged, "and finish that table-laying. Though God is the Father of all men, has He ever been accused of making all teeth in a mouth of equal length?"

Somebody opened the door, and two whiffs of air revived my desire for the top of the Mountain. I dropped my rucksack in a corner, where I could retrieve it in the morning, and left the hut.

The peak finished in a crown of boulders, with sufficient flat rock to carry the stone chapel, which stood darkly in the neighbourhood of a tall iron cross between the sombre instruments of the Passion. The chanting of human voices had floated down as encouragement during the last of the climb; later the lights of the sanctuary lamps gleamed through the window-slits in the chapel wall. Lastly, worshippers unable to press into the minute nave appeared clustering outside the door, or communing on ledges. The voices of chanting men warmed the loneliness; the gathering was jubilant. Had not the Virgin stood for three days and three nights on these very rocks, surrounded by angelic choirs, talking with the gaunt hermit, Maximos of Kapsokalyvia, who had been given the gift of flight to rush him up here to that joy?

I joined the group at the door, and, by a pressure never relaxed, passed slowly through the gowns and veiled hats, arriving in ten or fifteen minutes against the screen, no more than a dozen feet from the door. A simple man, advanced in years, conducted the service in hampering confinement. Congestion had prompted many to elbow out into the open, but this tireless old man remained at work from nightfall, and would be standing there to bless the grapes and distribute the bread at dawn.

It was Hilarion, Abbot of Karakallou.

There was no space for spectacle, little for simple ceremonial, and this place in the front rank of worshippers, won by steady pressure, was to become irksome. It seemed advisable to press gently backwards, which was in order, those stifling near the screen becoming in need of the night air, and the shiverers outside intending to warm up within. The night was spent moving in and out.

Hours later, a tender change in the sky warned us to bless the grapes. The bunches were borne to Hilarion in platters. Dawn fired our ardour, those outside seeking to enter the chapel, those within determining to stay. The vigil was ending; the fast was to break; joy mounted. Hilarion's final act was to distribute the blessed bread. We crowded out into the open munching that and the grapes.

A group had already lighted the traditional fire with sticks carried up overnight, informing the boats at sea that the grapes had been blessed. Men warmed at the flames while a mile below sheets of sea spread out on the reappearing map. Islands stood up; the three fingers of Athos, Longos, and Kassandra became joined to their palm, the remainder of Chalkidhiki. Blood was cool, appetite sharp; the hut with spread tables was a thousand feet below. More and more deserted the fire for the descent, which was not for the careless. A youthful deacon looked after Hilarion. The early light showed files of carefree monks picking the way down to the hut of the Panayia.

The Abbot was conducted to the top of the long table, but that was all the precedence insisted on. Important father elbowed lesser, and lowliest laymen took a place between. We stood for grace, then sat to eat free of a reader's homily. In half an hour we stood again—hands folded, heads bowed—for the abbatial thanks and blessing, before trooping outside.

Walkers slipped off ahead of the important, who demanded their mules. Hilarion and his deacon mounted, and a hammerheaded beast carried the sturdy old man off on the sliding descent to the lower rocks, a preliminary to the half-day ride to Karakallou.

Servants were still roping the chapel furniture and empty barrels to the baggage-mules when I joined in the flight. The way was wooded, the speedy soon left the slow behind, and I saw the last of them all by turning off at the Russian kelli of St. George.

That night spent on a rocky platform nearly seven thousand feet towards the sky remained with Hilarion after his crumbling mind had let other things go. Monks would continue to climb the peak in August, after his bones had been added to the monastic stack. An old man's easy tears watered his eyes at the reflection, and a soft hand pressed mine half a dozen times while we waited for vespers on the platform, among the drying tomatoes. Yet strip away that worn-out body and one must come on the hauberk of some sturdy pikeman of eternity.

When a veiled monk at last walked into the court with a semantron, Hilarion slowly found his feet, and drifted downstairs with the vagueness of the very old. He led me directly into the south choir, and he occupied the abbot's weekly stall against the bishop's throne. He was soon restless and, in intervals of taking his part in the service, pointed out a splendid needlework of the entombment of Christ above our heads, and next sent a monk behind the screen to bring out a carved crucifix of wood, a notable piece of work, for all the minute figures have character. He insisted on my carrying it to the light of a window, and I examined it with the full blast of the south choir in my ear. The fragile treasure had to remain in my hands until a monk's eye could be caught.

This church was built between 1548 and 1563. The murals belong to 1717. The ikon of the Apostles, by a priest Dionysios of Agrapha, was painted five years afterwards. The general impression of the interior was rich and satisfying, the screen intensifying this effect. The monastery has been dedicated to the Apostles Peter and Paul (festival June 29), and most novices take apostolic names. In the library is a thirteenth-century rolled parchment of St. John Chrysostom's Mass.

The monastery provided a neo-martyr in a certain Gideon, intimidated as a lad into becoming a Moslem at Valestino. Repentance drew him to Athos, where conscience would not leave him alone. Presently he left the Mountain to inform the Turks that he denied Islam. He was mocked at as a madman and sent back. But he left the Mountain a second time and, wearying Turkish patience, was chopped to pieces in 1818 at the Pasha of Thessaly's orders. His ikon is against the church's south-east column, and his relics are preserved.

The evening meal was eaten in the whitewashed refectory, and Hilarion took the head of a side table. As he had been relieved of some of his duties, his deputy struck the bell, and blessed us in passing out; but a row of three resumed their veils opposite the door to make obeisance to their Abbot on his departure, bending until their knuckles pressed the floor at their feet. The old man wandered humbly by, leaving his deputy to raise a hand in blessing. Thankful for what we had received, which had been the punctual octopus, we passed into the court.

I wandered into the Provata country the next day, where farm-houses and chapels shone among vineyards and hazel copses, and wells gave up chilled water to the bucket. Yet when I went into the chestnut forests I left behind man and all to do with him, nor can that upper country have changed much since the early hermits wandered there, munching raw chestnuts; and now and then came someone who had sat on a throne, only to find a sceptre a wearying staff to hold.

Below was the lonely tower of Morphonou on a rise, all left of the dead monastery of the Almafitans. I resolved to leave by the four-thousand-foot pass of the Iron Cross, which leads down to St. Paul's on the other sea, and I continued in the upper country, where a hollow in the slopes holds the isolated Rumanian skete of Lakkos. The huts lie within the influence of the peak, the bewitched men in them losing inclination to move away. A path rears over the Mountain's back to an iron cross marking the path leading down to St. Paul's. The other sea is in sight from up there, and cramped Dionysiou, on its rock above the shore, looks no bigger than a pea. So lonely a world that I have only once met a man on the path, but one drawing me back; for the taloned eagle and the beaked raven so frequently spread their wide wings in sight.

13

The Great Lavra: the Idiorrhythmic Monastery of the Great-Street-of-Cells

ONE SEPTEMBER DAY I boarded a motor-boat for Lavra. There were signs of a break in the weather, and the sea off Kapsokalyvia was confused enough to make the captain and his men gloomy about the chances of rounding Prodromou. However, with half a dozen monks and laymen urging boldness, and an engagement for next day to run an important elder from Lavra to Iviron, he agreed to try, and came dancing along the boat for fares, bawling we might still find ourselves landed back where we started.

Kapsokalyvia was made after a two-hour beat up the coast from Daphne, and Daphne after a two and a half hours from Prosphori. The wind freshened steadily, and a deep sea heave began lifting us after St. Anne's. Karoulia's cliffs looked uncompromising under the lowering sky; we moved into worse round Cape St. George, where pagan Nymphaion had stood.

The boat had filled up at Daphne with several monks and a layman. A muscular ikon painter, the colour drawn from his eyes by the sun, with a pupil who had deserted a monastery to study under him, and a nondescript individual in a monk's black hat who carried a pedlar's pack, were for Kapsokalyvia. The layman was a pious Athenian of the humbler sort, sightseeing in a blue suit and a brown hat, with a handkerchief as luggage. He drew out the handkerchief, unscrewed a twist of green tissue paper inside it, and exposed a small bone, fixing general attention; then lifted up handkerchief, tissue paper, and bone to the ikon-painter, who bent over, his colourless eyes peering through portholes in his upper beard.

"Simeon sold you that," he pronounced.

"The jaw of St. Arkadios," the Athenian replied, with the smirk of a man with a bargain.

"I've known Simeon of the Annunciation for years," the painter observed.

"Have I a holy relic of St. Arkadios here?" asked the Athenian, apprehension edging into his voice.

"Simeon comes across bones which he lays against a saint's bone, and he sells those bones. When he can."

"Come across what bones?"

"What he can in the forest. Hare bones. Bird bones. A man's everlastingly coming on bones in forests."

"But Father Simeon touches the saint's bones with them?" the Athenian urged.

"Simeon lays the bones he picks up on the glass of the reliquary top, if the sacristan lets him."

I knew the individual they were discussing, for I had turned up the year before at a kelli above crumbled Morphonou, late one evening. A junior in homespun knickerbockers and clumsy sandals offered the best he had, a room like a cellar, furnished with a mattress that made me choose the floor at bedtime. The chapel at the passage end supplied a knotted cord to guide the letterless monk in his prayers. No late sunbeams warmed those slopes, and I went outside to stand in the last of the evening light, and encountered the elder, emerging from the trees with hoe and spade, a kindly old man whose mind could be seen at work. Yet there was the substance in him to equip him for this solitude.

He told me that it was from this cottage a much-talked-of monk had lately gone over the frontier wall, claiming healing powers for some bones, which he laid against the bones of relics, and some pieces of wood, which he laid against fragments of the True Cross. The reliquary glass intervened. His personality was arresting, and reports spread of the sick improving, of horses and mules putting off their decrepitude for another winter. But grumblers appeared to complain of no adequate return for presents and fees, and it ended by gendarmes sending him packing with his bones.

"Such bones draw virtue to themselves through the reliquary glass?" the Athenian suggested half-heartedly.

"Those bones of Simeon's are unimportant," the painter answered, staring dubiously at the fragment, and only too soon it was to be seen that they were. The peddling kelliote jerked forward, asking:

"Are you in need of carved spoons? Or a rosary of seeds from the forest?"

The distraction allowed a gust of wind to whip relic and tissue-paper over the side. The kelliote bobbed back, amid general dismay except on the painter's part, who observed, rather labouring the point: "Simeon's bones are unimportant."

The mishap left our captain more than ever in two minds about venturing beyond Kapsokalyvia; but when we closed with the exposed landing-stage a deep-laden, broad-beamed boat was moving ahead on our course and gave some confidence.

She moved across to Karavostasi, the Bay of the Standing Ship. The ikon-painter peered after her, observing to the layman:

"The Virgin rooted the keel of St. Peter the Athonite's ship in these waters to indicate he must go ashore." The Athenian, holding his hat and blinking from spray, stood to survey the historic waste of waters; but a roll returned him to his seat. "St. Peter went up into the rocks guided by the All-Holy-One," the painter continued, elbowing past the captain, who was concentrating on holding the craft off the rocky landing-stage, "and men followed him to the Virgin's Garden."

The settlement of Kapsokalyvia was out of sight in the upper rocks. Painter and pupil leapt to shore across swirling water, followed by the pedlar, who sailed through the air with the bag of spoons and rosaries lodged like a snail's shell on his shoulders.

The captain took the tiller, his men pushed off, and we drove into increasing seas. There were a few minutes when it was possible to alter course and return, but we were soon committed. The evil coast round here grinds boats to pieces, and craft starting on the long, exposed run in a rising winter sea are condemned to finish the voyage or find a grave among the rocks. Monks and fishermen are drowned periodically, and we were to hear in the morning that the sand-freighter, leading us at the start and presently

PLATE 17   *A hermit "kissed by God" and his pet crow*

PLATE 18   *The entrance to the cave of St. Athanasios*

passed, had later filled, drowning one of the crew of three monks. Cliffs, towers, shelves of rock reach far out under water; waves lift and toss in any wind, and even in moderate weather there soon descends on anyone in a small craft a brooding sense of open sea. Passing steamers still sound their sirens off Karoulia in triumphant memory of the destruction of the Persian fleet by storm here, two thousand five hundred years ago.

We were committed to this hostile run, the motor-boat riding down into hissing valleys and up the long green shoulders of waves, kept well away from land by the captain, who confronted the confusion of waters with a crimson face in which the flame of concentration burned. She was never to take more than spray aboard, though continually diving into steeper seas as she flew up off one valley floor to rush down into another. Like this she passed under the great scree earthquake had created below Peter the Athonite's cave. Or the waves rolled at us in long walls, up and over which she climbed, monk and layman clinging and swaying. In a few minutes she was carried parallel with St. Athanasios' cave high in the cliff face, and we saw the chapel in the cavern mouth, beside the hermit's white lodge. That famous retreat, reigning over the solitude, inspired a buoyant deacon to raise his voice to the Ode to Athanasios; but at the word *thanatou*, death's genitive, which the singer was covering in quarter tones, our craft, entering yet shorter, steeper seas, smacked against them loudly enough to leave us afraid she must break in half. The deacon left off singing and widened his eyes with the rest of us. But she shook herself and ran on with the old hardihood. The confusion of waters worsened in drawing level with Prodromou and the cave of the Wicked Dead beyond; but after leaving behind that unholy place, Lavra harbour came in sight and within a few minutes the helmsman was running her towards land. Easier seas washed us into the calm of harbour, and we tumbled out on shore, thanking the Panayia and crossing ourselves queasily.

The fortress above the harbour, a tower and surrounding wall, had stood picturesquely crumbling until so unimaginatively restored quite lately that it may take a century acquiring the old charm. The gendarmerie using it shook off their melancholia and emerged to examine permits; but there was no malice in them, and they soon revealed themselves as exiled human beings beneath sun-scorched chevrons.

The deacon, who had borne his tossing well, now encouraged us up the hill with more of the Ode to Athanasios and passes of his umbrella. The captain gave the motor-boat over to his man in a series of shouts and bounced into place on my left, while the Athenian layman, less his relic, somewhat gloomily took the tail.

"The Great Lavra, the Mountain's senior house," I whispered back to him while waving at the heights. "It completes the pilgrimage."

"The country of our great father, St. Athanasios," the deacon seconded. "He went up and down this hill with his monks, drawing the stones that have stood for a thousand years as Lavra's walls. The Panayia herself talked with Athanasios by his well."

We were rising into a country of holly, arbutus, turkey oak, and the shrubs of a desolate land, the territory of that stout soldier of God and slave-driver of men, Athanasios of Tre-bizond, who became a Mountain hermit in 950. This path mounted towards the Lavra founded by him in 963. A shrine stood near the top, with a seat to pant on. Demons had prowled round here in the saint's day, and the shrine marks the traditional spot where they joined battle with him. The monks were dragging the stone basin, now in the library court, uphill behind bullocks to the unfinished monastery. A fountain plays in the basin to-day, and there are goldfish, but then it was a block of rough stone. The demons emerged out of a thicket where the shrine now stands, and broke a bullock's leg as a first act of hindrance, causing the small-spirited monks to shrink back; but the saint harnessed himself in the bellowing animal's place, and the transport of the stone continued. The fiends, crowding up, broke the saint's ankle in the ensuing struggle, whereupon the tortured man seized his iron-tipped staff (the same leaning against the screen in the Chapel of the Shearing) and laying about him right and left drove them off howling in fright. The saint's foot became printed in the basin's rim in the mêlée, where a cross marks the place. It is a mighty if indistinct footprint, though in murals Athanasios appears as an old fork-bearded recluse, bald but for a forelock.

"After Vespers," the deacon cried, getting his second wind and glancing at the recovering layman, "your lips will press a piece of the True Cross, the head of St. Basil the Great, the left hand of St. Chrysostomos."

The Athenian revived sufficiently to be encouraged on to his feet again, and we overcame what was left of the hill, turning at the top towards a triple-gated entrance among flowering oleander bushes. The prospect of slopes falling seaward behind the kiosk was wide, wild, and challenging. A yawning porter shuffled out of the lodge in slippers for our letters, and slithered on in the lead to a balconied guest-house, built as a hospital four hundred years earlier, but restored for guests after damage by earthquake.

The deacon noticed that the layman was impressed on entering this venerable house, and he remarked exuberantly to the porter:

"Our visitor has come all the way from Athens."

"Why should a man not come from Athens?" said the porter, still slithering forward, "since they come from Germany, France, England, America, from all those Frankish lands to put us about."

The monastery was dreaming out the siesta. Not a cat prowled. I waited for vespers resting my back against a balustrade overlooking the early eighteenth-century Chapel of the Panayia Koukouzelissa, and thinking of the story of the imperial singer, John Koukouzelis. The deacon as a singer himself said to the layman:

"Look at the chapel they built on the place where John Koukouzelis received a golden medal from the Panayia."

John Koukouzelis, son of an indigent widow, was born in the thirteenth century in Albania, when Lavra was coeno-bion. His outstanding voice attracted enough notice for him' to be accepted at the Imperial School of Singing in Constantinople. The name Koukouzelis, or Beans-and-Peas, stuck from the day he said in provincial speech that he was having beans-and-peas for dinner. The emperor heard the golden voice, and ordered the youth to marry and remain near the court. But marriage was far from the pious youth's intention, and he followed the Abbot of Lavra from Constantinople to Lavra's gates. He made friends with the monastic porter and offered his services as goatherd in hope of being shorn. The monastery needed a goatherd, and the emperor's singer was instructed in religion in the intervals of herding goats. One day, where the tall cross called Koukouzelis' stands up on the Lavra Kerasia road, the goatherd was so moved by the simplicity and happiness of his life that he burst into praises of Christ and Christ's Mother, filling the lonely waste with notes that caused the goats to stop feeding and prance round him. A hermit presently crept from a neighbouring cave, convinced that an angel was singing, to be disappointed at sight of the dusty goatherd. He realized that the goatherd must be the missing singer, and that meddlesome recluse lost no time in informing the Abbot, who wrung the young man's identity from him. He took the singer's part and pleaded with the emperor to release the shorn monk from his service.

Koukouzelis had the habit of standing day and night in front of the ikon now named after him, until he fell asleep on a certain Sunday of the Akathistos hymn. The Virgin marked the godly weariness by placing a gold coin in his right hand, saying:

"I shall not desert you while you sing to me."

He was allowed to foresee the hour of his death. They buried him in the chapel of the Archangels, now part of a kelli a few minutes from the monastery, while his cave can be seen in a shelving-in of the rock below the chapel of St. Kosmas and St. Damianos. The completion of this small chapel, partly of stones from a pagan building, was not easy, for every night demons destroyed work done by day until St. Athanasios solved the problem by completing all in a final twenty-four hours, and celebrating an immediate Liturgy to render them harmless.

We were sipping coffee when an Englishman appeared in the doorway to fall on me like a Robinson Crusoe on an unexpected ship. He was elderly and under the weather. The group turned as one man with the Greek's friendly interest in foreigners to watch the new-comer lay bare his terrible situation in a language they could not follow.

He had read about the Mountain for years, and had plunged with enthusiasm into the interior. He moved from house to house in a languageless state, daily more exhausted and upset by the food. He realized it would take him days to getaway, and he had become too weak to go anywhere. Antique parchments now merely swam before his eyes. The tentacles of an octopus, rising pinkly from green oil on his platter, made his stomach wince, and he had emulated the great hermits of history by seeking to sustain himself on the fruits of the field. But while those iron men had benefited by nuts and berries, he found that his desperate attacks on the vineyards entailed a terrible revenge, and he passed all night on his feet as well as all day.

"It may be the world's most interesting and beautiful place," he cried, "but I do not want it for my grave!"

"Many of the over-enthusiastic have nearly met their end here," I admitted, "though I have yet to hear of one actually leaving his bones on the Mountain. Visitors insist on taking Athonite life at a fast tempo, and pay for it."

"I shall remember the last ten days as the highlight of my travels; but the age of miracles has passed, even on this Mountain, and only a miracle can save me. The lumbago their beds have given me has left me too weak for the three days on a mule to Daphne."

"That's exactly where you're wrong," I answered; "the age of miracle has not passed on Athos. The man on my left is captain of a motor-boat, now in the harbour. He rounded the cape this afternoon on purpose to take one of the monks here along to Iviron early to-morrow. A miraculous chance. You can wait a month here for another motor-boat to turn up. He would certainly close with a reasonable offer to take you on from Iviron to Erissos, where there's a passable hotel, and a daily bus for Salonika. Shall I negotiate for the motor-boat?"

St. Athanasios the Athonite, who founded the Great Lavra in 963, had been hiding on the Mountain, disguised as a peasant to ensure the success of his retreat from the world. Nevertheless he was discovered by his friend, Nikephoros Phokas, soon to be emperor, who persuaded him to give his blessing to the campaign that wrested Crete back from the Saracens in 961. Athanasios blessed the enterprise in return for a promise by Nikephoros to take the vows, which the general broke on finding a throne within his grasp. The new emperor tried placating the cheated ascetic with an offer of funds for building the Lavra, and the future saint accepted them, tradition says, ungraciously. The Lavra was built, and administered so successfully by Athanasios on the Studium model as to end the old system of loosely-organized hermit communities throughout the peninsula.

John Tzimiskes, assassin of Nikephoros Phokas, further enriched the house. To-day it shelters a hundred and twenty-five monks, draws revenues from lands and forests, and has the prestige of seniority; nevertheless it has suffered the same ups and downs as other monasteries in its long history. From seven hundred monks in the sixteenth century it was reduced to five or six men at the beginning of the seventeenth, and was to fall for a time into such acute poverty as to part with its holy vessels.

Though the great house covers several acres, the interior court is so broken up by detached buildings that the eye is nowhere nourished on a sense of space. The court sloped eastward from our balcony, and the indifference of builders towards effect had left the prospect muddled and homely. All widened to give room to the Church of the Falling-asleep-of-the-Virgin, facing the sixteenth-century trapeza. The finest phiale, or basin for blessing the holy water, on the Mountain, stood between the two buildings in the neighbourhood of two venerable cypresses said to have been planted by St. Athanasios and his bursar, Euthymios, founder of Docheiariou.

On the court's south side tombs hold the bones of two seventeenth-century patriarchs, Antimos II and Dionysios III, and Jeremias III of the eighteenth century. The tombs are unremarkable, yet rouse the curiosity of most visitors.

The court broadened east of the church, and there was the goldfish basin, originally the unhewn stone monks were drawing uphill when attacked by the demons. Library and treasury were at that end; manuscript rooms and rooms for printed books adjoined each other. The library ranks as the Mountain's first, with seventeen hundred Greek manuscripts, including six hundred and fifty parchments, mellowed to an ivory hue.

I wandered towards the church at the sound of the semantron. The veiled monk ran his mallet up and down a slim handboard, his background the wide monolith basin of the phiale, out of which rose a gilded iron fountain ornamented with rams, bulls, and fabulous animals. A massive wooden semantron, dumb on all but great occasions, hung by chains nearby in the refectory porch. Gennadios, Archbishop of Serres, raised this building in 1512, and the entrance had been made more decorative in monkish taste by the inclusion of capitals from the pagan town of Athosa, believed to have stood here. The interior is impressive, murals carrying the eye up to a roof of noble timbers, laid in 1512. The abbatial seat is in an apse at the far end of the cruciform chamber; and lines of D-shaped marble tables, for half a dozen diners, form a cross within a cross. The customary poverty of window-space leaves this hall in twilight, and lest diners should let thought wander from life's impermanence, the grim sixteenth-century frescoes glimmer warningly.

Monks came through doorways and round corners, settling their veils. I found a stall in the south choir, and waited to distinguish details of the rich interior. The librarian settled in the next stall, laying his hands on the arms. He had no scholarly understanding of the valuable books and missals he kept, but was devoted to them, and lifted them down to show to the right sort of visitor with the pride of a parent showing off children. He loved to turn one large leaf over on its neighbour, letting in air and light upon old illuminated lettering, and disturbing the amiable ghosts of old scribes and painters; shades asking the charity of half an hour's attention to move again after centuries of death.

The church built by Athanasios immediately following 963 is still traceable in this later building, the pattern of which had become traditional for Athonite churches. A narthex, passed through to reach the naos, is believed to date from 1060, was rebuilt in 1814, and ineptly frescoed in 1852; but a pair of magnificent brazen doors open into the naos, rich with early sixteenth-century murals credited to Theophanes of Crete, and untouched by later hands, though damp has been at work. Apostles, martyrs, saints flowed up from where I stood, spreading over walls and ceiling, their restrained colouring travelling down again to a marble pavement worn by nine centuries of use, and giving way in the transeptal apses to a wall covering of Persian tile friezes.

The formal marble screen carried two pictures sheeted in silver enriched by precious stones, gifts of Michael IX: a Christ as Pantokrator of arresting expression, and a Virgin with countenance strongly projected in convex lines. A third noteworthy ikon by the bishop's throne struck the stark, satisfying note of the Phokas Bible and reliquary. All three pictures were remarkable for detachment and restraint.

Behind the screen, in the apse's extreme curve, stands an insignificant marble table so placed as to prevent a foot treading on the spot below. St. Athanasios and four workmen fell to their death from above, when the dome they were raising collapsed. The large ikon over the table is treasured as the personal property of Athanasios, and from the back of the altar rises a cross rich in the effective simplicity of line and jewelling of the finest Byzantine work.

A substantial fragment of the True Cross lies in the silver-gilt reliquary given by the monastery's co-founder, Nikephoros Phokas, a companion gift of the Bible in the treasury, possibly the choicest treasures of this house.

Athanasios' tomb is within the church, in the Chapel of the Forty Martyrs (frescoed 1578), behind a low slab on which the saint is said to have knelt in prayer. Oil from the lamp before it is credited with curative properties, and the tomb itself is supposed to have power to drive evil-doers away, flames once bursting out of it, according to story, when the Latinizers approached, intending desecration. For they were here to the monastery's cost and shame.

High up on the coastal cliff face, below the Rumanian skete of Prodromou, and unapproachable by land or sea, is the black mouth of a cave. Two other holes suggest other entrances into a concealed chamber. Lavra monks are said to keep some of their excommunicated fathers there in awful circumstances. When the thirteenth-century Latinizers descended on the Mountain, they found martyrs who refused their orders at Chilandari and Iviron, but not at Lavra. The time-serving monks of this house allowed the Latin rite to be performed, and a handful even assisted at it, though a mist rolled down over the monastery during the celebration of that Mass. Those apostates, dying when their time came, lay in the ground the customary three years; but on being dug up for stacking were found fresh as on the day of death, except swollen and blackened, after the manner of corpses visited by vampires. Hair and finger-nails had continued growing. The community kept the ghastly remains on their hands for some time; but when the bodies tenaciously rejected decomposition the situation could no longer be accepted, and the unholy corpses were borne away to this cave. There they still lie, I have been assured by a Father Niphon of Kapsokalyvia. They are wrapped round in their own hair like cocoons of silkworms, the curved fingernails penetrating through the backs of the closed hands. The cave is known as the Place of the Excommunicated

Ones, also as the Cave of the Wicked Dead, and the prudent boatman passing below does not neglect to cross himself.

Athanasios' broken body was entombed, and a chapel raised in the court, where a festival is held on the date of his death, July 5. The iron cross and collar he was accustomed to wear penitentially are kept beside the chapel screen, and novices have the heavy collar hung over their shoulders at their "shearing". Against the screen are also propped the two iron staffs of Athanasios. One, topped by a cross, was used on the demons breaking his ankle, and the other is the one with which he struck the rock at that point of the Karakallou road called the well of Athanasios.

Lavra has lasted a thousand years, but all went wrong at first. Materials, labour, and funds lacked. Athanasios was ready to give up, and tramped off to discuss affairs with the Protos at Karyes. After following the shore for a long time, bent in melancholy, he raised his eyes. A woman stood in the path. The Mountain was forbidden to women, therefore she must be a demon. The future saint made the sign of the cross to dispose of her. But the glorious apparition did not fade; she spoke to him and asked him why he was fleeing. He replied despair was the whip driving him, as his monks lacked the rudest necessities. She told him to return to the half-built monastery, because all would be supplied:

"For," the sweet Appearance said, "I am the Virgin." Athanasios prudently answered:

"Overlook it if I must ask for a sign before believing; for Satan's wiles are innumerable."

He was told to grasp his staff, utter the name of the Trinity, and strike at the rock beside the path, in the form of a cross. The answer would be a flow of water. He struck, and streams of crystal water gushed into sight; nor has the flow ceased.

Encouraged, he returned to the monastery and, in gratitude, built a road from Lavra to the well, a road still in use.

The Virgin is recognized as the monastery's ikonomissa or stewardess, and a shrine has been built to her under that name.

The Chapel of St. Nicholas, parallel with the Chapel of the Forty Martyrs, has a ceiling of lively sixteenth-century murals by the hand of Frangos Katellanos of Thebes in Boeotia, and a gilded seventeenth-century wooden screen. Certain forgotten monks, whose reflections were not illuminated by imagination's disturbing beam, placed here portraits of the Emperors Nikephoros and John Tzimiskes; soldiers both, and victorious ones; the first the monastery's co-founder with Athanasios, and the second its generous supporter; the second the slayer of the first. The pictures commemorate kindnesses to this house, murderous nephew beside murdered uncle; he who ruled greatly, and he who slew a patron barbarously and at a disadvantage, to fill the throne himself, and as ably.

One winter night the palace gates were treacherously opened to the assassins. Nikephoros Phokas slept away the last hours of his reign on a tiger-skin. He was kicked awake, and a sword-stroke opened his face. His legs were roped, and his bleeding body dragged to Tzimiskes, who taunted him, and in fury plucked out his beard. The Emperor looked up at the emperor-to-be, adulterous lover of his wife, Theophano, the tavern-keeper's fair and vicious daughter; she whose beauty lifted her from the tavern to share the couch of three successive emperors. Then Tzimiskes killed him with his sword. The pictures of murdered and murderer keep perpetual company, and are held in equal honour by the monks.

14

Prodromou: the Coenobitic Skete of the Forerunner

Kapsokalyvia: the Idiorrhythmic Skete of the Burnt Huts

IN THE MORNING I passed the charnel house where any passer could peer through a gate at a pyramid of bones and skulls. It is claimed that the remains of ten thousand monks are crumbling to dust at the foundations, and the pile is still rising on top.

A desolation of bushes stretched ahead towards the Cross of Koukouzelis. Several of the Mountain's hermits, among them Peter and Athanasios the Athonites and Maximos and Akakios the Kapsokalyvites, spent years here. The Rumanian skete of Prodromou occupied a headland a mile or two away. Weathering had already fitted this range of buildings into the landscape, though Rumanians first came to Athos in 1820 and obtained the kelli from Lavra. The kelli was promoted into a coenobitic skete about 1852, and a handful of monks enlarged it into the present range of buildings, dedicated to John the Baptist. The Rumanians, like the Russians, now get no novices, and some fifty only are left.

Eugenios, the guestmaster, a youngish man with lively brown eyes and a long, firm stride, enjoyed guests, and after giving me an airy bedroom took me outside, where the vineyards were in full bearing, and endless rows of vines black with the fleshy, strawberry-flavoured grapes which most travellers discover enthusiastically. We strolled off with our hands full, passing the shrine where Prodromou's Virgin Not-made-by-Hands is set up at the annual open-air service on the way to Athanasios' cave, striking the cliff-edge at a point where a flight of two hundred or so wide steps led rather airily down to the cave hung between sky and sea in the cliff-face.

"One behind the other, Father."

We began to leave the wide world above for a world of nesting birds and scuttling lizards. Guardians of the cave had built a cottage in the cavern mouth, and the present hermit had dug a pocket-handkerchief garden on a shelving of the rock ledge. Cave and cottage rose towards our descending feet, as did the hermit, lame in one leg. He was able to stare far down on a sea across which he never sailed.

"By the prayers of the fathers," Eugenios murmured, and received the traditional "Amen" with permission to pass on into the cave, which sheltered two chapels, the inner said to be the one used by Athanasios, and warmed by successive hermits reading their offices.

A thousand years before, heavenly agency had revealed to Athanasios that this cliff held a cave sheltering a powerful ikon. When that Alexandrian harlot who was to become St. Mary of Egypt could no longer ignore conscience's loudening voice, it was this ikon that addressed her in Jerusalem, at the feast of the Elevation of the Cross, and directed her to repent beyond Jordan. She obeyed, to be lost in the desert for forty-seven years, until, naked and monkey-like, she was found by the anchoret Zosimos. He prepared her for death, and she died at an hour when a roaming lion drew near, and was instructed by Zosimos to employ his mighty paws and bury the withered body once so much desired.

Her ikon passed miraculously oversea, and was undiscovered until Athanasios received heavenly instruction, and crossed the few miles of rough country from the Great Lavra to find this cave and the ikon inside. He carried it back to the Lavra; but it returned to the cave three times. He then built the inner chapel, and the ikon to-day is between the screens of the two chapels; the inner one dedicated to the Panayia, the outer to St. Nicholas. It became his habit to retreat to this cave during fasts.

This ikon, or a copy of it, is shown at Jerusalem, but who can say which is the copy and which the original?

We left the limping hermit digging, and reascended the steps. Eugenios walked a short way, led more by faith than landmark, and found a ladder as a stairway down to a ledge overhanging the void. I take it the ladder was secured to the face of the cliff, though it seemed hanging against it. The lower end rested on the ledge. The ledge began an easy descent to a new cave, with a hut and chapel dedicated to the nativity of Christ. The founder of the Rumanian skete had spent his last years down here, and two hermits now occupied it. One recluse was absent, but his companion, a scrubby-bearded man wearing steel-rimmed glasses, crouched over a pot of weeds boiling into soup. He drew aside for us to pass beyond to the chapel, on the farther side of which a crumbling stairway on struts led dizzily away somewhere.

Eugenios crossed himself in the chapel, hurried to the end of a short prayer, crossed himself again, and out we went to find the hermit, Nestor, still on his hunkers before the bubbling pot. This time he looked round with worldly alertness, and indeed if he were unspotted his absent partner could hardly have been, for a half-grown kitten waltzed into the hut chasing its tail. The guestmaster stared, and sailed down on it like a vulture out of the sky.

"My little bird," he gurgled. "Ten days lost little bird!"

The hermit considered the scene over his glasses.

"My little bird!" the guestmaster crooned on, burying the kitten to its whiskers in his beard, "and this pair stole you and said jackals had eaten you."

"That's our kitten," Nestor stated in a forthright fashion. "Theodotos found it on top, and brought it down a week ago."

"My little cat, which I fed from the first week, and to be assured the jackals had eaten you! Up you come to our daylight."

"You'll be taking away what we've been feeding a week," Nestor warned, raising his voice.

"What fat have your lizards?"

"Put down our kitten."

I determined to keep in the lead in the retreat along the cliff edge, all too well aware of a rearguard action of words fought to the very foot of

that ladder overhanging the void. Up I scrambled first, and on my heels
Eugenios jerked into sight, kitten on shoulder.

"God has added five fingers to nearly all hands," he observed on top,
twitching his cassock to shake Nestor out of mind. "But some know how to
stretch them farther than others."

Eugenios rapped the semantron for vespers. The Church of the
Epiphany, finished in the eighteen-sixties, already has a damaged nave and
ceiling. The monks claim that the faces of their most important ikon, a
large, modern Virgin and Child on the north-east pillar, were miraculously
painted. The prior of that time was unable to buy an historic ikon after
completing the church, and ordered a studio picture from the best artist in
Rumania. The man's hand trembled when he worked on it, which might
have been the result of secret sinning, and it was decided the painter should
recite the canon in church before attempting the holy faces. This he did;
but on the picture being uncovered for a fresh start, the faces were found
to have been completed by divine art.

There are two unusual murals: the monk crucified, and pigfaced
St. Christopher.

The house is bone poor. The majority of monks are primitive Rumanian
peasants, though I shared an evening stroll with an educated French-
speaking father. The day was closing in shadows, and the vineyards seemed
an unsubstantial conquest of the surrounding wilderness. The farthest sky
was torn with wind.

"Youth," he mused, as we wandered through the grapes, eating what we
liked, "so soon gone. The importance of oneself to oneself; but a more
moving way of living than later. If one could only store the fuel of youth to
burn under the chilly enthusiasms of age! Did we have so many saints in
early days because life was still young here? Think how our life was once
torn to pieces by the schism over the light on Mount Tabor."

He had touched on the fourteenth-century dispute over the uncreated
light on Mount Tabor, originating through a fasting Athonite monk, during
contemplation of the interior of his navel, believing he recognized the
divine light of Mount Tabor, and thus proving to himself the "light was
uncreated and of the essence of God". The news spread; the experiment
was shared. But opponents of the idea arose, and an important Calabrian

monk, Barlaam, declaimed against the converts. The rising fury of the controversy necessitated the calling of several synods during the first half of the fourteenth century, and the Archbishop of Salonika, Gregorios Palamas, who had taken up the cause of the "navel-souled ones", engineered the anathematizing of Barlaam and his supporters, so that today Barlaam's name heads the list read out on Orthodoxy Sunday of those anathematized, though he was to be pardoned for his errors.

"It tore our quiet to pieces," Pachomios murmured, flitting forward through the vines, "and now not a monk in fifty, outside those sometimes peeping into our libraries, has ever heard of it."

"They've even forgotten to undamn Barlaam," I pointed out.

The prior was the last to come in from the fields, and the wind rose with a moan in the first moments of complete dark, bringing a few splashes of rain. At last the missing man came through the shadows, hoe in hand. He stood in the court sniffing out the change in weather like the peasant he had been in Rumania before taking the habit. At the end he turned to me with an invitation to supper. The table was completely covered with platters of beans and stock-fish, a tureen of vegetable soup, and a good rough red wine. After crossing himself Methodios bowed his huge frame over the plate and munched. He gave the impression of unusual peasant strength, though sixty-five years old.

Rain was beating against the window by midnight, but it was possible to leave for Kapsokalyvia under a clearing sky in the morning. The way was by the wooden Cross of Koukouzelis, standing against the skyline where the Lavra path turned righthanded to run by St. Peter's cave to Kerasia. A signpost marked the split in the paths to Kerasia and Kapsokalyvia.

The upper path continued through rustling chestnut woods to Kerasia under the peak, passing almost at once above the hermitage attached to the cave inhabited for fifty years by St. Peter the Athonite, the earliest recorded solitary. There the hunter found him. The cave is closed now. Some say the 1905 earthquake destroyed it; others that the Lavra monks closed it after some monks had sinned there. Father Athanasios of St. Anne's, on the contrary, assured me that Peter the Athonite had difficulties during his lifetime in controlling a local howling of demons. These have ever since hung about the locality and now, in the days of lesser men, cannot be so authoritatively commanded. It is therefore wiser that none should visit the place, which has been closed. He told me the fiends can occasionally be heard giving tongue inside by those incautiously standing above.

I took the lower path, a thread in a dozen threads leading into scrub. It must be understood the exact path continues by that great rock at the start of the scree on which a cross is set, and the walker must take the direction of that cross before plunging down. From there the path is too defined to lose again, and follows the crown of a slope falling hundreds of feet to sea, to the edge of a majestic scree widened by the 1905 earthquake, when the land roared and slid, and a bounding rock blotted out a boat and crew in the distant water. The path persists across this spectacular barrenness, and at the far end leads out of sight to the kelli of St. Neilos under rustling trees.

On the way across this desolation I picked up the frail, piercing, distant notes of one "kissed by God". At the end of the ribbon of path which challenged the scree was approaching a hermit wild as the scene he intruded on, probably endeavouring by his chant to keep chained in their cavern those very demons claiming this territory as early as St. Peter the Athonite's day. The bonnet of the God-kissed man was crushed, his grey hair dangling, his cloak as stained with bivouacs as any campaigner's cloak. He nailed me to the path with a dark glance, swung a veined hand round the sea's rim to draw my sight along it, and cried he had seen a monster move out there for which God had not yet found time to produce a duplicate.

"When did you see it?" I demanded.

"At the moment the sun stood up there," he cried, marking out 8 a.m. in the sky. A glance at my watch informed me I had missed leviathan, or was it kraken, by fourteen minutes.

I plodded through bushes up the slopes towards the green of tall trees, and slid off my rucksack in the doorway of St. Neilos' kelli. Both kelliotes were in the vineyard beyond the cottage, loading a panniered mule with grapes. Going round to buy a hatful, I was told to take all I wanted for "a blessing", a way of leaving me to offer what I liked; and the monks sent me back to the cottage door with half a dozen black and white bunches, and later came out of the hut with raki, and water from a deep spring. St. Peter the Athonite had mounted over these rocks eleven hundred years before, on the way to the cave across the scree, the single man on the wolf-prowled peninsula.

Centuries later one Neilos the Flowing-with-Myrrh settled here, to make his way on the eve of death down to a cave five minutes away. There was time to look in on his hermit successor. A path crossed the vineyard to the cliff's edge, going over into the void in a flight of steps, finally reaching a rocky ledge in the fall of the precipice where the present hermit carved beside a chapel and whitened recess enclosing the saint's empty sarcophagus. Lodge and chapel hung between earth and sky like a birdcage against a house wall.

The old man, who had taken the name of Neilos, after his canonized predecessor, was crouched in the open with his back turned, at work on a matchbox-sized Crucifixion. I took the trifling carving away with me, together with a second piece chosen from a heap poured out of a soiled calico bag. Neilos used hollyoak and boxwood, spending three or four days on a piece of work, and expecting less than a shilling a day payment; a journeyman artist, slavishly duplicating a few subjects, which habit was helping him to repeat in spite of failing eyesight. The work was marred by the association of two traditions, the severity of the sterner masters of the Byzantine School, and that Raphaelesque geniality afterwards brought to the Mountain by the Russians.

The old hermit had withered up into a tiny man. The eyes peering into mine were too colourless to be called grey, and his rags too unimportant, except as coverings, to be spoken of as clothing. The silvery peak faced us, at no great distance, harsh and difficult, disciplining to the spirit; and hundreds of feet under our sill ran the rocky, forested valley leading to the Bay of Karavostasi (Standing Ship), the gloomy ravine up which Peter the Athonite had clambered in search of his cave.

St. Peter was to pass on without finding this ledge of rock or the true cave a little above it, which remained unknown until occupied by St. Neilos the Flowing-with-Myrrh. Neilos died and was entombed here, and, according to story, myrrh presently streamed from the body down the rock-face, tempting mariners into the bay to recover it for sale to the pious. The tomb is now empty, and St. Neilos' bones have been carried off as relics. The sarcophagus fills one end of a miserable room where the present hermit sleeps.

"How many find the way down to you?" I asked.

"The kelliotes above when they wish."

"Are those sacks near the tomb all you've got for a winter night?"

"Winter's expected to be cold. You find me a hale old man."

He pushed the twigs together on an open-air hearth of two stones and, blowing a thin flame through them, balanced a pot of water on top. A meagre tree, dropped as a seedling from somewhere, roofed this kitchen. At the first bubbles the anchoret sprinkled dried herbs on the water, and offered me the finished brew, with a crust that could have broken my teeth, to steep in it. These rusks, baksilaria, are dried in the monasteries for recluses, who eke them out with the roots grubbed up. A friend, usually the solitary's confessor, carried a bag of them to the hermit to save him contacting the world, and I once shared a boat with a monk taking two or three rations to solitaries at the Mountain end.

"How often do you go up the steps?"

"When I must find new herbs."

"Nothing else takes you?"

"Why should I go up?"

If all necessary to him was to be face to face with the harsh peak, snowy for the greater part of the year, the answer was reasonable.

"You've been here for a great many years, I know."

"Thirty-eight or forty-eight; I'm not sure."

"Never needing a companion?" I persisted. Did his answering glance suggest there had never been lack of companionship?

As I looked at him I was struck by the outward sameness of all recluses. All were dirty, though not necessarily verminous, being clothed in wrappings and roughened by exposure. An age-old gown, or sacks stitched together; shabby sandals or bare, hardened feet—that was all. Poverty, combining with renunciation, erased all personality. The live plant, patience, had withered into the dried specimen, resignation. The heroic resistance to heat and cold, into the nullity of indifference. All extreme solitaries are outwardly the same: negative, unremarkable; and I was looking down on a gentle, bent, possibly anaemic old man. Was he succeeding in a quest set himself? That part of him, the hunter, had retreated inwards from the impertinence of the curious. Yet he had the power to make me half envious.

I drank a pannikin of the thin tea brewed me, plucked from a bush, and re-climbed to the cliff's edge, turning once for a farewell wave. But there was only his back to salute as he crouched carving.

A path to Kapsokalyvia from the kelli above curved and fell into the valley below the cave. Few men can have ventured off it into the thickets right and left. Within the next hour I had rounded a shoulder above the water and entered the idiorrhythmic settlement of Kapsokalyvia, dedicated to the Holy Trinity; forty cottages with chapels and orchards centred round a church, in the overlordship of the Great Lavra. The settlement, an eighteenth-century foundation, appeared to be barely won from nature at a distance; but there was plenty of evidence on the spot that men had laboured at the paths between cottages, and building the terraces enabling gardens to stay in being. Until a certain Paisios who restored Xenophontos in 1784 and became its abbot saw to matters, the place was nearly unapproachable, though it had been founded some time before by a mighty ascetic, St. Akakios, and centuries earlier a solitary of even larger stature had given the locality its name of the place of the Burnt Huts.

The fourteenth-century hermit, Maximos, had come to these ravines where only the birds, the grunting of wild swine, and the crash and whisper of the sea were to distract him from listening to heavenly instruction. He lay down at night in the cloak used by day, and in order to be taken for a madman rather than pointed to as an example he would set fire to his bough shelters, earning the neighbourhood the name of Kapsokalyvia or the Burnt Huts. Falling into ecstasy on a certain All Saints Sunday, he was called from church by the Virgin to join her on the peak of Athos. Three times he doubted the summons; but on Whitsunday the command was not to be disobeyed. Lifting his eyes to the peak, he became aware of the Virgin's presence with the Babe, and her choir of angels. He broke laws of gravity, and rushed through air to join her, and remained three nights and days in her company; plagued by Satan, anxious to drive him away, but fed with heavenly bread. From that time he was often mantled in light "not of earth" when in prayer. He lived to be ninety-five.

A later saint, Akakios the Younger, turned the rocks into a settlement before his death in 1730. The world had known him as Athanasios, but he wandered about the Mountain as Akakios the Harmless One, eventually retiring into Maximos' cave. The horizontal saplings of his bed are still in place; but he preferred to sleep standing, and may be the man who strung a rope across his cave and leaned against that for a bed, for stories are told of such a man. He often went to the door naked, to preserve his single possession, a cloak. He built the hut of boulders, still beside the cave, with his own hands; for men came great distances to talk with him and expected shelter. He read men's hearts, and so inspired disciples that three died as martyrs: Romanos in 1694, Nikodemos in 1722, and the Russian Pachomios or Prokopios in 1730.

He ended by attracting a group to the neighbourhood, and it was necessary to find permanent water, which was discovered at a spot known as the Well of Akakios just above the settlement, where the finest drinking-water on the Mountain still sweeps out of a tunnel.

The murals tell stories of these saints. The bell-tower was a gift of Joakeim III, who lived here in retirement, and cleared the present path to the peak. The guesthouse was by the church, and the guestmaster had his beans ready by the time I had washed. It was a day of abstinence and the beans were served without oil; a platter of them, sliced and boiled, making lunch. A lantern-jawed layman, in a threadbare city suit and worn boots, sat down with me. His neck rose out of a collar-band instead of a collar, and both hands emerged from frayed sleeve cuffs.

We turned over the beans absent-mindedly to the grinding of the guestmaster's coffee-mill. My fellow muncher told me he lived by selling political pamphlets. His eyes hardened to the glare of a hovering bird of prey which had marked a movement in the bushes. This salesman of pamphlets and I were the sole guests in a settlement only an ibex could leave in a hurry. The inevitable moment of purchase was ahead.

He pushed the pamphlet towards me, and between munches let me know the state of sales on the Mountain. Monks have the same violent political feelings as other Greeks, but none of them had felt strongly enough to give five drachmas for a leaflet which was expensive at one. He had returned after clambering all over his switchback settlement with as many pamphlets as he had gone out with.

"What sort of people live here?" he hissed. "Zealots they call themselves! You see my boots? Their flint roads have cut them to pieces! Can I find a cobbler to mend them? They will only patch the shoes of monks! The one at St. Anne's would not pick up an awl for an outsider! A zealot is what he's called!"

He manoeuvred a fork of beans into his mouth and pushed the leaflets nearer.

"You'll want one to read through. You'll want to pass them on to friends. There are reductions on numbers. A reduction on twenty-five. A further reduction on fifty. You may know a schoolmaster ready to distribute them to his pupils. Our national hymn is on the other side."

Just as it seemed less a matter whether I should buy than how few I should buy, intervention came from the guestmaster's corner. A windy sigh crossed the room, and Evlogios dropped the brass coffee-mill into his black lap, exclaiming:

"What a nation they must be!"

"Yes, Father?" I asked.

"What do you know of Hungarians?"

"Their capital's beautiful, their land's rich. Have you met any?"

"One. And such a man!"

"Indeed?"

"He came last week from Lavra on the way to St. Anne's. It was a hot day. What did he do?"

"What?"

"That man climbed up to the cistern, which fills straight from our saint's fountain and gives the holy water to the church, and the skete its drinking-water, and he bathed in it!"

"The act of a hot and ignorant man. But done innocently, Father. He wouldn't be thinking what sort of water it was."

"Our holy water!"

"And the drinking-water," I murmured, stretching over the water-jug towards the wine. "How was it settled?"

"We sent him off without bread and olives, and emptied the cistern. It's a large cistern; but a body in the holy water!"

"Not to be considered. He was a tired Hungarian, Father, and without any imagination."

"As I said," my fellow muncher interrupted, "overleaf is our national hymn."

I paid calls after the siesta, and turned in to the kelli of St. John the Divine. The chapel murals are accepted as the finest in the settlement. This kelli was the scene of a miraculous direction on May 8, 1800, feast of the Evangelist. Three monks occupied the cottage at the time. The two younger, flushed with wine after breaking the fast, disputed over who had the more important seat in heaven, John the Forerunner, or that favoured John who received the Virgin into his house. A wineglass, knocked off the table in the heat of argument, was broken into two jagged pieces. The elder of the house, struck by an idea, ordered the two halves to be picked up and weighed. They were found to be of exactly equal weight; plainly indicating both saints were equal in heaven. The rebuked squabblers glued the pieces together and set them in a silver filigree cup, which I took out of a drawer in the chapel while my host read an account of the incident from a volume kept there.

The cave used by Maximos and later by Akakios was in the neighbourhood, kept carelessly, with a heap of rubbish and some broken gardening tools in the mouth.

The community gathered at nightfall for a vigil, and veiled figures chanted until morning. I was with them far into the night, part of the time with monks who watched outside on the rocks of the two dead saints.

15

Kerasia

St. Basil's

Karoulia, or the Pulleys

The Idiorrhythmic Skete of St. Anne's

New Skete

THE SUN WAS LOW when I left the following afternoon, though it had been a nice point deciding how far to let it sink before starting, for to be overtaken by dark was to risk a night among the rocks. The path entered overhanging forest near St. Akakios' spring, and then stood on end. The settlement remained in sight for long afterwards, pressed down among ravines. The only change in these woods and rocks since the hermits found them was the connecting thread of a mule-path. Solitaries lived here unsuspected; in caves, in cabins only differing from caves to the extent that the tenant has retreated into a recess between boulders, levered other rocks over as roofing, and fixed a door. These anchorets rose with the birds when dawn was breaking, and lay down when they roosted. A rosary, sacks for bedding, a water-jar, matches, and a pot for boiling a herb soup completed their property.

Occasionally three or four laps of the track were folded above one another, and beside one of these I interred a bundle of leaflets. The path eventually came out beside a kelli where a hunchbacked father invited me to dine off the magnificent figs splitting on his trees.

The peak dominated this high country, and the march over a second easier shoulder was towards its roots. Trees dwindled into bushes, the landscape tamed. Finding a more productive territory up here than on the granite slopes below where the soil had to be carried in baskets, man had scratched at every fold in the soil, and several dilapidated Greek, Russian and Bulgar farm-houses stood in chestnut plantations.

At dusk I pulled up at a Greek house not far from the Russian St. George's. The long wooden cottage, watered by three fountains running into a trough, was attractive from a distance, but turned into a dismal abode. Peach, apricot, fig, and walnut trees fell in slopes into the distances below.

The locked cottage was barred like a prison. A cold evening was growing colder, and I was in a shirt saturated with sweat. Occasionally a ripened chestnut thumped to the ground. At last an old man with a beard on the moult and a dusty habit led a mule out of the dusk to the trough. He promised me lodging when his elder, Trophimos, arrived to unlock the doors. After stabling the mule he returned and sank on a stone, while the chestnuts continued to drop. A minute or an hour were one to him, though not to me, for I was slowly freezing.

"Can't you sit down?" he asked.

"It's warmer standing without a jacket."

"Though one can see you're not a poor man, you are coat-less."

"The slopes lower down are warm. There's no need for a jacket down there yet."

"Ah-ha, how is a man to foresee next day? Where he will be and what he will need? Ah-ee, what can a man know of next day?"

Five tangle-haired monks filed up from the forest in the halfdark, two elderly, and three ragged youths slouching under axes and bulging sacks. The elder unlocked the door and the pinpoint light of a taper guided us along the dark passage. Trophimos opened the most dismal room I had ever passed a night in, with floorboards penetrated by grass, and a mattress in the corner spread with chaff-bags stitched together. Hosts of vermin might be lying in ambush.

"We've nothing here. Why didn't you go to St. George's?" he said, lighting a taper for me. "No one comes here. Travellers sleep at St. George's. This kelli was rich in the Russian day. Now the Russians have gone, and Greeks are poor."

"If monks aren't afraid of poverty, those calling on them shouldn't be, Elder," I said stoutly.

"Poverty or wealth is with God. There's firewood under our trees. And fruit on the branches."

I stumbled at his heels to the passage end, past open doorways revealing small floors spread with walnuts and watermelons. The polished chapel we entered contrasted with this animal poverty. All was complete: screen and the holy table; stalls; the reading desk; costly silver-sheeted wall ikons, some of them Russian, it having been a Russian house. A becoming dignity descended on the worshippers after those ragged gardeners had cloaked and veiled themselves.

I left at dawn. The cold, unsunned air was soon alight with day. A gush of water near the road, the murmuring leafiness of trees, made an oasis in this desert stretch, for nothing could be more pitilessly barren than the peak. It was near at hand, the Chapel of the Transfiguration on the summit, a lowly tabernacle, raised by enthusiastic hands.

The lower peak of Carmel rose directly in my way, as harsh as the greater one, and crowned with a chapel to Elijah, saint of mountaineers, with a path to the top trodden at the annual festival. Men seldom tarry on these storm-ridden peaks. Suns blaze on them, frosts split their crevices. Young monks sometimes climb the higher peak of the Transfiguration, unlock the chapel door, light the dead lamps, and recite a few prayers.

Forest closed round the neighbourhood of the pass. I entered trees, but there was no more climbing. The path continued at this level towards the white rock incised with a cross, traditionally by St. Athanasios' own finger. A right-hand fork led on to St. Anne's. Those tracks which tempt the walker to the left drop in wild falls to St. Basil's, Katounakia, Little St. Anne's, and Karoulia or the Pulleys. These settlements are perched on the cliffs, and the nesting hermits have carved out stairways along the cliff-face for their bird feet, have looped ropes and chains as banisters, and hauled their provisions up the precipices to their larders with pulleys. Their hut chapels stood in soil pockets built by the basketful in the cliff-faces, and vegetables enticed eked out their few stores. Some painted ikons; some carved; the humblest lived by boiling down deer's horn to mould crosses for the Karyes souvenir shops, and by stringing rosaries of forest seeds.

Karoulia is still spectacular from a boat. A precipice of hermit eyries joined by chain-and-rope banisters, with its roots everlastingly chid by waves. It is still spectacular, but not as it was a few years before someone moved with the times sufficiently to scratch a track from top to bottom to allow a loaded mule to slither down, and his driver to follow, after crossing himself. This path has done away with the lower chains by which the caller hauled himself out of the boat up to those heights, and by so much has the power to astonish been lost to the world.

Father Nikon, charming, educated, a Russian, and once a man of the world, survives there in his chapel cell, lying down to sleep with a stone for a pillow and the skulls of seventeen of his predecessors staring at him from a shelf. There he shed his association with courts and kings, and gained an ease of soul that shines from him. He is possibly the last of the educated solitaries left on the Mountain, and to spend an hour or two in his company is something out of this world. Only the stouthearted can face the chains leading down to his eyrie.

A letterless kelliote came out of bushes ahead of me and poised himself for the descent, when my call held him back like a bird or a bat stayed from launching into air. He carried a light staff.

"A long way to the bottom?" I said.

He looked more like a bird; nor answered. Would he launch himself? Would he stayed poised?

"Have you come far?" I asked; "I have to get to St. Anne's."

"I've been selling work we've finished with two others."

"I hope you did well."

"Well enough to buy what we lacked. The others took it to Karoulia by boat. Why do you need to go on this path?" Because of his pose I could only think of birds:

"Hawks and eagles use this way, and why shouldn't I?"

He was gone, slithering down through bushes towards the first of the great slopes, steadying himself with his staff. The branches closed behind him and stopped trembling. What can the outmoded humanity of the Mountain illustrate? This, possibly: that like Noah's raven "which went forth to and fro" without profit the mind goes out to find no foothold; but like Noah's dove the heart presently comes winging back with "an olive leaf pluckt off".

The Mountain satisfies many types of monks; but not in the same way, and the content of monks is often underlined by the misery of travellers.

It was a highway to quicken the mind, and I continued among rocks and trees, looking far down on leagues of sparkling salt water uncut by a keel, as far as the rock St. Athanasios incised with a cross a thousand years ago. At last, far below, was Lavra's idiorrhythmic skete of St. Anne, founded in the seventeenth century and holding festival on December 9.

The rough track was as difficult to descend as to climb, but the skete's fertility was striking after the long morning in the grey rocks. Streams gurgled beside footpaths and through gardens, crossed the road on aqueducts of hollowed tree-trunks. But the general need of clambering called for resolution in visiting a next-door neighbour. Level ground had been hammered out round the church, a gathering ground for monks, and to afford a stranger a seat to bring his lungs to rest.

This skete increased in importance late in the seventeenth century under a certain Dionysios, who retired here from the patriarchal throne. It was dedicated to St. Anne at that time, after the acquisition of St. Anne's left foot from a church in Erzerum, which was in danger of passing into Turkish hands. An ikon of St. Anne in the church is said to supply nursing mothers with milk, should the husband pray before it.

A hundred and fifty monks occupied the sixty cottages. To each cottage its trade. Men painted ikons, carved enkolpia, or whittled more modestly at wooden spoons and eucharistic bread-stamps. Groups lived by knitting the coarse woollen socks able to survive for a time the rub of a monk's shoe, and I passed six placid fathers under a fig tree; two bowing overwhirring spinning-wheels, and each spinner with a pair of monks feeding a serpentine length of wool to the wheel.

Arsenios came beaming out of his cottage, and waved me into a workroom where there was a knitting-machine with a half-finished sock.

"I've kept my word, Father, and come to see you; but why settle in the highest cottage of all?"

From his high window the track could be seen until it joined a wider path, which fell towards a neighbouring settlement beside the sea known as New Skete, founded in the eighteenth century, an idiorrhythmic settlement dependent on St. Paul's, and dedicated to the birth of the Virgin. Some way down, the path passed under an archway acting as boundary mark between the lands of Lavra, a two-days march behind us, and St. Paul's an hour farther on. Arsenios came to look over my shoulder after putting on tea. Though the more famous saints were relics for centuries, they were as real to him as his next-door neighbours, and he enjoyed even the shabbier sort of anecdote about them.

"Athanasios of Lavra and Paul of St. Paul's agreed to come to a decision about their boundaries," he chuckled. "Both saints were to celebrate the Liturgy in their monasteries before setting out, and the boundary was to be where they met. But Athanasios had the wily idea of saying Mass the night before, and when poor Paul came out of church at the usual time he was only able to get an hour along the road before running into Athanasios. That's how Lavra has so much and St. Paul so little."

No one can visit St. Anne's without hearing tales of Bishop Hierotheos, for it is there he lives in a cottage on the way to the shore. Monks enjoy talking about him, and chuckling with delight Arsenios told me about the young man from Chester, which I cannot resist repeating.

One very hot day a man from Chester toiled over the rocky, switchback mountain roads. He carried a heavy rucksack, and just as he thought he could not possibly travel farther two dusty old monks caught him up and cried a greeting. He was a Byzantine scholar and so knew modern Greek, and he promptly transferred his rucksack from his own back to that of one of the monks. After a few miles they came to cross-roads which proved the parting of the ways, and so the young man from Chester received back his rucksack. He felt in his pocket and pulled out some Greek notes, but the man who had carried the rucksack stopped him with a gesture:

"My boy," he said, "you do not tip a bishop!"

16

St. Paul's: the Coenobitic Monastery of St. Paul of Xeropotamou

I LEFT THE VILLAGE in December 1939 after the Second World War broke out, and for the whole of the war I worked with the Poles; first in Rumania and afterwards in Cyprus and Palestine. In November 1944 I returned to Greece from Alexandria, attached to British Military Liaison. The retreating Germans had left an unpoliced country in the hands of the guerrilla forces acting as the military arm of the Greek Communists, who had started to govern the land through village committees which they had carefully organized during the occupation.

Fighting broke out in Athens soon after my arrival in Salonika and British troops intervened on behalf of the Greek Government, which was still in exile. The guerrilla forces fought back, but were defeated by the British. This intervention led to the return of the Greek Government, and eventually the King. King George had in fact insisted that he return with the army, but was not allowed to do so by the Allied Governments, who could not be convinced that the people wanted him. Finally elections and a referendum were held to decide the matter.

Communist guerrillas operating from the northern frontiers, and constantly assisted by the neighbouring countries, with the exception of Turkey, menaced Greece for several years, throwing it into a state approaching civil war. Not until 1950 was the distracted land able to take up something like normal life again, and only then was it possible for me to return to my old home.

The locality had suffered severely in the war years, and the aftermath. Erissos, after numerous guerrilla raids, became an armed camp behind barbed wire. The valuable forest land of Cholomonda had been slowly destroyed by manoeuvring forces. As Government troops won an ascendancy, the guerrillas degenerated into bandits foraging for supplies, and villagers were forced to graze their cattle close to home for greater security. This was not only harmful to the crowded livestock, but it ruined pastures and vineyards. Men who worked all day became a civil guard all night and patrolled the roads with guns in their hands. Wood-cutters and tobacco-pickers went to work supported by civil armed guards.

The tragic years had changed the small village of Prosphori, which had been renamed Ouranoupolis. Some men had died fighting, others by murder. The tide of Communist belief had left debris in receding. Fewer went to church, though the community gathered to the great festivals of the year. There was more freedom among the young people. Everyone was more restless. Poverty was the same, and because of increasing numbers by the natural cause of birth, there were fewer opportunities. Bloody crimes, committed in the name of politics, divided households. Village life retained its likeness to Gospel conditions: hatred of petty officials; the tax-collector; customs officials. A widow without a son old enough to protect her interests was in a hopeless position. Immediate jealousy flared up against anyone showing signs of success.

One of the main escape routes for British, Australian, and New Zealand soldiers had been through Chalkidhiki to the Holy Mountain. Weatherbeaten peasants, coming up to shake hands after the long absence, told me of being startled outside the village during the German occupation by heads rising cautiously out of bushes; heads joined to emaciated bodies in the rags of foreign uniforms. Food would be taken to them at night, and a guide led them safely past the village, a hazardous task, for the village was policed by German soldiers.

The Germans did not interfere much with the monks during the years of occupation. Occasionally a few visited the monasteries to examine the murals, libraries, and treasures. Most monks sympathized

PLATE 19   *The court of the monastery of Karakallou: not one of the greater
monasteries, but one of the friendliest*

PLATE 20   *The cross on the summit of the Holy Mountain*

with the Allies, and the majority of monasteries offered fugitive soldiers shelter and food. Indeed, some remained weeks and months in lonely cottages in the woods until they could be got away in boats. Odd fugitives reached the crags at the end of the peninsula and, in tattered cassocks and sweeping beards, were accepted by the Germans as one more dubiously clean holy man. A few of these did not get away until after the war. I was told that the top storey of the little hotel at Daphne was strictly reserved for escaping officers, and was often full, while German soldiers slept below.

The Mountain suffered under the communist ascendancy following the German withdrawal, for trained committees took it over at once. Terrorism, ridicule, and lack of sympathy caused a number of monks to break their vows and leave the Mountain. The slender food-stores of undefended Athos later became a temptation to the guerrillas in their own years of adversity. In 1947 the animals from the crowded villages were driven by an arrangement between the Greek Government and the Holy Assembly on to the Mountain, as being safer from bandits. Livestock estimated at seventy thousand head, mostly goats, remained inside the frontier for two years, doing enormous damage. Wolves followed these droves of animals to the new grazing grounds. Wire entanglements were stretched across Xerxes' Canal, and the ground between the fences was mined. The livestock left Athos in the autumn of 1949 by a gateway, after the military situation turned in favour of the Government. The wolves were left behind the fence. These animals increased to a menace until a large bounty tempted hunters to reduce them—but not before they had done considerable damage to the few remaining animals of the village of Prosphori. One night in June 1951 two women watched from their window a wolf eating a donkey that had been tethered in the street close to their house in the middle of the village. This was the last donkey to be eaten, but by no means the first.

In December 1948 guerrillas raided the Mountain in force, supported by twenty-five armed women who ignored the rule forbidding them. Karyes was occupied for a few hours, and long-range volleys exchanged with the gendarmerie. Stocks of flour and other provisions were carried off on the captured mules, and two hundred head of livestock driven away.

August 1951 saw me at Karyes renewing a permit for the Mountain, and as the visit coincided with a biennial conference of the abbots of the coenobia and the trustees of the idiorrhythmic houses I ran across a score of old friends. Two I had known best, Prokopios of Dionysiou and Meletios of Vatopedi, were dead. David of Kastamonitou was there, and has reached sufficient importance to be sent into the world to represent the monasteries when business required it. Mention was made of the great period of Athos; of ten thousand monks on the Mountain half a century before. These had dwindled to half by the outbreak of the Second World War, and the number had further declined to three thousand when Italy attacked Greece. There were fewer than two thousand three hundred a year after the close of the Second World War, and in October 1951 I was told by the General Secretary of the Mountain that numbers continued to fall, and there were at this date one thousand nine hundred and eighty-one registered names, with an additional eighty monks not on the books.

Next morning I went to Daphne, and from there along the coast by boat to St. Paul's. The rough ground where I landed towards evening was flat compared with the surroundings, yet I began an uphill advance, putting wild pigeons to flight within a stone's throw of two muleteers repairing pack-saddles near a cottage.

The long rays of the sun at this hour mellowed the harsh ravine, left barren as far as the monastery by the loss of some vineyards swept away in the melting snow of a severe winter. Monks have found marble fragments which suggest a pagan settlement here, but only a community with sombre minds could be imagined living in the oppressive influence of the ravines. The monastery stood against a background of precipices.

The usual interior court brought into being by rectangular lines of dwellings differed to the extent of a towering crenellated wall, raised against winter blasts which swept from the peak.

A modern memorial, replacing an earlier one which was washed away by flood, commemorated a miracle. Maria, daughter of the Serbian prince George Brankovitch, and wife of Sultan Murad II, mounted to this spot from the shore in the fifteenth century. She carried in her arms a gift of the gold, frankincense, and myrrh brought by the three Magi to Christ's manger. She climbed until halted at this spot by a voice "not of earth":

"Take not another step. Another Queen than you is here; the Queen of heaven." The rebuked Sultana stood still, and waited for the monks to come down and relieve her of the precious gift, still treasured in the church above.

An old monk sat on a boulder, and watched me draw near.

"You're tired?" I asked, stopping by him.

"I'm an old man, and so I'm sitting. Are you he who has returned to the village down the coast?" And then he began talking of the murders connected with my home, a tragedy that greatly saddened me, for five people had been led out and killed. It had made a terrible impression on the Mountain, as one of the murdered was a small boy of eleven. I got away from him at last and continued the journey uphill.

This well-kept house, planned with broad, airy passages outside the rooms, had a good name with visitors. Wide spaces of the earth had benefited by the coming of the D.D.T. age, and among them Greece. A Flit-gun figured largely in the monasteries, though it might be empty, and the sight of it gave confidence to the traveller.

One account speaks of this house beginning as a cell dependent on Xeropotamou, and not gaining independence before 1414; a variant history reduces it to the rank of cell dependent on Xeropotamou after destruction in the fourteenth century. Xeropotamou, from poverty, presently sold it to influential Serbian monks, who renewed its independence in 1404.

The monks of to-day claim as founder a hermit contemporary of St. Athanasios, Paul, who first brought Xeropotamou into being, and then found the way here and settled in the forbidding rock passage behind the monastery known as his cave. At the time of his arrival, the ruins of a monastery dedicated to the Presentation of the Virgin stood on the spot now occupied by St. Paul's, and when a voice "not of earth" addressed the solitary in his cave from the Chapel of St. George, which was built on a wall even then in existence, instructing him to build, he obeyed by founding the present house. St. George himself had called to the future saint, promising Paul the abbatial staff of the new house.

St. Paul's, periodically served by Serb and Bulgar monks, received benefactions in the fifteenth century, George Brankovitch, the outstanding Serb sovereign, raising a church to St. George in 1447.

The Rumanian princes came forward during the sixteenth and seventeenth centuries with money, and Russian help was obtained in the eighteenth. Two sketes belonged to St. Paul's: that of the Nativity of the Blessed Virgin (New Skete), and the Rumanian St. Dimitrios of the Ravine.

The dominating keep dates from 1522, and the present fine church of the Purification of the Virgin (patronal feast February 2) was completed about 1844. All else, other than St. George's chapel, dates after a disastrous fire in 1902. The church is still unfrescoed, though decorative use has been made of the grey marble of the Mountain. Maria's gift of the Magi's gold, frankincense, and myrrh, a piece of the True Cross marked by a nail, an ikon of the Virgin ikonoclasts were unable to burn, once belonging to the Empress Theodora, are safeguarded within, together with one of the Mountain's loveliest altar crosses, a silver-gilt and gem-adorned wooden cross with fifty-six miniatures, thirteen of which are now missing, scenes from the Saviour of man's ministry, painted by a master.

The murals in St. George's chapel, painted in 1423 by a certain Andronikos of Byzantium, rank with the Mountain's best in vigour and clarity of colour. The barrel-vaulted chapel on the monastery's outer wall is probably the remains of an earlier monastery incorporated at the foundation of the present house, and from this chapel St. George is said to have called to the saint, who crouched in his cave nearby. Paul appears in these frescoes as a man with a meagre beard, in allusion to a false tradition that he was a eunuch.

A vault under the chapel flooring is often shown to visitors as the saint's cave, for he occupied it after deserting the rock passage in the neighbouring ravine. The chapel was then entered from the outside wall, and pilgrims attracted by Paul's austerity climbed up past his retreat to converse with the solitary on the way to worship. But where the roots of the cliff meet the monastery is the shelter the saint was occupying when addressed by St. George, as grim as any abode chosen by the Mountain's great ascetics; a rock passage too low for standing, where the dweller shares the floor with trickling water; a place for the bow-legged toad.

17

Dionysiou: the Coenobitic Monastery of Dionysios of Kastoria

Gregoriou: the Coenobitic Monastery of Gregory of Sinai

Simopetra: the Coenobitic Monastery of the Rock of Simon

WHEN I GOT TO Dionysiou, the boat which carried me along the coast in the tail of a storm practically tossed me on to the jetty. I hurried to the sheltered road to get out of the gale, and settled on some coping to recover breath. My previous visit had been before the war, but so unchanged was the scene, so great the sudden quiet, that I felt I was waking from some dream and that everything was still at the day when Marko's octopus boat had settled me on the beach below ten or twelve years ago.

He helped to pitch a small tent for me late in the evening, near a timber shed, and I left him fishing for supper while I mounted this steep road to return a monk a packet of handwritten Easter charts and tables, a pet child that had brought him disappointment; for Athenian publishers had seen no profit in them, and the monastic committee had declined to pay for the printing. The system foretold the dates of Orthodox Easters for all time.

The handwriting and the beautiful spidery diagrams charmed; one hoped the charts would at least find a way into the library. This seemed worth pointing out when we met in the guestroom above.

"Monks and visitors will enjoy looking them over," I said.

"To smile over as a curiosity when I'd hoped they'd be useful. Well, if time honours my tables to that extent, I needn't mourn the lost hours so deeply."

We stood near a window, on a sloping floor, for the wooden struts supporting this overhanging guestroom had contracted. Evening light winked down through the water and revealed the sea bed. This was the scene of the shark story of Athos. A monk was bathing and was seized by a shark close to the shore, under the eyes of the fathers, who crossed themselves at these windows as they watched. They shouted to the monk, who was swallowed to the armpits, to delay matters by stretching his arms to form a cross. Which he did, and stuck like this until fresh instructions reached him to join his hands over his head to facilitate swallowing, for the shark seemed unwilling to disgorge him. He immediately disappeared.

The shark continued to cruise the neighbourhood, and so the fathers were tempted to the extravagance of a goat. The bait was seized and the shark dragged ashore, to be buried by book and taper, with the monk inside. The tragedy is clear in detail, though dates alternate between centuries ago and a few years.

The outer stairway into the court led past a door in the keep. In the heart of this tower, built before a disastrous fire in 1535, stairs wound up to a valuable library under the roof, where a possibly seventh-century parchment of the Gospels in uncials is shown to visitors. Additional books have been found since the cataloguing of the library by Lambros.

The big church badly restricted the court. A shabby door opened in the side of the court, near the bottom of the steps. Few notice it; fewer still open it; yet it encloses the natural rock, sanctified by a lamp burning before an ikon of John the Baptist, to whom the house is dedicated. The fourteenth-century ascetic, Dionysios of Kastoria, retired to a cave behind Philotheou, at the time Bulgarian, and disputed so violently with the Bulgars in trying to reinstate the Greeks, that they bound him to a cypress tree in Philotheou's court. The tree has grown no bark on that side since.

Nevertheless Dionysios expelled the Bulgars, and remained in the monastery until his brother, Theodosios, arrived about 1375 to become abbot. Dionysios then withdrew to a cave in the twin peaks overlooking the rock supporting the monastery of his name. One evening, while staring seawards, the solitary noticed a fire burning on a great rock overhanging the water. The unfed flame licked skywards, and flared like a mighty torch for nights to come. He finally interpreted the message. The rock must be covered with a monastery. Monks have since arranged the simple shrine on the point of rock where the flames were seen; the rock is revealed by opening this door.

Dionysios' brother Theodosios, now Metropolitan of Trebizond, interested his imperial master, John Alexios Komnenos of Trebizond, in the idea of building a new monastery on Athos, and the ruler's magnificent chrysobull is in existence in the monastery. The monastery's treasury has several locks, the keys of which are kept by separate monks, and these individuals have to be hunted down all over the grounds, and hunted patiently, before the ceremony of opening the door can take place. Glass cases protect a great deal of finery and treasure from the past, and this chamber safeguards the bull, a brilliantly illuminated parchment twice as long as a tall monk in his hat, and eighteen inches wide. Christ extends both hands to bless Alexios and his Empress Theodora, and the imperial scarlet enriches parchment already emblazoned with golden and ultramarine capitals, within borders of noble design.

Though the monastery (patronal feast June 24) was not founded until late in the fourteenth century, no house is more suggestive of age, a reason being the buildings have escaped fire for the last four centuries. It gained its present ranking of fifth place in the sixteenth century, after fire ruined Xeropotamou. In the same century its own turn came to be fireswept; but the generosity of a voivode of Wallachia and his family brought life, and it was rebuilt within a few years. Much built then stands to-day.

Belfry and tower antedate the fire. The church seems to have been begun in 1547, during the rebuilding. From the shrine some of the cloister murals were to be seen, leading left to refectory and kitchen and, right hand, round to the church door.

The sixteenth-century murals are sometimes amusing, and sometimes warning. Monks passing from church to trapeza brush them with their gowns. The big refectory, redolent of oil and garlic, is shaped as a headless cross, and is well lighted in terms of Athonite lighting. The luminous colours of a hundred wall-pictures, and the pulpit's brilliant tints, combine in making the place striking, especially at midday when the yellow sunlight floats captive in the distant roof beams.

Monks claim that the murals of the Church of John the Baptist are the work of Zorzi. The south-east column supports an ikon of the Forerunner, saved from the sixteenth-century fire, and at the festivals of Christmas, Epiphany, Easter, and the patronal feast a silver lamp from the treasury is hung before it. A Greek, assaulted by a Turkish robber long ago, killed his attacker and seized his silver-mounted weapons. He presented this ikon with a lamp beaten out of the silver.

A reliquary contains the Forerunner's right hand, procured after the monastery had lost that saint's head to pirates. A portion of the True Cross is preserved, together with a fragment of St. Peter's prison chains; and in an unusual silver reliquary much admired by visitors—a five-domed church remarkable for magnificent tracery—are laid away many of the bones of that St. Niphon who occupied the patriarchal throne in Constantinople during the fifteenth century, to exchange it in the end for a cave. He served here as woodman and muleteer, revealing his identity on his deathbed in 1508. His cave is close to the monastery, and his tomb farther round the same hillside.

An ikon said to be painted by St. Luke is in the Akathistos chapel, in the church's north-west corner. The monks say that the Patriarch Sergius carried it round the walls of Constantinople during the siege of the city by the Avars in 626. In gratitude for the enemy's withdrawal, Sergius composed the Akathistos hymn to the Virgin. None may remain seated while it is being chanted. The ikon reached Trebizond, and was handed by Alexios II to Dionysiou. Dionysiou's monks daily chant the hymn before the ikon. A monk who recovered his lost sight through its offices has sheeted it in gold.

The ikon fell into the hands of pirates in 1592. The Virgin appeared to the captain of the ship three times in dreams telling him to put back to land. When he disobeyed, she raised a shrieking storm. Wind howled, and water ran on deck; but the cabin filled with the fragrance of myrrh from the stolen ikon, winning it the title of Myrovlitissa, or Flowing-with-myrrh-One. The wind dropped to a breeze as the ship put about. The ship arrived at Dionysiou with a repentant crew, one of whom was shorn later.

The ikon again fell into the hands of pirates in 1767, but was recovered and taken to Skopelos, where the islanders would not let it go until the place had been chastened with plague.

I passed through a door in the thickness of the wall. Fifteen or twenty monks were taking an airing. It was impossible to forget Nikander, absent from the porter's lodge after lending it the glory of learning. The dead porter had held two doctorates, and spoken three languages. He asked for the post in old age to test himself in humility. He had been wise and friendly, with an enjoyable trace of acid in his make-up. He was interested in the outside world to the end, without wishing to return to it.

To look up from the boathouse was to see the monastery against the sky like a poised bird. Unscalable walls rose off unscalable rock; and the strut-supported living-rooms swung out floor by floor farther over space, relying on those walls. The valley narrowed in rising, meeting the sky at last in twin peaks, shaped like human knuckles. Those peaks Dionysios had stared down from towards the torch of fire were remote and a trifle disturbing. No wonder solitaries heard sometimes the "howling of demons", and to this day fervently believe in them. There is the story of a monk who believed he had made a pact with the devil, and threw himself from a window on the date of its maturity, leaving a pathetic record of his wickedness in writing.

The caller toiled up from the beach; but went down to the boathouse in five minutes.

"Did you get hold of fish, Marko?" I asked as I arrived.

He surprised me with half a dozen, cleaned and laid out for frying. There was the making of a sound meal in sight. Bread and cheese in good supply; then two men with guns and a dead hare came out of the bushes. I bought the hare and invited them to join us, and presently fish and hare were grilling and frying side by side over red embers. A movement brought a monk into the firelight to join the party. He had expected to go without supper in his boat, until he recognized me. He was a gloomy fellow from a farm down the coast, an overseer of labourers. Some years ago he had rowed at dead of night into Prosphori with a labourer who was unconscious. He told me that the man had had a bad fall, and he left him at the little village tavern and departed in his boat as he had come. Next morning the man still showed signs of concussion and I suggested sending for the doctor; but the taverner objected. He said labourers' heads soon recovered. The second day the man had recovered sufficiently to demand a gendarme. The injury was not the result of a fall. The labourer had got drunk and had blasphemed against the Virgin, whereupon the monk had caught up a lump of wood and struck him over the head. Sufficient religious fervour had been in the blow to crack his skull. That night the monk returned, collected the man and rowed away with him. The taverner went to the skete some days afterwards and returned with a barrel of wine for his discretion. He had sent for the monk instead of for the gendarme. The striker of that godly clout was on the other side of my fire.

A moon as round as a copper cauldron and the colour of one was launched off the horizon into the sky. We had sucked our bones by this time, watched by the dogs with lifted ears. The moon mounted higher over the waters and put out the stars. A jackal howled.

"Winter's on the way," I said.

"Who minds the sneaking jackal?" Andreas, seller of the hare, cried boisterously.

"Hear the lynx howl," his friend followed up. "Where the lynx howls the wolf doesn't walk. Who ever had lamps in his house like a lynx's eyes? That beast isn't really of this earth."

"There are wolves, droves, packs in winter near my village, beyond Florina," Andreas claimed. "They've teeth but not brains. When the wolf and fox co-operate, it's the wolf provides the strength and the fox lends his brains."

"Should my grandfather want to save himself from a wolf," cried the partner, "he ties a rope round his waist and lets the end drag. No wolf would come near it thinking it a great serpent."

"We've our own way of hunting," Andreas interrupted; "the hunter takes a few sheep bells up a tree with him, settles on a bough and shakes them. The wolves draw near the tree, expecting sheep."

"How many fell to your gun last time?" I asked.

Andreas' face split open into a bray.

"What a night to have chosen! When I tried getting down I'd frozen to the tree. The branch pulled the pants off me, and my skin went with them."

Marko's grin had been widening.

"A jackal can howl. A lynx howls. But what howl like a mad dog's?"

"Now they send you to a hospital and treat you with a syringe, and you never get the madness," the monk observed knowledgably, "though can any but the Panayia say you would have sickened?"

"It was not that way in my grandmother's day," Marko asserted roughly. "They carried you round the village, chanting certain words. If you were no better after that they threw water over you to kill you at once and stop your sufferings."

"Or they took a mirror off the wall," the monk added, returning to the days before he took the habit, "and held that square of glass up in front of the sufferer, who thought it was water and died at once."

The hunter's partner leant back against his tree trunk, replete and satisfied. The monk rose to his feet muttering and crossed himself. "I'm going down to my boat."

"Bed for me too," I agreed.

That had been when I was last this way twelve years before. I broke the spell of memory and breasted the steep ascent to call on my old friend the Abbot Gabriel.

Gabriel was taking the air in the sheltered gossiping ground outside the monastery gates, and the warmth of his greeting was still ringing in my ears as we walked into the court and up steps to a small room overlooking the sea, to talk till vespers of the fugitive soldiers and guerrilla troubles. Both Dionysiou and St. Paul's have lively tales to tell of the fugitive soldiers and German search-parties. Sometimes hunters and hunted occupied neighbouring rooms and only the adroit cunning of Gabriel prevented a discovery. He was an able abbot, but he was aware of the twilight closing over the land. We lingered looking at the cloister murals after vespers, and he raised his black staff to point out how the old painter, centuries ahead of time, had drawn the mushroom-like burst of an atom bomb in a demon's mouth, and has foreshadowed the aeroplanes of this age in the shape of crouching fiends.

St. Anne's post-boat picked me up next morning on the run to Daphne. One of the Lavra committee-men sat beside me. He was going to meet a timber merchant in the hope of selling a wood concession to him. He told me that it was difficult sometimes, as caiques had to pay such high wages there was no profit on timber, and also that both wood and charcoal were used less each year and petroleum, gas, and electric fires became the fashion. Good for the trees, but bad for the pockets of the monks, he said.

Gregoriou, like Dionysiou, stood on a rocky headland, wetted by sea. Its beginnings seem to have been late in the thirteenth century, and the name most associated with the foundation is that of Gregory, a monk of Sinai who called on the help of disciples. The house ranked last but one in the typikon of 1394, and is still unimportant. It was burned down about 1500; but the reigning hospodar of Moldo-Wallachia came forward with help. A second fire ruined it in or about 1761, and this time its sacristan, a certain John Longbeard, persuaded the Turkish sultan and the Wallachians to send funds to restore it.

The monastery dates from after this disaster. The north and south ranges of cells were built in 1776 and 1783 respectively, and most of the rest in the last decade of the nineteenth century. Among the earliest of the buildings is the Church of St. Nicholas (patronal feast December 6), which was frescoed throughout at the end of the eighteenth century. Several large and ancient ikons have a place in the small nave, and a gilded and painted wooden screen gives an effect of luxury; the approach through frescoed anti-churches heightens the sense of crowded colour.

Treasure of treasures is rightly considered the late seventeenth-century or early eighteenth-century ikon, the Panayia Galaktotrophousa or Virgin-giving-suck, a brooding mother of lifesize and dark tones, holding her breast to the Babe's lips with a right hand, and with her left supporting the tender body against hers. The flowered design of coif and gown makes this picture a work of detail, delicacy, and harmonious balance of colour.

The approach from Dionysiou presents a façade supporting a building which seems larger than it really is. Behind a wall a palm tree droops in exile, a landmark which has been there for years. The motor-boat closed with the quay close to a layman slapping an octopus on the cement. A kelliote suggested to a companion that they buy it. He was like a housewife hesitating before a tender chicken:

"It's already well beaten."

The road to Simopetra began as a track on the left, crossing desolate country before rearing up in the air. The port's boathouse and cottages clung together timidly in a waste of menacing boulders. There is said to have been a temple of Poseidon here in pagan days, but no monk I have talked to has been able to point to one stone of it. A string of mules stood on the quay, jangling their bells, stamping and flicking their tails, while labourers loaded them with manure under the eye of the rat-whiskered Father Andronikos, who added his shouts to theirs as he swept the leavings together. A gipsy blacksmith, black as a boot, leaned against a wall. He grinned at our boatload and seemed prepared to continue leaning; but he suddenly came together at the joints, and withdrew to a shed at a walk degenerating to a flight. One of the most capable of managing elders was advancing down the slope from the monastery gates. The elder came striding, and the rat-whiskered overseer modulated his shouts."

Good morning, Elder," I said. "I'm pulling myself together for the climb to Simopetra."

"You'd be wise to get up there before the sun's any higher." He smiled at me, but his mind was on the labourers. "We're manuring our gardens— a heavy work with our reduced numbers. But hard work doesn't call for noisy work. We're told St. Tryphon loved and looked after gardens and orchards; but we don't hear he shouted all the time!"

"Do you feel your numbers are reduced because of changing ideas and ideals in the world?"

"Some of the fault is our own, to do with internal management. A few monasteries are able to draw sufficient novices."

"They told me at St. Anne's kellia once selling for eighty or a hundred gold pounds are to be had for a tenth of that."

"Yes, I've heard that." Then he turned once more to his labourers, and I listened to his cutting remarks as I started up the path to Simopetra.

All must feel astonished who pass under Simon's Rock in a boat and stare up at that eyrie of men for the first time. The human eye takes in that boldness, though the camera's mechanical eye foreshortens distance and produces disappointing pictures. Men stepping on to those distant balconies, and eyeing the void through gaps in the flooring, sometimes step back hastily into the rooms behind, with heads swimming from the dizzy height.

After twenty minutes' climb two paths join near a shrine with an ikon of the Virgin with St. Anne and St. Joachim. There is a seat, and an inscription tells of an incident when the original builders were toiling up and down under blocks of stone. An exhausted monk, in despair at this spot, asked when his labours were to be rewarded, or was Kang David correct in pointing out that endeavour was likely to be vain? A voice "not of earth" informed him that the monk who toiled uncomplainingly and learnt obedience would in good time wear a crown of the kind worn by martyrs of the faith. I did not sit down so much to meditate on toil's reward as to get my breath back.

I attacked the remainder of the path after some moments' rest, and was rewarded by the gradual descent of the monastery out of the sky. The kitchen gardens sank to my level, cabbage beds spread round Simon's Rock; off the rock rose the foundations of the house, and high up in the house's face projected the hanging balconies. Ahead was an aqueduct bringing water from the well of Simon on a haunch of hill, and a fountain and seat stood a hundred yards from the entrance. The monks had done wisely placing tap and seat for the restoration of pilgrims arriving from below.

The house is said to have been founded about 1363 by a hermit, St. Simon the Flowing-with-Myrrh, whose cave is beside the path on the Daphne road, five minutes from the monastery. One Christmas night the solitary was kneeling at its mouth, at prayer in his world of rocks, when a new and astonishing star became a point of such golden glory in the firmament as to leave no doubt in his mind that it was the identical star of Bethlehem that had burned in the sky centuries before, to guide three kings

PLATE 21 *The hero of the cigarette-papers raid*

PLATE 22   *Land view of Simopetra on its high rock; and* (below)
St. Paul's Monastery

to a manger. The hermit, pondering on its possible message, watched it shine down on the rock where the monastery now stands, and finally interpretation was granted him. Simon received divine instruction to raise a monastery there to God's glory.

The place looked impossible and, failing in faith, he started building beside his easier cave; but the stones placed by day fell down at night. He gave up in despair and began building on the rock, where he found all difficulties were overcome, though builders suffered at the start from giddiness. However, one labourer slipped over the precipice one day while taking a cup of wine from Simon, and landed unhurt on the rocks with the wine unspilt. Then the inconvenience of giddiness passed.

Simon discovered a patron in John Ugljesa of Serbia, after the hermit's prayers had cured the despot's sick daughter. In another account the building had been begun earlier, and the Serbian marshal, a great benefactor of Athos, enriched it about 1334. The house, dedicated to the Nativity of Christ, was first called New Bethlehem, and only later the Rock of Simon. Corruption has since caused it to be more commonly known as Asimopetra, shortened to Simopetra, the Silver Rock.

A monk once assured me that the monastery need not fear earthquake, which many sightseers keep in mind; but it has suffered from disastrous fires, and in 1581 was completely destroyed, the bodies of thirty monks who had jumped from the windows littering the rocks below. The abbot arrived at Xenophontos with a band of survivors. Funds were raised in Bucharest for repairs. Fresh rebuilding followed a fire in 1635. The house was closed from poverty in the middle of the eighteenth century, and was again abandoned in the troubles of 1821, remaining empty until 1828. A new fire in 1891 destroyed so much, including the library, that little more than the relics and holy vessels were saved. This time Russia provided restoration funds.

The new church dedicated to the Nativity of Christ (patronal feast December 25) was built in 1893, and the other buildings are little older. The arsenal on shore dates from 1567.

I spent a few minutes on the seat before moving to the gate, where the porter had come out to watch my advance.

"Good morning, Father. With you at last!"

He led me along rock passages frescoed with saints and demons that had had their eyes scratched out by Turkish soldiers quartered here after the 1821 rising. He gave me over to the guestmaster, who led me to a reception room from which I went out on to the highest of the balconies, where wider heaven was spread above wide sea. The faint smoke of a steamer en route to Cavalla floated off the point of Longos.

A fleshy Father Barlaam and a bony Father Athanasios sat on a bench by the door, and Barlaam patted it to show a place was left. We sat and watched the steamer.

The coastal steamers of years ago were so unassuming. The miniature St. George nosed along the coast, stopping off Prosphori on Thursdays; a suggestion of St. George's dragon about her on winter nights, when lighted from bow to stern. A stride took the first-class passenger from the isolation of the single stateroom under the bridge into a group of squatting peasants returning from sitting in town with the long patience of the poor outside some doctor's or lawyer's door. For years she steamed past Prosphori's tower, guided, said her captain, by the light of the sanctuary lamp in the chapel. She hooted until boats went out to her. The placid captain, who had put up a notice in her saloon forbidding passengers to take the Virgin's name in vain, died of appendicitis during a bad storm, when he sheltered in the bay of an unhabited island.

A second small steamer took her place. Her master had a large dog to keep him company on the bridge. He died in his ship like his predecessor, for she went aground during a long storm, on to a sand-bank built by wind and waves in a few hours. His frozen body was found next morning on the bridge, with his living dog beside it. The dog was rescued. Then road communication opened up with Salonika.

"And now the age of motor-boats," Barlaam complained, chiming his thoughts with mine, and fading out a dream.

Was it that? Was the Mountain suffering from the motorboat age, and all it represented?

It was no longer secure in the old sense of the word from the outside world. Society no longer had sympathy with the monastic way of life. The modern man demanded speed, noise, change.

The tourist was ousting the pilgrim of the past, who arrived after difficulty, in the mood to venerate. The sightseer now caught a bus across the mountains, or came in his own car to Erissos, and ran up and down either coast of the Mountain in a motor-boat. With him came the post, newspapers, and his own sceptical mind prepared to smile at what he found there, rather than regard a little enviously a single-mindedness beyond his own duplication. The Communists had heaped anti-religious argument and ridicule on humble old men without education or wits sufficiently nimble to reply to them. All this led to something intelligent monks constantly underline, that the ailing community could only be restored to health by men of education, conviction, and good will taking the habit. Newcomers with gifts of leadership and purpose must be found to take the age-old vows of stability, obedience, poverty, and chastity. But in this motor-boat age is it possible to find numbers of men whose fullest way of self-expression in the world is to be found by withdrawing from it?

Appendix

THE PRIMITIVE PERIOD on Athos of hermit solitaries and hermit communities was brought to an end when St. Athanasios, the Athonite, founded the Great Lavra in A.D. 963. To-day there are twenty monasteries on the Mountain, and their various sketes, kellia, etc.

Eleven monasteries follow the coenobitic rule, nine the idiorrhythmic rule, as follows:

COENOBITIC MONASTERIES	IDIORRHYTHMIC MONASTERIES
Dionysiou	Chilandari
Esphigmenou	Docheiariou
Gregoriou	Iviron
Karakallou	Lavra
Kastamonitou	Pantokratoros
Koutloumousiou	Philotheou
Simopetra	Stavronikita
St. Panteleimon	Vatopedi
St. Paul's	Xeropotamou
Xenophontos	
Zographou	

COENOBITIC RULE

The coenobitic rule insists on absolute spiritual obedience to an abbot, elected for life at a meeting of all monks of six years' standing in the monastery. He should be past his fortieth year, and an educated man (not insisted on) with executive ability. Spiritually he is absolute, but in administrative matters has the help of two or three trustees (epitropi) chosen by all, or by the "Elders' Assembly" of eight or ten senior monks (gerontia). The monastery dispenses property, clothing, and food, and meals are eaten in common.

IDIORRHYTHMIC MONASTERIES

The idiorrhythmic monasteries, on the other hand, first appearing in the fifteenth century, are directed by two annually changed trustees, helped by the Assembly of ten or fifteen leading monks (proestameni), whose decisions they enforce, and from among whom they are chosen. A spiritual man (pneu- matikos) is engaged for spiritual guidance. A definite class distinction appears in these houses, the "assembly" coming from the upper ranks and apportioning labour to the lower. Individuals retain personal property, eat their meals in their cells, which may be apartments of two or three rooms, and are left to their own judgment concerning personal austerity. A few hold paid appointments.

The coenobitic considers the idiorrhythmic rule lax, and is answered that the latter allows opportunity for severer individual discipline. This may be the ideal; but the greater austerity obtained in the coenobia, leaving the individualistic and better off to enter the idiorrhythmic monastery.

NOVICES

The man from the "world" who is drawn to the idea of becoming a monk on Athos usually visits several monasteries, before choosing one. He then presents himself to the Committee. Applicants who come at the suggestion of a relative find the way smoothed for them. The applicant must not be less than eighteen years of age, must belong to the Eastern Orthodox Church, and must be applying of his own free will.

A young monk may serve an elder in the idiorrhythmic houses, and in return be instructed in religion by him. Other men, required for specific work and possibly invited, may be quickly accepted and shorn. Personal property should be disposed of, for the monastery automatically inherits from the monk.

The novice is likely to be appointed to some humble post, such as kitchen help. On completing the probationary period (usually three years) he is shorn, becoming a wearer-of-the-gown. The officiating priest calls him into church, offers thanks for his rescue, then cuts a few hairs crosswise from his head, in the name of the Trinity, and covers the shorn head with the monastic hat, draping the cloak about his shoulders. The "beginner" takes no vows, but states he intends continuing in the monastic state and will keep the rules of the monastery. If he wishes he may remain permanently in the lowest degree, and may choose to do so.

If he seeks advancement, he presently becomes a monk-of-the-little-habit by taking the vows of stability, obedience, poverty, and chastity. The vow of stability binds him to monastic life. He is stripped of outer garments at the church door, then passes in to prostrate himself at the altar before his abbot, while the choirs chant. In a series of questions and answers, between abbot, priest, and himself on his knees, he makes it plain he takes the vows of his free will, underlining this by handing the priest the scissors for the second crosswise shearing. He has now died to the world, and receives a first name identical in initial with the rejected Christian name. The new name has been borne by a dead saint, and is to be an inspiration. The name of the monastery becomes his surname.

There is a third grade of monk-of-the-great-habit, which many never enter, others only in old age. A stricter discipline is demanded. More prayer, more silence, stricter fasting. He is buried in his full habit.

SERVICES

It is usual for monks to be called from bed at eleven p.m. for an hour's private prayer, and later in the small hours to be summoned to church for matins and the singing of the hours. The Liturgy follows, timed to be celebrated when the gates are opened. Thus summer hours are earlier than winter. The main meal of the day follows, from which the monks rise to undertake the tasks set them, reassembling in church at three p.m. or five p.m. for nones and vespers, according to the time of the year. Then supper and compline between six and seven. Afterwards bed when the monk wishes.

Services are directed from the south choir by a "typikaris". Monks occupy stalls allotted them, and though public opinion is the judge in idiorrhythmic houses as to whether these stalls are occupied sufficiently, the abbots of the coenobitic houses inspect the stalls during the services to mark down absentees.

VIGILS

The Eastern Orthodox Church recognizes more than fifty vigils calling for continuous services throughout an evening, the night, and the following morning. One of these vigils may include little vespers, great vespers, matins, the first, second and third hours, and an elaborate liturgy.

FASTS

A single oil-less meal is eaten towards noon in the coenobia on Mondays, Wednesdays, and Fridays; and two meals on other days. The fare is vegetarian, with an allowance of bread and wine. Sometimes fish appears, but never meat. The idiorrhythmic rule requires abstinence from cheese, butter, and meat on Wednesdays and Fridays. Meat is allowed on other days, but may not be cooked in the monastic kitchen. Neither meat, fish, cheese, butter, nor eggs are permitted during the forty days of Lent ending in Easter. This fast begins after Quinquagesima on Monday with a preliminary week of abstinence, known as "cheese week", and many monks let nothing pass their lips during the last days of the fast. A like abstinence obtains during the Lent of the Apostles Peter and Paul, from Monday after All Saints Day to June 28; during the fourteen-day Lent of the Mother of God, from August 1 to 14; and during the Christmas Lent, beginning on November 15, and ending on the night of Christmas Eve.

MONASTERY PLAN

The Mountain's monasteries conform closely to general plan. A church stands apart in the court created by four rectangular lines of two-, three-, and four-storeyed buildings. Cells and living-rooms of the monks open off the long corridors of the upper storeys, as generally do the offices and guestrooms. Kitchens, storehouses, and workshops are at ground level, with doors and windows into the court. The basin for blessing the holy water on the first of the month stands in the neighbourhood of the church, and the refectory is frequently built opposite the church's west door to allow the monks to pass in from outside. The outer walls are windowless near the ground, and windows are barred when they begin. The tower or keep rises above all, a final refuge in unsettled times; now, as often as not, housing the libraries' yellowing parchments.

MONASTIC CHURCHES

Monasteries differ in detail while conforming to type, and so do their churches. A closed rood-screen divides chancel from nave, and behind it the "holy table" or altar stands free before the apse. North and south are generally smaller companion apses; the northern for the preparation of the elements, the southern serving as vestry and treasury. Where nave and transepts intersect rises a central dome, supported on four pillars leaving the pavement below. The bishop's throne stands under the south-west column. North and south choirs are in the transepts. The nave ends in a western wall usually entered through the narthex, divided into eso-narthex and exo-narthex, the latter often an open loggia. Thus sanctity increases as a church is penetrated, traceable to the age of three categories in the Christian community; those who minister; those who are baptized and admitted to communion; the repentant and cut off from communion and anxious to be received again. Unbaptized, eager to learn about Christ, stood in these last. The first class had access to the sanctuary, the second to the nave, the third to the narthex.

Church differences are in degree rather than in kind, tradition even ordering the murals. Christ, as the Almighty, invariably stares down from the drum of the dome, and the four apostles, pillars of the Church, appear where the dome rests on its four supporting pillars. The screen carries ikons of Christ, the Virgin, John, the Forerunner, and the Archangel Gabriel; the Virgin enthroned and bearing the Infant, Jesus, is above the naos doors; the two narthexes have scenes from the life of the Virgin and the prophets, and in the pronaos are warnings from the apocalypse and the Day of Judgement, for those remaining outside the Church.

The Author

SYDNEY LOCH WAS A Scotsman. Widely travelled, he had sailed round the three famous capes which give the right to those who have rounded all three to add "God bless her", when toasting the Queen.

At the age of seventeen he went to Australia. He had £20 with which to start life, but felt the world was his. He worked as a jackaroo on several sheep-stations, and spent his holidays astride a horse exploring country farther out, or in a pearling lugger off Darwin and Thursday Island.

At the outbreak of the First World War he joined up with the Australians and was in the landing at Gallipoli. Towards the end of that campaign he developed typhoid, but before he reported sick was wounded. After a long illness in Egypt he was returned to Australia. He wrote *Straits Impregnable*, which was one of the best of the books on Gallipoli. His strength was slow in returning, and so he sailed round the Horn in a windjammer in order to get back condition. The voyage took nine months and nearly ended disastrously on two occasions. He sighted another ship once. He was in Dublin doing journalistic work during the last months of the British régime. Then the terrible plight of the Poles in Eastern Europe captured his imagination, and he joined a Quaker unit for relief and reconstruction. He visited Russia during the aftermath of the revolution.

The vast movement of Greeks from Asia Minor to Greece began under the League of Nations, and he went to Greece, working with the American Farm School, and the Quakers.

In 1928 he revisited Poland on behalf of the Quakers, and in that same year found and settled in Prosphori Tower on the Athos Peninsula, where he worked on a scheme of his own for bettering village conditions.

In 1932 an earthquake completely destroyed Erissos, the local town, and badly shook the monastic world of Athos. Sydney Loch was the first to get to Erissos with first aid, and worked among the wounded and dying for thirty hours before other relief came with the British Navy. He then acted as interpreter to doctors and demolition units.

At the outbreak of the Second World War he was asked by the Quakers to go to the help of the Poles who were then streaming into Rumania. The Polish Relief Fund provided the money, which was raised through the Lord Mayor of London. Poles poured into Hungary and Rumania; then down through Turkey to Cyprus and Palestine. Sydney Loch was with them on their long journey. Other streams went through Jugoslavia and Greece, making their way to France before that country fell. After Germany occupied Hungary and Rumania the Poles travelled from Siberia and Russia into Iran and Iraq. Thousands went to Palestine, were reconditioned and drafted into the army, or sent on to other countries. It was a full-time job, and during the entire war he took no holiday. In spite of the Polish work on his hands he found time to organize relief for those Greeks who got to Palestine from the islands.

In 1944 he returned to Greece with the first British Military Liaison unit. Once there he worked on relief, taking supplies to villages behind the guerrilla (communist) lines. He worked at the American Farm School which he had taken over at the request of the Board of Trustees in America, in the absence as prisoners of war of the Director and his wife, Mr. and Mrs. Charles House, who were his friends through all his long years in Greece.

At the end of the guerrilla warfare in 1952 he returned to Prosphori.

In this book he goes deeper into the life of the monastic world than any other author: he is concerned with library and treasury, but also with the people living on the Mountain. The monks, the fishermen, and charcoal-burners were his friends. He has met hermits on their own ground, and realized the spiritual urge and powers of self-discipline which drove them to solitude and perched them on windswept cliffs. Seldom has a layman been greeted with such affection in monastery or hut.

He died suddenly in February 1954, sitting over his fire, ten minutes after going out into the snow to identify a pelican which the peasants had brought in. He had that day finished typing out the sixth chapter of the book; but he had completed the manuscript.

He was awarded the Polish Gold Cross of Merit, was made a Freeman of Erissos, and in the district where he lived are to be found streets and squares named after him.

All the photographs were taken by him, with the exception of three.

He was married in 1919, and his wife shared his adventurous life with him. After his death she remained on at Prosphori in order to edit and type the book in the atmosphere in which it was written.

J. M. L.

Index